Introduction to Political Economy

To my wife, Rayzil, mother of all my children

Introduction to Political Economy

E. J. Mishan

Hutchinson
London Melbourne Sydney Auckland Johannesburg

Hutchinson & Co. (Publishers)
An imprint of the Hutchinson Publishing Group
17–21 Conway Street, London, W1P 5HL

Hutchinson Group (Australia) Pty Ltd
30–32 Cremorne Street, Richmond South, Victoria 3121
PO Box 151, Broadway, New South Wales 2007

Hutchinson Group (NZ) Ltd
32–34 View Road, PO Box 40–086, Glenfield, Auckland 10

Hutchinson Group (SA) (Pty) Ltd
PO Box 337, Bergvlei 2012, South Africa

First published 1982

Typeset by Preface Ltd, Salisbury, Wilts.

Printed in Great Britain by The Anchor Press Ltd
and bound by Wm Brendon & Son Ltd
both of Tiptree, Essex

British Library Cataloguing in Publication Data
Mishan, Ezra
Introduction to political economy
1.Welfare economics
I. Title
330.15′5 HB99.3

ISBN 0 09 145390 9 cased
0 09 145391 7 paper

Contents

Part One

The agenda of political economy

1 Introductory observations

The term 'political economy' continues to be used in a number of related senses. For instance, what we refer to today as economics was generally known as political economy during the nineteenth century – not inappropriately since it was a mixture of the descriptive and the prescriptive. Economic doctrines and economic maxims went together. During this period, moreover, the notion of immutable economic laws was widespread. The object was to discover them, and from them to derive principles of sound economic policy.

This notion of immutable laws has evolved into the conception of economics as a discipline that is held today by a number of prominent economists, a conception of economics as a body of general principles by which one can determine only the broad direction of price and quantity adjustments in response to significant changes in technology, in institutions, in people's wants and in government policies. When this conception of economics is allied to the liberal doctrine arguing for carefully defined and limited powers of government and, consequently, an antagonism to the expansion of bureaucratic power and continual intervention in the economy, it can boast a following not only among businessmen but also among some distinguished academic economists. Certainly over the last decade or so there has been growing support for the idea of removing encumbrances placed by ambitious governments and bureaucrats on the free operation of a market economy. Support is particularly strong among economists for whom a market economy is equated with a competitive capitalist economy or, put another way, with a decentralized private enterprise economy whose interdependent activities are co-ordinated by a universal pricing system.

So regarded, the changing prices of goods and resources are the signals by which a mass of information about what people want and what can be made available is disseminated through the economy. The faith in a competitive capitalist economy of this sort draws upon a number of considerations. The first is related to the aspect of a Burkean political philosophy that favours traditional and proven institutions, among which the market is one able to trace its origins to Antiquity. Another is the belief that a private enterprise economy, as distinct from a collectively planned economy, not only offers a wider range of choices to individuals in the selection both of goods and of vocational opportunities, but also acts to safeguard the political freedom of the individual.[1]* A third consideration is that, seen as an institution for catering to the material wants of individuals and for encouraging innovation both in goods and in productive methods, it is more efficient than the alternative system of centralized planning characteristic of communist countries.

Hayek, in particular, has repeatedly emphasized and elaborated on the 'invisible hand' theme[2] – that each person, in pursuit only of his own gain is led by a providential mechanism (the 'invisible hand') to promoting the general interest. This seemingly miraculous phenomenon is, of course, the decentralized market economy which brings together and transmits the information diffused among millions of people in the effective and economic form of price changes, these price changes being, as indicated, the signals that guide the economic system's productive and distribution activities so as to meet the changing material wants of people.

Concentrating on this third consideration, the efficiency of the signals may be regarded as turning only on relaying information about market conditions, and may therefore be judged by the infrequency and the limited duration of surpluses and shortages of goods and resources. Allowing as a judgement of fact about the working of alternative institutions, that the competitive capitalist system is the more responsive to changing conditions of demand and supply than is a centrally planned economy, the support of the market economy entails a value judgement that efficiency in this sense – the more rapid adjustment to changes in demand and supply – is a good thing. And, it may reasonably be urged that this value judgement, in addition to that which favours personal freedom, is one that is shared by the public at large.

*Superior figures refer to the Notes on pages 249–58.

It would be absurd to deny that this conception of economics, of the competitive market, and the conclusions derived therefrom, can legitimately be described as a branch of political economy. If I choose not to treat it in full here it is simply because the emphasis in such a study is on the political rather than on the economic, whereas in the bulk of this text I propose to place the emphasis on the economic.

Moreover, a treatment of the three considerations adduced in favour of a competitive capitalist economy, and in favour also of defined and specific restrictions on government activity, involves very limited analysis and very much description and illustration, historical and hypothetical, of the intricate interdependencies of a market economy; and, as a corollary, illustrations also of the detrimental effects of persistent government intervention in its misconceived attempts to plan for the 'needs of the people'. Such a treatment can hardly avoid taking on the complexion of an essay in persuasion, which is contrary to my main intent in this book. The reader who is interested in this sort of political economy – and I hope there are many of them – cannot do better than go back to the original sources (including Adam Smith's *Wealth of Nations*) where the case for a competitive capitalist economy is lucidly and cogently argued. The present volume, however, is reserved for an introduction to the modern development of normative economics, which is clearly associated with the mainstream of positive economics, plus a fairly radical critique of the relevance of that development in so far as it is regarded as an instrument for social improvement.

It is interesting in passing, however, to reflect that the proponents of a competitive market economy, taken as a whole, who value this institution as a means of dispersing information, of facilitating adjustment to changing conditions of demand and supply, and of encouraging innovation, tend to dissociate themselves from an interest in modern theoretical welfare economics, in particular from propositions about the norms of resource allocation. This dissociation, however, is not easy to maintain. The information that is amassed and dispersed through the market mechanism produces continual changes in the allocation of the resources available to the economy. If it is argued that the competitive market is more efficient than the centrally planned economy, the question naturally arises: efficient by what criterion? I dare say that the proponents of the competitive market economy would like to confine the term efficiency to the economy's performance in adjusting smoothly to changes in the conditions of demand and supply – measured, perhaps, by its success in avoiding prolonged shortages or surpluses.

But if one presses the question, what is wrong with an economic system that does not adjust smoothly in this way, I fancy that it would be hard to offer a convincing answer without drawing on aspects of a normative theory of allocation. There are, surely, inseverable links between efficiency as conceived, on the one hand, by such political economists (as the continuing reallocation of resources in response to changes in demand and supply conditions) and efficiency as conceived, on the other hand, by the normative economist (as a criterion for ranking alternative allocations for any given demand and supply situation). After all, what should it matter if the market failed to eliminate a shortage of goods if it could be shown by normative allocation criteria that such goods ought not to be produced anyway? As we shall see later, the implied belief of such political economists that people's valuations should count, irrespective of the distribution of income, is a value judgement that is one of the maxims of modern normative economics.

Be that as it may, it was well after the turn of the century that a distinction was consciously drawn between on the one hand, an economics viewed as a positive science, one yielding hypotheses about the working of the economy which in principle could be tested against the facts, and a political economy on the other, from which maxims of economic policy might be deduced. In fact, the subject matter of political economy in this latter sense is today sometimes taught explicitly as a normative subject under the title of the 'theory of economic policy'. At all events, by the middle of the twentieth century, the distinction between a positive (or descriptive) economics and a normative (or prescriptive) economics was well established – even though, occasionally, authors of positive economics textbooks may be found approving some economic institutions and practices and condemning others.

However, the matter does not end there. For within this explicitly normative part of the subject – and quite apart from the doctrines discussed above (and chiefly linked today with the names of Friedman and Hayek) – a dichotomy has been evident for some time. As a result, the term 'political economy' is often associated with the specific advice given by one or more economists (usually having strong convictions) to governments or to the public at large either on broad policy issues or on particular proposals. This advice, which appears as policy conclusions, rests upon judgements of values and judgements of facts (facts both of economic behaviour and of political responses) which are particular to the writer(s) and are not necessarily shared by other economists or by the community at large. Much of this sort of political economy – which we might call *personal* political economy – is the stuff that appears in newspapers, magazines, bank reviews, pamphlets and popular books.[3]

The other interpretation of a prescriptive economics that is comprehended by the term 'political economy' has been given the more general name of 'normative economics', although the term 'welfare economics' (following the title of Pigou's celebrated work of 1920, *The Economics of Welfare*, is more popular today. The aim of this welfare economics, which is not quite as comprehensive in scope as normative economics, is better understood by the more explicit 'economic theory of social welfare'. Stated thus, it suggests that economists seek to build a body of prescriptive generalizations resting on widely accepted value judgements and assumptions of economic behaviour.

For reasons indicated, we shall not be directly concerned in this book with the political economy of a competitive market system or with the movement seeking to restrict the role of the state and so to enlarge the area of the private sector. None the less, Part Five, which breaks out of the conventional framework of assumptions in which modern normative economics is developed, does attempt to assess some of the claims made for the market, especially in the light of post-war developments. As for the writings of the more personal sort of political economy, much of them directed towards the economic problems that beset the poorer countries of the world, they do not lend themselves easily to a textbook treatment other than a taxonomic one. However, although these writers of political economy are inspired by a personal philosophy and, perhaps, by a world view, they do indeed borrow propositions from the more formalized treatment of normative economics. Their recourse to the more familiar allocative propositions however, does not preclude injections of their own personal value judgements into their arguments. For example, they may confidently assert that a movement towards freer international trade is so advantageous that one should not carp at some incidental increase in the instability of employment and industrial readjustments. But such an assertion cannot be derived from the corpus of modern welfare economics even if the increment of free trade and of instability could be specified exactly.

In sum, a personal political economy is an art – a somewhat opinionated art – in which standard economic techniques and normative propositions form only a part. With enough experience, and with enough conviction or folly, a person may come to write political economy of this personal sort. But, in the nature of things, it cannot be imparted to the student. In contrast, welfare economics, as commonly understood, *can* be imparted to the student, as I hope to convince you.

I should not want to leave you with the impression, however, that there is a settled or monolithic view covering every aspect of welfare economics. Controversies still persist, as indeed they do in positive economics. But such differences that continue to exist are *not* the result – as they often are in controversies arising from different personal political economics – of differences in personal judgements, whether of facts or of values. They arise either from intellectual error or from misconception, such differences being properly regarded as normal and inevitable consequences of the continuing development of a discipline that aims, ideally, to reach a synthesis and, more immediately, to extend the area of agreement among scholars.

In its more general treatment welfare economics may be said to embrace two interrelated aspects, those of resource allocation on the one hand and distribution on the other. Most students have an idea of what is meant by resource allocation – loosely speaking, the amounts of the various goods that should be produced with the resources available to us – but non-economists may misunderstand the meaning of distribution in this context. It has nothing to do with the distribution trades, or with the marketing or retailing of goods. The term refers only to the distribution or the sharing of the products of industry. A more 'progressive' distribution is one in which a greater proportion of aggregate income goes to the 'poor', as a result of which the structure of income looks more equal or, at any rate, less unequal.

Although, as mentioned, resource allocation and distribution are interrelated aspects of the subject, each can be treated separately from the other, at least provisionally. After we have covered some ground, I shall indicate how distributional considerations affect allocative propositions and how allocative considerations affect distribution. But for the present we are to concentrate on allocation alone, simply because economists have a great deal to say about allocating resources and very little to say about distribution (except in so far as it is related to the study of allocation).

Assuming welfare economics to be a successful discipline, it would enable us to say to society, 'Organize the economy in this way rather than that!', or, more modestly, 'Better build a bridge than a ferry service!', 'The tax on gasoline should be increased by 14.6 cents per gallon.' (Bear in mind that figures *beyond* the decimal point impress the public with your expertise far more than the figures before it.)

Such statements are clearly prescriptive, or 'ought' statements, and the temptation to utter a few pertinent if perfunctory remarks about them is not to be resisted.

Elementary treatises on ethics sometimes draw a distinction between a 'conditional imperative' and a 'categorical imperative'. An example of the conditional imperative is the statement, 'I ought to visit granny more often – if I expect her to leave me a tidy sum in her will.' An example of the categorical imperative is the statement: 'Thou shalt not bear false witness.'

The example above of an ought statement that is a conditional imperative shows it to be a rule of expediency. Euphemistically, perhaps, we could view it as an example of enlightened self-interest. I begin with the thought of the joy to me of having some of granny's money. Being 'enlightened' (which in economics usually means shrewd), I calculate that my chances of obtaining some of granny's money would be much improved if I ingratiated myself with the dear old lady by visiting her frequently and showing an interest (which doubtless I feel) in her failing health. I conclude without hesitation that I ought to visit her more often – before it is too late.

The example of the categorical imperative is not one of expediency or enlightened self-interest. Indeed, it is altogether possible that, were I to consult my immediate self-interest, I might discover that I could materially benefit by circulating falsehoods about a particular person. Yet the biblical injunction forbids me to do so.

And a good society would regard it as a binding rule irrespective of self-interest or inclination. Of course, you can try to justify the categorical imperative as an application of the golden rule: not to do to others that which you would not want them to do to you. But if, notwithstanding, you would also go so far as to question the universal validity of the golden rule, what then?

Allowing that human beings are imperfect creatures, subject to temptations and mischievous impulses, I might observe that a peaceful and stable society would not be possible if such a moral law, among others, were not binding on people. You might agree with my judgement of the consequences of a rejection of such moral laws, but then go on to question the advantages of living in a peaceful and stable society. Should I then seek to persuade you, drawing on historical experience and the resources of imagination, that a peaceful and stable society was generally a desirable thing, you might press further questions upon me. And so we could go on indefinitely.

But we need not enter the realm of moral philosophy here. For the purposes of welfare economics, it is not necessary to establish that prescriptive or ought statements are unquestionable and universal moral imperatives. In any case, there can be conflicts of the moral law which may be resolved by reference to an accepted hierarchy of moral propriety or by reference to particular circumstances. All we need to know if our Welfare Economics is to be a valid instrument for allocative (and distributional) prescription is that the basic ethical premises on which it is raised would command a consensus in the particular society for which it is intended. The question ultimately is a factual one. It is a question about the interpretation of one or more ethical premises that are particular to the Western type of liberal democracy. For without such ethical premises, there cannot be a welfare economics with authority to prescribe for this type of society.

But just what are these ethical premises? Now if you are an impatient person there is nothing to prevent you turning at once to Chapter 3 for the answer. My advice, however, is that you heed the small voice of intellectual conscience and attend first to two considerations that sometimes deter students from taking a serious interest in the subject.

The first consideration takes shape as the 'social welfare function', mentioned below. The second, which is the subject matter of the following chapter, is a short account of the arguments of those who oppose in principle the very notion of a welfare economics.

The term 'social welfare function' originated in a celebrated paper by Bergson (1938). To visualize it, imagine all conceivable 'economic situations', arranged in a person's mind so distinctly that if any of a number of alternative economic situations are proposed the person has no difficulty in placing them in order of preference. Since a typical economic situation in this context is taken to consist of a collection of many goods (possibly enough to exhaust the producing capacity of the economy) plus a particular distribution of each of these goods among the members of society, the concept of a social welfare function strikes one as formidable. No living person can reasonably be expected to have such a blueprint at the back of his mind, even though he may have clear and consistent ideas when it comes to ranking two or three relatively simple economic situations.

But let this difficulty go for the present by imagining that we inhabit a world in which men have such remarkable powers that they all walk about with fully blown social welfare functions hovering at the back of their minds, ready to be consulted at a moment's notice. How does the concept help? Bergson himself used the idea of a social welfare function simply to shed light on the contemporary controversy about certain propositions in welfare economics. Putting it crudely, if the A school of thought held proposition X to be valid while the B school of thought held X to be invalid, the discrepancy can be explained by the fact that school A embraces a social welfare function that is different in one or two particulars from the social welfare function embraced by the B school. No need to quarrel about an issue if differences could be attributed to the adherence of different social welfare functions.

Not surprisingly, the term 'social welfare function' acquired a vogue among the economic fraternity. Worse, students of economics who found themselves floundering in controversy with others were apt to write the whole thing off by blandly exclaiming that 'it all depends upon your social welfare function'.

However, the peccadillos of students are less interesting here than the uses made of this billowing concept by academic economists. It lent itself nicely to evading the question of the broad ethical judgements on which a welfare economics has to be founded. One could have a sort of 'open-ended' welfare economics, taking shape as a taxonomic exercise: you name your own social welfare function and derive your own prescriptive propositions!

But no economist concerned with prescribing for social welfare can remain content with so complacent a formula. The question of co-ordinating the divergent social welfare functions of different individuals into some sort of blueprint for society was bound to arise, and indeed was raised by Arrow (1951). More explicitly, the problem is that of moving from any given number of individual social welare functions to a social welfare function for society as a whole – allowing ourselves to be guided in this task by a number of 'reasonable' rules. Arrow, who proposed the 'reasonable' rules, maintained that it was, in fact, impossible – or rather impossible for all conceivable cases. Even the traditional majority-rule method of ranking alternative situations could lead to intransitivity: thus, using majority rule, situation A could be preferred to B, and B preferred to C, yet by the same majority rule C would be preferred to A.[4]

Arrow's monograph caused a great stir when it appeared in 1951 – not so much, in my opinion, because it threatened the foundations of welfare economics, even though there were economists at the time who affirmed as much. The stir arose from those economists who fancied their skill in symbolic logic and were quick to grasp the paper-publishing opportunities in the new territory pioneered by Arrow. And, as is usual in such cases, the slighter the arguments the thicker became the mathematic foliage.

The relevance of the ensuing social welfare function literature for welfare economics is dubious. The notion of deriving a social welfare function for society as a whole from the array of individual social welfare functions is in fact more of political than of economic interest. In his introduction to Graaff's *Theoretical Welfare Economics* (1957), Samuelson aptly refers to the social welfare function literature as 'welfare politics' rather than welfare economics. Certainly, thinking in terms of the simpler ordering of a manageable number of alternative situations, there is some incentive to examine, and to devise, political procedures or constitutions that produce satisfactory collective decisions from the decisions of individual citizens.[5]

Be this as it may, economists have continued to offer economic advice when it is demanded – and, often enough, when it is not. Indeed, they still make use of traditional allocation rules, which can be traced back to the so-called neo-classical revolution of the 1870s and were clearly and elegantly formulated in Pigou's *Economics of Welfare* (1946). Moreover, the immense economic literature on 'spillover effects' or 'spillovers' – the effects of pollutants, noise, congestion, etc., on productivity and welfare (which are the subject of Part Three) – builds upon the traditional allocation rules. Since these rules derive from the premises of welfare economics, the subject would appear to be alive and thriving.

So much by way of sceptical survey. The question we must address at various places in this volume is whether welfare economics, as understood today, and especially the allocative propositions it yields, can indeed by justified by reference to an ethical consensus. Even if we conclude that it can, there is still an important question to be faced: just how useful to modern society is the prescriptive knowledge that the economist brings to bear on social problems? The issue will be given expanded, albeit opinionated, treatment in Part Five.

In the chapters which follow, it is possible, for the most part, to use as close synonyms the terms 'political economy', 'normative economics', 'welfare economics' and 'allocation economics', without risk of confusion. At some points in the exposition, however, a distinction may have to be made and the precise meaning of the term has to be borne in mind. The context, in such cases, will generally ensure that the student will not feel uncertain about the meaning of the term – assuming that he has understood the distinctions in question. At all events, the summary below is no more than a ready reminder of the definitions I have used in this chapter.

Political economy is the hold-all term for all economics directed towards appraising or prescribing general economic policies or specific economic proposals, irrespective of whether the statements rest ultimately on value judgements that are personal to the writer, or are common to a political group or are believed to be widely accepted by the community at large.

Normative economics may be described as that part of political economy which lends itself to academic discipline in as much as it draws on both the value judgements of the community at large and on the axioms and theorems of positive economics. Thus the propositions of normative economics are *relevant* to society only in so far as the premises on which they are based form a part of the ethical consensus. They are *valid* under that condition only in so far as the axioms and theorems from which they are deduced adequately describe the real world.

Welfare economics, which is an abbreviation of the economic theory of social welfare, is used by economists as a more popular synonym for normative economics. In fact its scope is narrower since, as distinct from normative economics, it covers only norms of allocation and distribution. Normative economics, however, is understood to have regard also to considerations bearing on equity where equity may have no direct or necessary relation to distribution.

Allocation economics, finally, which is a part of welfare economics, comprises by far the greater part of welfare economics as measured by the attention it attracts in the economic literature. In addition, it is the more traditional, the more fascinating and easily the more practical part of welfare economics as well as, for that matter, of normative economics. For these reasons this book is devoted chiefly to elucidating the central ideas and implications of allocation economics. Questions of distribution and of equity are touched upon occasionally from Part Three onwards, and with particular emphasis in Part Five.

2 The resistance to a prescriptive economics

First a word on what we are *not* talking about. There are economists, some of them Marxists, who to this day declare that a positive economics, regarded as a scientific study, does not exist except as a bourgeois illusion; that, indeed, what is spoken of as mainstream economics (as taught in the better universities of the West) is fraught with value judgements which, apparently, the economics profession conspires to ignore.

If this belief is tantamount to saying that the choice of areas of investigation, the choice of theories and therefore, also, of basic postulates are effectively determined or greatly influenced by the prevailing institutions (say, the 'class structure' and form of government), and by the economic and social problems arising therefrom, or by the belief systems and popular culture of a civilisation at some point in time, well and good. Few would want to dispute so broad and plausible an argument. Indeed, conjecture about the connections between the changing social and economic environment on the one hand, and the development of economic theory on the other, is a legitimate and fascinating branch of economic study.

Again, if this belief is taken to mean, as it occasionally does, that contemporary economic theories are developed with an eye to realizing ends which economists, influenced by the spirit of the times, believe to be urgent or desirable, no exception need be taken to it. For example, it may reasonably be argued that theories of income and employment presupposed that a high level of employment was a good thing, and that theories of economic growth were inspired by the belief that a high rate of economic growth was or should be a paramount objective of economic policy.

Certainly if the assertion that positive economics, or economics generally, is value-laden is understood in either of these ways, few orthodox economists would trouble to challenge it. From either interpretation it follows that no science whatever is 'value free'.

For all that, whatever the motivations of economic theorists and whatever the social forces that give direction to their thought, they are quite able to construct models of the economy that in principle at least can be tested against real world data. Whether a particular theory is general or limited, whether it is important or trivial, whether it is likely to be ephemeral or enduring: these are obviously important considerations in any overall judgement of its worth. But the judgement we reach in these respects has nothing to do with whether a theory (or model) is a scientific economic one, the criterion of its scientific status being that its implications can be tested for their correspondence with the relevant activity in the real world.

Be that as it may, the debate about whether positive economics and other sciences are implicitly value-ridden in the senses indicated above, or in some other (possibly related) sense, interesting though it may be, is one that I shall deliberately skirt since it falls outside the agenda of this volume. The questions raised by this debate are, in short, quite separate from those raised in this chapter; namely, whether it is advisable to continue to develop an explicitly normative economics, as distinct from and in addition to a positive economics as understood by the profession. Put differently, the issue broached in this chapter is whether economists, in addition to seeking to improve their skills in predicting the course of economic events – either generally or conditionally – may also legitimately claim to be able to advise the public on the soundness or otherwise of economic policies or proposals by reference to normative criteria, and particularly by reference to a criterion of economic efficiency.

Now if you think about it for a few minutes you may be inclined to conclude that the study of *positive* economics alone – in which study we ought properly to include not only theoretical analysis but also the quantitative techniques through which empirical relationships are established – has, of itself, little practical value for society. There is, of course, the cynical consideration that the popularity of economics is a blessing in disguise since it offers employment opportunities to highly trained and imaginative men who might else be adding to the mischief created by enthusiastic atomic physicists and microbiologists. But in the interests of discipline we must brush aside such irreverent surmises, and continue with out initial reflection on the practical uses of positive economics.

You might feel that unless the study of economics eventually produces advice about how to 'run the economy', or how best to allocate our resources, it is a sterile discipline. But the fact is that very few professional economists, even among those who are primarily interested in its normative aspects, would regard the study of positive economics by itself as necessarily a sterile activity. Assuming that the accumulation of empirical knowledge over time is not entirely ephemeral and unreliable, a knowledge of positive economics enables one to avoid gross errors at least. Moreover, if the ends of economic policy are agreed upon by the community, the economist should have some ideas of the ways and means by which those ends can be realized most economically. For there are always alternative ways of achieving desired ends and the economist can be of service in showing what courses are to be avoided and what to be followed.

Yet even in cases where the ends of economic policy are given to the economist, we are entitled to ask whether the choice of a method for realizing them does not itself turn ultimately on some criterion of economic efficiency. For if the answer is yes, then again we are invoking the services of a normative economics. In fact the answer is yes, and before concluding I hope to convince you of this.

Nevertheless, we have to face the fact that economists, good ones too, have argued otherwise and from time to time have expressed the opinion that the profession should confine itself to the study of positive economics. Reading such matter, the impressionable student may be lcft with the feeling that overt recourse to value judgements involves nothing less than an indecent surrender of one's methodological chastity. Such is the power of 'scientific chauvinism'.

Without further condescension, however, let us briefly examine the arguments of some of those unyielding 'positivists' who question the propriety and usefulness of a normative economics and, more particularly, of an allocative economics. (Remember, a normative economics also covers norms of distribution and of equity. But by far the greater part is about allocation.)

First, it has been alleged (Archibald 1959) that what passes for normative, or rather for welfare economics, is not in fact normative, or at least need not be normative. Furthermore, according to this argument, controversies about welfare economics are 'essentialist', or metaphysical, inasmuch as there can be no one correct index of social well being. Therefore what passes for welfare economics should be regarded as a positive study; it should concern itself with the economic analysis and the techniques necessary to discover how some interesting (though apparently arbitrary) welfare index responds to particular economic policies.

Some minor concession can be made to this view of things. If we start with an economic definition of social welfare then, to be sure, there is something to be said for trying to discover whether economists' proposals for increasing social welfare as defined are valid; that is, if their advice were followed, whether the particular index of social welfare could be observed to rise. Thus a test of the economists' welfare propositions is, in principle, possible and, to that extent, the testing procedure of positive economics is invoked.

What has to be rejected, however, is the notion that controversies about welfare economics are 'essentialist' just because there can be no 'true' index of social welfare. The claim that there can be any number of different definitions, and therefore indices, of social welfare, is undeniable but not pertinent to the main issue. The impression conveyed by such an allegation is that welfare economics is actually a sophisticated game which an economist may play with any welfare definition that happens to catch his fancy. Far from being arbitrary or capricious, however, the definition of social welfare can be acceptable as a foundation for the subject *only* if it is an appropriate one for the particular society to which the economist is to address his welfare prescriptions. To be more precise, if the economist's welfare prescriptions are to be taken seriously by society, the ethical premises on which his criteria rest must accord with those held by society at large; this view will be elaborated in Chapter 3.

A second source of dissatisfaction with welfare economics is that none of its propositions can be shown to be generally valid. Indeed, as is often alleged, welfare economists resort to criteria that appear to be self-contradictory (Graaff 1957; Nath 1964). This latter apparent paradox will be discussed in Part Four, where I will also argue that there is a necessary connection between changes in prices and changes in distribution.

The more general dissatisfaction stemming from the lack of generality of the propositions of welfare economics (and we shall confirm as much later) is no more warranted than a dissatisfaction with the lack of generality in positive economics. The trouble with what are called 'general propositions' is that they are commonly but unreasonably conceived of as meaningful propositions which should hold true in all circumstances – that is to say, whatever the assumptions about the nature of technology, institutions or people's behaviour.

But this notion of generality is impossible. In an economic universe that can take any shape imaginable any result becomes possible. In such a universe we cannot sensibly expect any meaningful implication to remain constant. When there are no empirical bounds to the assumptions an economist may build into his model, he cannot reasonably hope to derive unambiguous implications.

It follows that only as we investigate more closely the actual nature of the economic universe, and in this way *exclude* certain forms of economic behaviour and certain forms of technology and institutions from our models, shall we be able to derive defensible and unambiguous propositions in either positive or normative economics.

Finally, it has been argued that even if the propositions of welfare economics were to become generally valid and welfare criteria unambiguous, a normative economics would be unnecessary. It would be unnecessary simply because we can, and should, leave all the decisions about economic policy to a political authority – in the West, one that is shaped by the democratic process. This attack on normative economics is too common to be associated with any particular group, although it has been forcibly expressed by Tinbergen (1952). But its implications are pretty drastic. For if it is believed that all economic decisions have to derive their sanction from the democratic process, then any of the consequences of implementing such economic decisions may properly be criticized by the economist only in his role as citizen.

This is bad enough, but further thought suggests that this maxim is even more restrictive than is generally recognized. For one thing, economists would have to jettison some of their favourite techniques, such as traffic control and pricing, mathematical programming, cost benefit analysis and the like, since all of them derive their rationale from a criterion of economic efficiency, one found in the area of welfare economics. For another, the pro-market element in the profession, and it is large enough to encompass many of the foremost economists, would be harder put to justify its general approval of a competitive pricing system, or some system of ideal pricing, without recourse to such a criterion of efficiency.

What is more, the view of the economist as a consultant who provides information but avoids recommendation is not only unduly modest; it is hardly practicable. Granted that the economist is honest and competent, his presentation of a list of the economic implications of each of the alternative policies under consideration is almost certain to baffle the politician. In consequence, the economist is almost sure to be instructed by the politician to somehow 'organize' the mass of data he has produced so as to make it more digestible, and to provide some method of selection and arrangement to better enable the politician to reach a decision on the 'best' policy to adopt. Such requests, however, unavoidably place arbitrary power in the hands of the advising economist. If he is not to be arbitrary, he will resort to the standard norms of allocation.

Finally, whatever takes place in the real world, the crucial issue of principle is whether there can be, and whether there ought to be, economic criteria that are entirely independent of political decisions. If it can cogently be argued that there can, and ought to, be such criteria then there is nothing absurd or perverse in the economist's declaring a policy to be economically inefficient even though it is approved by the electorate. I shall go into this more in Chapter 3.

3 The nature of the economist's efficiency criterion

Welfare economics is that branch of economics that has for its agenda the study of criteria for ranking alternative economic situations along the scale of better or worse. Such a statement is both descriptive and definitional. And if I happen to think it wonderfully illuminating and you happen to think otherwise, our difference may be explained by the fact that I have been dabbling in the subject for some twenty years. Let me concede, therefore, that it may not be quite so crystal clear to you as I imagine it is to me, especially if you are new to economics. So a little elaboration may help.

Imagine yourself to be in a position where you have to choose one of the two options presented to you. Three examples of such options could be (1) a specific housing development for the worthy poor, close to the sea, or alternatively a housing development costing just as much but located in the suburbs of town X; (2) no intervention in the existing pattern of international trade or else a reduction of all tariffs on manufactures of 50 per cent; (3) the construction of a large airport near Blimpsby or else, using the same money, the construction of two smaller airports, one near Fogbury and the other near Smiggleton-by-the-Sea.

In each of these three examples two alternatives only are offered, each alternative being an economic situation. It often happens, as in example 2, that one of the alternative economic situations is no more than continuing with the *status quo*. In such cases, as you may know, the government is likely to call upon economists to undertake a cost–benefit analysis, a technique that draws its inspiration from, and may properly be regarded as an application of, the concepts and propositions of welfare economics.

In some cases, however, there may be three or more alternatives. And I would not have made so obvious a remark were it not for the need to draw your attention in passing to questions of consistency and of 'transitivity'. This is best done by considering any *three* alternative economic situations which we designate as I, II and III. These three alternative situations can, however, be reduced to two *new* alternative situations, as in example 3 above, by identifying economic situation I as the situation currently in existence. Situation II may then be taken to differ from the existing situation I in offering the community an additional 10,000 tons of beef each year along with an annual reduction of 100,000 tons of wheat, whereas economic situation III differs from the existing situation I by offering the community instead an additional 100,000 tons of wheat each year along with an annual reduction of 10,000 tons of beef. If by some given criterion situation II is ranked above I, we should be rather put out to discover that in some mysterious way the same criterion could be made to rank I above II. In fact economists once did write as if something just like this was the case, as a result of which welfare economics was thought to be an elusive and mysterious subject. The explanation of this seeming paradox is, however, as already hinted earlier, quite straightforward. There is really no inconsistency after all, as will be made plain in Part Four.

'Transitivity' is no more than an extension of consistency to three or more alternatives. If by a given criterion we rank economic situation III above II (and by the same criterion we *cannot* consistently also rank II above III), and rank II above I (and, once more, by the same criterion we *cannot* consistently rank I above II), we produce the ranking III, II, I – III preferred to II preferred to I. Yet by the same criterion we have adopted it may turn out, none the less, that alternative I is preferred to III. We seem to be going in circles.

In economics it is common to start with the supposition that each individual is consistent and transitive in his rankings, at least over some period during which his tastes remain unchanged. For each person then intransitivity or inconsistency is ruled out *by assumption*. But when we apply a chosen criterion to a community of individuals (each one of which is, as stated, assumed to be consistent and transitive in his own ranking, or ordering, of all conceivable alternatives) we cannot take it for granted that the resultant rankings for the community will always be consistent and transitive also. We are obliged to examine our chosen criterion carefully to discover whether it can be made to yield apparently inconsistent or intransitive rankings.[1] Unless we can show that the seeming inconsistency and/or intransitivity is not real after all, but only illusory, we shall have to find ways of guarding against such defects if we are not to discard the criterion in question as being unreliable.

Having pointed out in Chapter 1 that welfare economics as commonly understood encompasses considerations both of resource allocation and distributional justice, and also that by far the greater part of the subject addresses itself to resource allocation, we restrict ourselves in what follows to the rationale of the standard norms of resource allocation. Thus we are to discuss a justification for the criterion which ranks alternative economic situations *without* reference to distributional merit. I know from experience that some students get restive when I make this point explicit. They are prone to conclude that I am not much interested in questions of distributional justice or that I am effectively relegating them to an inferior role in the economic theory of social welfare.

Let me assure you that this is not true. I can readily conceive of economic conditions under which distributional considerations are paramount and, for good measure, of economic conditions under which the question of justice, *other* than distributional justice, is far more important than that of resource allocation. A cursory glance through Part Five should be enough to persuade you that in this introductory volume to political economy I have no intention of neglecting issues bearing on distribution, equity and many other factors associated with what is truly but tiresomely called the quality of life.

Above all, bear in mind one thing. You will not be able to hold your own in argument with the economists until you understand their language and the ideas behind their ways of looking at the world. Since their ways of looking at the world are strongly influenced by norms of resource allocation, it is a matter of prudence that you exercise patience for the time being and open yourself to the reception of their ideas – or, rather, to my exposition of them.

We might as well plunge in at the deep end since, where the rationale of allocative criteria is concerned, the deep end is not that deep after all. Its depth may be gauged by the general statement that in all allocative techniques used by economists the effective criterion turns on nothing more than the magnitude of the money value of the change in question. Put this way the criterion we are about to describe and justify seems to smack merely of good business. Maybe, but the criterion of the economist is more encompassing: whatever the change in economic situations we are contemplating, it is the money value of *everybody's* welfare which has to be aggregated – not merely that of the owners of the businesses or industries affected, nor only, in addition, those of their customers or their employees. What is more, the sanction behind the economic criterion is different from the profit criterion of a private enterprise.

The exposition that follows is restricted to an economic context described by economists as 'comparative statics' – a comparison between one possible equilibrium situation with that of another or with other possible equilibrium situations. (What is meant by an equilibrium is taken up in Chapter 6. For the present you may think about it as a state in which all price and quantity adjustments have been made, so that the particular set of prices and quantities that prevail during this state can be taken as the economic characteristics of the equilibrium situation being compared.)

Let us then begin with an existing equilibrium situation I, but with the option of reorganizing the economy in some particulars so as to reach a new equilibrium II. The change contemplated may be small (say, an additional yard of cloth is to be produced in situation II along with a reduction of some other thing) or it may be large (say, a bridge is to be built and other designated goods reduced, or the use of aerosols is to be banned and the production of other goods increased). In general, any such change affects the welfare of one or more or all persons in the community, and affects each one for better or for worse. Manifestly such a change has distributional effects. Yet quite irrespective of the pattern of the distributional change in the community's welfare, the economist vaunts a criterion by which he can pronounce on the economic efficiency alone of the movement from I to II.

At first blush, this criterion looks like the very soul of simplicity. It is supposed that the change in the welfare experienced by each person in the community – which community is often taken to be coterminous with the national state – can be reduced by him to a money equivalent which we designate as v. For example, if the change from economic situation I to economic situation II makes person A better off to such an extent that he is willing, at most, to pay $20 for it, his particular v is equal to $20. If this same change from I to II makes another person B worse off, but a sum of $15 will just be enough to reconcile him to the change, the value of his loss is reckoned as $15. A third person C can be wholly indifferent to the change, his v, therefore, being equal to zero. And so we could go on assessing the vs of every person in the community.

However, let there be but three persons in the community, A, B and C, as above. The algebraic sum of their individual vs – using a plus sign for a gain in welfare and a minus sign for a loss – would be +$20, −$15, and $0, respectively, or an algebraic total of +$5. This algebraic total of the individual vs, equal here to +$5, can be represented by a capital V and interpreted as the 'net social benefit' accruing to this three-person society of the change from I to II.

Thus, if this V is positive, as it is in the above example, the economist affirms that situation II is economically *more efficient* than situation I. In the absence of any other considerations he would prescribe a movement from I to II. If, in contrast, this V were negative – say it were equal to −$10 instead of the +$5 above – the movement from I to II would be regarded as one inflicting a 'net social loss' on the community equal to $10. Such a movement from I to II would not then be prescribed by the economist.

In essence, this algebraic total V is the allocative measure used by economists in ranking two or more alternative economic situations. And the art consists in discovering ways of capturing the data comprised in V by direct and indirect methods.

The comparison of the alternative situations I and II by this V criterion might be seen as no more than one made in response to a specific demand of the political decision-making process. Yet the fact is that economists attach to it more significance than that. For if a project confidently calculated by economists to confer a large positive V on the community were none the less rejected by the legislature, they would feel justified in asserting that, notwithstanding political opinion on the matter, the project in question would indeed confer a net social benefit. Put otherwise, if a situation II were judged by economists to be valued in the aggregate by the community higher than a situation I, they would affirm II to be economically the more efficient of the two situations even though there were a unanimous vote in favour of I.

What emerges incidentally from the above paragraphs may be

expressed by the statement that the 'objective' data for the economist are the subjective valuations of the individuals comprising society.

So much for the operative economic criterion. We have now to consider the sanctions on which it rests. Since the sanctions for the normative economist's criterion depend ultimately on an ethical consensus, it follows that it is *not* the fact itself of an *actual* increase in society's welfare – allowing, for argument's sake, that it could be satisfactorily defined, detected and measured – that is to underwrite the criterion. Rather it is society's fundamental beliefs about what *ought* to count as a contribution to society's welfare. It follows that the normative economist should not seek to determine in some 'objective' way whether, or by how much, the actual welfare of society has changed or may be changed. Inasmuch as he is to prescribe allocative changes for a particular society, his criterion must be such as to affirm a change for an increase in social welfare when, and only when, this society *in its ethical capacity* also regards the change as one conferring an increase in its welfare.

Now the basic ethical premises that have to be ascribed to a society for which the algebraic magnitude of V qualifies as the measuring rod of social welfare are not difficult to discover. Yet you are always to bear in mind that there can also be a number of fundamental beliefs about what is right and proper, or wrong and improper, which may occasionally conflict with and, indeed, override these basic ethical premises, in which cases they qualify the applicability of the economist's criterion or nullify it. Instances of possible conflict between the operative economic criterion, itself derivable from an ethical consensus, and other ethical imperatives of society are discussed in Chapter 17.

4 The rationale of the economist's efficiency criterion

The first ethical premise to which society must subscribe if the economist's use of V as a ranking device is to be upheld is that the welfare of each person in society is to count, and nothing more is to count. The phrase 'nothing more is to count' is appended to the sentence in order to obviate any 'transcendental' or 'holistic' interpretation of society's welfare. In other words, no abstraction such as the 'general good' and no such entity as the 'state' is to be considered in addition to the welfare of the individuals comprising society. This provision accords with the philosophic position sometimes referred to as methodological individualism, which is associated historically with the rise of liberalism.

The second ethical premise on which the economist's use of V has to rest is one requiring that the valuation of the change in each individual's welfare be that placed on it by the individual himself. If, for example, the economic change in question confers on him a net benefit that he values at \$15, society is also to reckon the benefit *to him* from the change as worth \$15, no more and no less.

This second premise is likely to commend itself to a society that believes, as a matter of right, that each person should be treated as if he knows better than others what a thing is worth to him. Even though it is widely acknowledged that, in fact, each adult in the community does not by any means always know what is best for him, especially when the choices facing him are complex, and that indeed others may often know better than he, a libertarian society would still subscribe to this premise.

Moreover, if the application of this premise is not to be frequently suspended, it is essential that no exemption be made in consequence of people's imperfect state of knowledge. Whatever the information in a person's possession at the moment of choice, it is to be deemed sufficient to warrant society's accepting his own valuation of the net benefit or loss as better representing its worth to him than any valuation determined by others.

The third and final premise to which society has to subscribe if this V is to be used as a ranking device may seem, at first glance, difficult to accept. Bearing in mind that all significant economic changes affect a large number of people in society, a possible criterion that would attract widespread support would be that of an actual 'Pareto improvement', named, not surprisingly, after the scholar Vilfredo Pareto (1848–1923), an Italian economist and sociologist. This Pareto improvement is defined as a change from which no member of society becomes worse off and at least one becomes better off. This agreeable criterion, as defined, is somewhat long-winded; we shall henceforth speak of a Pareto improvement as a change that makes 'everyone' better off (using the inverted commas to remind us that it is a shorthand for the more precise definition above).

But changes that meet the criterion of an actual Pareto improvement are not likely to be common in the world we live in. If the economist were to adopt this criterion, few economic changes would qualify for approval. Bearing in mind that nearly all economic changes that are the subject of public discussion are expected to raise the welfare level of some persons and lower it for others, the economist is impelled to rationalize his use of V as a criterion of economic efficiency if he is not to remain mute most of the time.

Now the use of V as a criterion may be interpreted as implying the acceptance *not* of an actual Pareto improvement but of a *potential* Pareto improvement. To understand this term consider the example in the preceding chapter in which the change contemplated produces a net social benefit of $5. It is manifest that from person A's gain of $20, a transfer of, say $17 to person B would leave them both better off. Assuming that such transfers are quite costless, person A is still left with a net gain of $3 whereas person B, who loses $15 from the change, is left with a net gain of $2 once he receives the $17 from A. Both A and B are thereby made better off by this change while person C remains unaffected. Therefore if the change in question, yielding a net benefit of $5, is actually undertaken, it will meet the *potential* Pareto improvement. For although the change does not *actually* make 'everyone' better off, a costless transfer of money from gainer A to loser B *could* indeed make both A and B better off, while person C's welfare remains unchanged.

Expressed more generally, an economic change that yields a

positive V, and is interpreted therefore as a positive net social benefit, is one that meets a *potential* Pareto improvement: gainers from the movement could so compensate losers as to make 'everyone' in the community better off.

And there you have it. The economist, then, who ranks an economic situation II above I because the V corresponding to the change from I to II is positive has to justify his judgement by affirming that the change from I to II is one that meets the potential Pareto improvement criterion – or, more briefly, the Pareto criterion.[1] Alternatively, he may assert that II is 'economically more efficient' than I, or else that the situation II produces a 'higher real income' than I.

The question that now presents itself is whether there is consensus on the Pareto criterion.

On first reflection you may reasonably doubt whether the Pareto criterion, as just described, is one that is likely to attract widespread support. We may suppose it easy enough to secure general agreement that an economic change that actually does make 'everyone' better off is a desirable change. It is much less certain that there would be a general agreement in favour of an economic change which, although it would make a number of people worse off, would be able to make 'everyone' better off only if a redistribution from the gainers to the losers were a costless operation; as it never is costless, the desirable redistribution is unlikely to accompany the change.

None the less, an economic change that meets a Pareto criterion (a *potential* Pareto improvement, remember!) might well qualify for society's seal of approval by virtue of any one or all of the following beliefs about the working of the economy:

(a) that economic changes which meet a Pareto criterion are not, in fact, likely to have significant 'regressive' distributional effects – that is to say, they are not likely to make the distribution of real income less equal, or more unequal, than it is;
(b) that the existing tax structure provides adequate safeguards against the occurrence of regressive distributional effects;
(c) that over time a succession of economic changes introduced by reference to the Pareto criterion is, in any case, unlikely to result in regressive distributional effects of any importance;
(d) that a succession of economic changes which meets the

> Pareto criterion has a better chance of raising society's standard of living over time than a succession of changes sanctioned by any other criterion.

At all events, if we do decide to adopt this Pareto criterion in ranking alternatives in order to explore the implications further, then the term 'economic efficiency' has a clear meaning. What is more, it has a meaning that is entirely independent of political objectives and political outcomes. Thus, if a correct calculation of all the welfare effects involved reveals that the alternative situation II has a higher aggregate valuation than does the existing situation I so that the movement from I to II yields a positive V, then situation II is held to be economically more efficient that I – even if it turns out that voters on balance, or even unanimously, prefer situation I to II.

Some simplifications have been used in the above exposition for pedagogic reasons. It is a matter of prudence that I point them out.

First, as expounded above, the Pareto criterion appears to be unambiguous. But this is because I have deliberately omitted two considerations each of which, by itself, can cause ambiguity. The first consideration has, until recently, been a source of endless debate among economists. It is not hard to show that beginning with a situation I, a movement to II meets a Pareto criterion and that, when II is adopted, a movement from II to I also meets that same Pareto criterion.

Since this seeming inconsistency or paradox is central to the long debate in the literature on welfare economics,[2] we shall examine it closely in Part Four. Until then you may let your mind vaguely anticipate the explanation by recognizing that the magnitude of the V in question depends also upon the prices of the two different collections of goods that are associated respectively with the two economic situations I and II. And, as it happens, the prices which come with the I collection of goods will generally be different from the prices which come with the II collection. It may transpire then that at the set of prices associated with the I collection of goods, collection II is valued higher than collection I, while the set of prices associated with the II collection of goods, collection I is valued higher than collection II.

The second consideration is comparable in effect: that is, successive applications of the Pareto criterion can again lead to ambiguity, but not for the same reason. It was assumed above that whatever the prices prevailing in the two situations under comparison, they are prices common to all the individuals. Thus if the market price for good x happens to be $2, we are able to say that it is worth (at least) $2 to each person who buys some of good x. If we now remove this assumption that the price of each good is the same for all individuals and assume, instead, that there is no market price whatever for the good in question, the context turns out to be one in which the Pareto criterion can again prove to be ambiguous – but for quite a different reason. For in this new context, each person has to place a value himself on some aspect of the change in question as it affects his own level of welfare. But the truthful answer he gives depends upon how the question is formulated. If the change is favourable to him we may discover that the most he will pay for it is $110. It does not surprise the economist, however, if the same person cannot be bribed to forgo the change for a sum smaller than $150. If this sort of response does not surprise you either, you will readily perceive the possibilities of contradictory rankings of two situations according to the questions we put to the two groups of people – gainers and losers – in contemplating the movement from one situation to the other. However, if this sort of response does not seem plausible to you, I bid you be patient until we come to Part Three where I undertake to demonstrate its plausibility.

There is, finally, an observation I had better make now lest some of the more sophisticated economics students unwarrantably conclude that I have omitted an important criticism of the Pareto criterion and that I have failed to mention an alternative approach. This alternative approach stems from the neoclassic school[3] which traces its origins to the so-called marginal revolution of the 1870s. Since I will have something to say about this way of interpreting the economic universe in the chapter on distribution, I shall not broach it here. However, I will mention that the neoclassic approach comprehends a common distributional criticism of the Pareto criterion, to the effect that the use of V alone as a ranking device implies that an additional dollar to the rich affords as much satisfaction as an additional dollar to the poor, which is contrary to common sense.

But this criticism itself is unacceptable. For it entails an *interpretation* of the rationale of V as a ranking device which is different from the rationale argued above (pages 35–6). I myself do *not* believe that an additional dollar to the rich affords as much utility as an additional dollar to the poor. And if such a belief were necessary to the acceptance of V as a ranking device, I and other economists would promptly repudiate it.

The four beliefs about the working of the economy, however, offer a rationalization of quite a different sort, and one more readily acceptable. At any rate we shall provisionally continue to accept the interpretation of V as one implying 'hypothetical compensation' – that is, we shall continue to rank according to the algebraic magnitude of V on the Pareto criterion as defined and on the rationalization mentioned – if only to explore the resulting notion of economic efficiency more closely.

5 Things to come: a preview

On the principle of surveying the territory before making the journey, let me indicate briefly the main features of the landscape and the route we shall be taking.

With respect to the main features of the landscape, a twofold division lends itself admirably to splitting the subject into four distinct though related areas of investigation. The first division of the subject is that which separates its treatment into a 'general' economic context on the one hand, and a 'partial' economic context on the other. In this connection, the term 'general' is used to suggest a concern with the economy as a whole. We do not – indeed, we cannot – describe in detail the working of the actual economy of a country. What we do is to exercise our minds on a drastically simplified model of the economy, one which may have no more than two kinds of goods, two prices and two persons. Yet even so simplified a model reveals important relationships which can be generalized to many goods, prices and persons.

The term 'partial', in contrast to 'general', correctly suggests that only a part, usually a very small part of the economy is to engage our attention. So small is this segment of the economy that the particular changes contemplated are supposed to take effect wholly within that segment and to have negligible repercussions on the remainder of the economy. In sum, we virtually ignore the remainder of the economy when we focus on a small segment of it, as we do in 'partial economic analysis'.

The second useful division in a study of normative economics is that between a 'best' position on the one hand, and an improved or better position on the other. A best position is sometimes referred to as an 'ideal' or, more commonly today, as an 'optimal' position, one that we shall define presently. As for a better position which involves the ranking or comparison of alternative positions, the higher or (in the case of three or more situations) highest ranking alternative may not, in fact, be a best or optimal position.

This two-way division – general versus partial on the one hand, best and comparative on the other – results in four possible paired combinations, each pair, as it happens, corresponding to a distinct area of study. The four areas are:

1 general and optimum;
2 general and comparative;
3 partial and optimum;
4 partial and comparative.

The chapters of Part Two are devoted to outlining the concepts used and the conclusions reached within the area of partial economics. Chapter 7 discusses the characteristics of partial economic analysis, its limitations and its more familiar uses. Chapter 8 introduces the most crucial of concepts among the selection used by normative economics, namely those of 'social value' and of 'opportunity cost'. In Chapters 9 and 10 the more popular instances of (3) and (4) above are given extended treatment. Thus Chapter 9 addresses itself to what is known in economic parlance as 'consumer surplus', while Chapter 10 on 'economic rent' essays a symmetrical treatment of another aspect of the same economic phenomenon, a measure of the change in welfare resulting from a change in price or availability.

Making use of the twin concepts of consumer surplus and rent, we go on in Chapter 11 to offer a simplified and provisional vindication of the allocative merit of a competitive market, following which we assess the applicability of the marginal cost-pricing rule. The final chapter on 'Second Best' in economics is inserted at this stage as a sort of caveat to be borne in mind when using partial economic analysis.

Part Three, which discusses what economists call 'external effects' or 'spillover effects' (or just 'spillovers'), is divided into four chapters. Post-war concern with environmental pollution, along with other developments, has produced a burgeoning literature which has made a significant contribution to society's understanding of the issues and has gone some way, therefore, to justify the development of normative economics.

Finally the last chapter in Part Three is, in effect, a symmetric extension of the four chapters on externalities. For while the external effects can meaningfully be described as 'public bads', this last chapter deals with 'public goods' – bearing in mind, however, that the public good in question is often introduced to overcome the public bads that result from technical innovation and the spread of industry. It will become clear that many of the known difficulties in the literature on so-called public goods can be traced to semantic confusion and faulty definition.

We turn in Part Four to resource allocation within a general context, so coming to grips with both categories (3) and (4) above. After a preliminary chapter on the uses of a general economic context, the characteristics of an overall optimal position for the economy are described in Chapter 20. The concept of an efficient distribution of any given collection of goods in Chapter 21, useful in itself, is also a prerequisite to the understanding of the apparent paradox which can be generated by successive applications of the Pareto criterion, a subject taken up in Chapter 22. Pushing the argument further in Chapter 23 may lead to the cynical conclusion that the notion of Pareto optimality (or an ideal allocation) is fatally flawed, a conclusion that is reinforced by noting in Chapter 24 the way in which the apparent paradox is resolved.

Part Five, on the sources of economic failure in a technological age, marks the point where the book's more formal exposition of the subject, constrained as it is by the accepted economic framework, perforce gives way to informal reflection. Working within the boundaries of his discipline confines and distorts the light the economist can shed on real social problems. When we come to the larger questions of social welfare, this light will be found to be either illuminating the wrong areas too powerfully or illuminating the right areas too faintly.

Thus a genuine concern with the welfare of modern society and with the contribution to its understanding that he may make will sorely tempt the thoughtful economist to move from the comparative safety of the demarcated area of his subject into new and uncharted territory. But speculative though such an excursion must be, the range of factors connected with social welfare are too important to neglect, even in an introductory volume. In the event, a personal opinion which raises issues, as well as hackles, has more to be said for it than discreet silence.

The five chapters in this final part are, then, admittedly polemical from a professional perspective, but if they act to dispel complacency among students of economics about the virtues of a competitive market economy, or about the power of economics to resolve the many social problems created by technological innovation, they will have served a useful purpose.

6 The basic economic assumptions

In all the chapters that follow on the economics of allocation you will do well to bear in mind the limitations of the assumptions, or suppositions, to be mentioned below. All of them are commonly although not invariably used in economic textbooks. Some are always used, some occasionally, some provisionally, while others are chosen from a number of alternatives specifically to yield implications illustrating a particular case. In addition there are assumptions, the appropriateness of which are in continuing controversy, though we shall not bother ourselves about them here.

From time to time, I shall want to remind you of a particular supposition and to emphasize its importance, perhaps by showing what happens when we adopt instead some other supposition. But since it is entirely possible that at some later stage in the exposition you will feel a bit uncertain of the assumptions appropriate to the argument, it is useful to have them all – or, rather, all the common ones – in this chapter for ready reference.

Behavioural assumptions

The first set of assumptions are about the psychology or behaviour of the individual 'economic man'. Few economists, I assure you, believe that all of the assumed psychological or behavioural characteristics to be mentioned are generally true of ordinary men and women. Our excuse for adopting them is the belief that when built into economic theories, results can be deduced that correspond in some degree with features of the real world. Put differently, the economist believes he can predict economic events, or the outcome of economic forms of interaction, better by using these particular assumptions in his theories than by using others which may, in fact, look more plausible. The list of behavioural assumptions includes insatiability, rationality, unchanged tastes and sufficient knowledge.

Insatiability

This must *not* be taken to mean that there is no limit to the amount of one or more particular goods a person can absorb within a period of time. A person may dote on fresh strawberries but the amount of them he can eat in a day or a week is biologically limited. And before that limit is reached you would certainly have to bribe him to continue stuffing himself with strawberries.

Insatiability – more formally referred to as the postulate of non-satiation – carries a more credible interpretation: that the individual will always prefer more goods in general to fewer, and larger amounts to smaller. In the formal arguments it is axiomatic that our economic man will prefer a larger batch of goods to a smaller batch. This comes almost to the same thing as saying that, given the prices of all goods, he will prefer to have a larger money income than a smaller. (I say 'almost' because in the simpler normative models, movement to a batch that has more of *every* good is correctly taken to confer on him an unambiguous increase of welfare – even though he might be yet better off if, at the given prices, he were allowed to choose a batch with *less* of one or of several of the goods in question.)

Our economic man is not, of course, obliged to consume all that he buys within a given time span. He can use his money to buy houses, land, securities, government bonds, and to give sums to charity or preservation societies. But however he uses his money, the economist assumes that he always prefers to have more of it than less.

So interpreted, you will agree that this first assumption, at least, is far from being implausible. If anything, it is a reasonably accurate description of people's attitudes in today's secular and affluent societies. For that reason you are unlikely to forget it.

Rationality

In economics this is generally taken to mean that the individual is consistent and transitive in his choices or preferences. Thus, if person A prefers the II batch of goods to the I batch, he does not at the same time prefer the I batch to the II. And if he prefers batch III to II to I, then he necessarily prefers III to I.

Unchanged tastes

This assumption is linked to the preceding one. For if it appears that, over time, the individual makes an inconsistent or intransitive choice, it may be explained as arising simply from a change in his tastes.

This assumption of unchanged tastes is, however, vital to normative economics. For so long as each person orders his preferences in exactly the same way, the economist hopes to prescribe means of increasing social welfare by reference to the economic criterion adopted. If, instead, tastes are known to have changed, the economist's prescriptions, based as they are upon a given pattern of preferences, are at least suspect. He can do no more than start all over again, and hope to prescribe within the context of the new pattern of preferences. Put differently, the economist cannot satisfactorily compare the welfare of the same person at two different points of time unless his tastes remain unchanged over that period of time. (It may be just worth remarking that clear evidence of a change in tastes is the observation that *with unchanged income and prices* the individual now chooses to buy a different batch of goods to that previously bought.)

It is reasonable to believe that this assumption of unchanged tastes is less realistic in an affluent society, in which the continuing introduction of new goods and the resources of commercial advertising act to change people's tastes in numberless ways over relatively short periods of time, than it is in more primitive or traditional societies where most of the goods are staple products and respect for custom and propriety acts to stabilize choice.

Sufficient knowledge

Some textbooks are careless enough to specify an assumption of 'perfect knowledge', influenced possibly by the term 'perfect competition' or 'perfect mobility'. These latter terms are, however, precisely defined in contradistinction to 'perfect knowledge'.

Although the term 'sufficient knowledge' is, perhaps, somewhat equivocal, it serves to remind us of the point made in Chapter 3. namely that no person's choices or valuations be disregarded on the grounds that he does *not* have sufficient knowledge of the market. Privately, you and I might agree that when it comes to choosing a winter coat Joe Bloggs hasn't got a clue. But as normative economists we have to go along with the assumption that Joe Bloggs's choice of a winter coat gives him more satisfaction than any other coat of that price which you, I or anyone else would prescribe for him. If this were not so, then we should have to suppose that society would also be ready to accept as an improvement in the social welfare the occasional overriding of some people's choices of market goods by reference to the opinions of others.

In general, then, as stated earlier, the normative economist believes that he is only reflecting fundamental beliefs in the Western democracies when he states that each person is to be treated as if that person himself knows his own wants better than others know them.

Technical assumptions

The second set of assumptions are of a technical nature and are more likely to be used provisionally as simplifications which can later be removed or modified. Five will suffice for our purposes.

Constant returns to scale in production

This means that in the production of any good, say cloth x, a doubling of all the market inputs results in a doubling of the output of cloth – given time for full adjustment. We shall use as a synonym for input the more formal term 'factor of production', or more briefly 'factor', which is sometimes defined as the services of a particular resource. Thus, using the broadest classification, we could denominate manpower, capital and land as the resources of an economy. The services of each of these – respectively labour services, the services of capital and the services of land – would be the factors of production corresponding to these three resources.

The implication of constant returns to scale is that if the market prices of the factors of production – the services of labour, capital and land – remain unchanged over the period of time that concerns us, the average production cost of cloth (when fully adjusted) would also remain unchanged irrespective of the amount produced.

It is common enough in the literature, when talking of factors, or factors of production or inputs, to omit the words *services of*, and talk of labour, capital and land, it being understood in the context that the services of these resources are implied.

Different factor proportions for different goods

Each of the goods produced in the economy is supposed to employ factors in different proportions. This assumption looks pretty far-fetched if we think of the modern economy which produces scores of thousands of different items. It looks a lot more reasonable, however, if we group these many items into a number of broad categories. And when we construct really simplified models of the economy – the simplest being that of a two-good economy – it is realistic and revealing to make this assumption.

If, for example, in this simplest of imaginary economies the two goods are labelled grain and manufactures, each good being produced with the two factors, land and labour only, then the amount of grain that costs $1 to produce uses, we shall suppose, 60 cents' worth of land and 40 cents' worth of labour at current market prices. On the other hand, the amount of manufactures that cost $1 to produce uses, say, 20 cents' worth of land and 80 cents' worth of labour at current market prices. The economist, given this data, says that the production of grain is 'land-intensive' compared with the production of manufactures since, at the given factor prices, a larger proportion of land is used in grain production than in the production of manufactures. By the same logic, we should say that the production of manufactures is 'labour-intensive' as compared with the production of grain.

When there are three or more goods, they can be ranked either in order of labour-intensivity or in order of land-intensivity; otherwise, we can compare the factor-intensivity of one good with the average factor-intensivity of all goods. (Three or more factors require a somewhat more elaborate scheme, but do not fundamentally affect the broad conclusions reached with two factors of production.)

Equally efficient factors

This assumption, that a member or unit of one factor class, say labour, is just as efficient as any other, quite obviously does not accord with the facts. One coal-face miner does not generally produce as much coal in an hour as another working under identical conditions – and so it is in all but the most highly automated tasks. Yet it is believed convenient to use this simplification since quite often allowances for differences in efficiency involve fairly straightforward adjustments to our main conclusions.

Fixed amounts of factors in the economy

Again, this is sometimes a useful simplification. But it is rather restrictive for a normative economics, bearing in mind that by factors we mean the inputs or services of resources. Thus, if there are 100 men and no more available for work in an island economy along, say, with a big machine, the situation is that of fixity of *resources*; not of factors. The availability of the factors themselves – the services of the resources – can be varied a great deal up to some limiting point. In the limiting case, the 100 men may not choose to work at all. We may suppose they survive comfortably on the fruits and berries gathered by their wives and children. But they may work all together for 3000 hours or for 5000, or for even longer, each week. Thus, the assumption of fixed amounts of factors, applied to the manpower available, would require that these 100 men offer to work exactly the same number of hours per week for the period of time under consideration. What is more, in such cases, there is often an implicit assumption that they are all equally efficient also, so that the contribution per worker per week is the same for all workers.

This restrictive assumption is, however, often relaxed, especially within a partial context in normative economics, in order to allow for variations in the amount of labour offered in response to changes in the real wage and, in particular, to define the conditions for optimality whenever the worker has complete choice of the amount of labour he will offer at the going wage. In fact, a relation between the amount of labour offered by the individual worker and the market wage is explicitly postulated in Chapter 10 on economic rent.

A given state of technology

This assumption that the technology does not change over a period under scrutiny is optional, depending as it does on the particular inquiry we have in mind. In welfare economics, for example, a change in technology, usually to a more productive technology, is a change the economist has frequently to examine. It takes the form, among other things, of a fall in the unit cost of production of one or more goods, yielding a social benefit that the economist seeks to measure. For the problems that arise in welfare economics, or allocation economics, this assumption of given technology is best related to the point of time from which we take our bearings and our departure. Needless to say, in a technological society technology is the one thing we all expect will change over time; some of us, in our innocence, continue to suppose that this change is (on balance) socially beneficial.

Institutional assumptions

Finally, there are two institutional assumptions of a simple nature to consider.

Constant population

Although manifestly untrue, for a short period of time this assumption will not seriously mislead us. Moreover, adjustments can easily be made for small changes in population which occur over a short number of years, at least under certain conditions. For a period that spans a number of generations, however, problems arise quite apart from the virtual certainty of changes in tastes that take place in today's affluent societies.[1]

Transactions costs are negligible

The term 'transactions costs' can be extended to cover all costs connected with negotiations between the interested parties, all capital and administrative costs involved in controlling or regulating an industry, the costs of calculating and changing taxes, subsidies, grants, etc., the costs of protecting private property, enforcing contracts and much else including, sometimes, the apprehensiveness associated with changes of organization and the law, and the pangs of vexation arising from the extension of bungling bureaucracies. These sorts of costs are characterized by their not taking form as market prices of the goods or bads which form part of our model but which are none the less real in the sense that they do use up economic inputs.

It goes without saying that this assumption is wholly false. But is is important to adopt it provisionally, and for a great part of the exposition, simply as a pedagogic device. Such transactions costs are usually difficult to measure. They do not lend themelves to theoretical elegance. But when it comes to choice of economic organization, especially where the issue is that of correcting outputs or inputs for spillover effects, transactions costs are of essential importance.

Two things remain to be said. First, that the three behavioural assumptions mentioned have a strategic importance, especially in normative economics, that does not extend to the technical and institutional assumptions. As stated, the latter are less rigid, and more optional and provisional.

Second, in the interests of ease of exposition and of getting to the heart of the matter as quickly as possible, I remind the reader that I shall continue to leave out certain refinements and qualifications that would otherwise blur the outlines of the argument. However, I do mention the more important of these refinements and qualifications every so often at the end of a chapter, and sometimes I will illustrate briefly the difference they make to the propositions and conclusions reached.

At the end of each of the next three parts of the book, moreover, there will be references to additional reading matter (much of it, I confess, to be found in textbooks and papers of mine) for the more specialized student and for those who feel an urge to follow some particular strand of investigation.

Part Two

Allocation within a partial economic context

7 Uses and limitations of a partial economic context

When an economist examines a problem within a partial economic context, he focuses his attention on one or more segments or sectors of the economy. The sector in question may be an industry broadly defined; it may be a couple of interacting firms; or it may be a particular investment project being mooted by the government. The essential feature of partial economic analysis is that, being directed towards a very small part of the total economy, it considers it reasonable to ignore the repercussions on the remainder of the economy of the particular adjustments being contemplated in the relatively small segment or sector of the economy. To be more explicit, these repercussions are imagined to spread themselves so thinly over the rest of the economy that for all practical purposes they can be ignored.

It is, of course, always possible that the repercussions from the intervention in a small segment of the economy do not spread themselves evenly over the economy. Some may fall rather heavily on one or other segments. And if so, then it is essential to take these effects into account in the partial economic analysis.

In *positive* economic analysis within partial economics, the economist pays most attention to changes in prices and quantities that result from some force 'outside' the economic system. Such an outside force is referred to in the jargon as an 'exogenous' change. Examples would be a spontaneous change in the conditions of demand, a change in technology, the introduction or removal of a tax or a rationing scheme by the government, or some public spending or investment. In *normative* economics also attention is paid to the movements in prices and quantities that result from some exogenous change. But in order to assess the welfare significance of such a change or to measure the net social benefit arising therefrom, the normative economist requires additional data.

Within a partial economic context, problems can be treated within either a 'comparative statics' framework or a 'dynamic' framework, the difference between these two methods of analysis lying in their use of time. Let us consider them in turn.

Comparative statics

Comparative statics is restricted to a comparison of two (or more) alternative economic situations, each situation corresponding to the same segment of the economy at two (or more) different points of time. Alternatively, two (or more) differently located segments of the economy may be compared at a given point in time.

Restricting ourselves to the former sense of comparative statics, the comparison of two situations can be likened to two snapshots of that particular segment of the economy taken at two different points of time, separated by an interval of months or years, or else – and this is more common – by some hypothetical time interval necessary to make the transition from an initial equilibrium to a new equilibrium, one corresponding to some change in the conditions of demand and/or supply.

The features in the snapshots that matter to the economist are, as mentioned, prices and quantities. The snapshot reveals the price, or prices, prevailing at that moment of time along with the amount or amounts of goods being produced. The amounts in question are measured as *flows* – so many units bought or sold per week or year. Thus, much as a glance at the speedometer of an automobile tells you that at that particular instant it is travelling at, say, 50 miles per hour, so also does a glance at the features of one of the economic situations in a model of comparative statics tell you that at the given point in time 10,000 yards of cloth per week are being produced. If you were simply tracing events in this particular segment of the economy over chronological time you could measure the variations in the number of yards of cloth per week at the end of each day, each week, each month or each year.

However, in comparative statics you are not concerned much with tracing the movement of prices and quantities over chronological time. You are generally comparing two alternative *equilibrium* situations, and paying little heed to the actual time it might take to move from one equilibrium to the other. But let us clarify the term 'equilibrium'.

In physics an equilibrium position is determined by a constellation of forces. Once attained, the equilibrium position is one from which, in the absence of a change in designated forces, there is no tendency to depart. If the equilibrium, moreover, is a *stable* equilibrium, then a random displacement from the given equilibrium position results in movements that return it to that equilibrium position. The simplest example is a stone suspended by a string from a hook in a beam. The force exerted on the stone is, we suppose, only gravity. The equilibrium position of the stone is one that is vertically beneath the hook. The equilibrium is stable since, if it is disturbed by your finger, it will swing to and fro and in ever smaller movements and – in the absence of further disturbance – return to its original equilibrium position.

In comparative statics, economists tend to concentrate on positions of stable equilibrium (unstable equilibrium being of more interest in certain dynamic problems). The analogy with physics is quite useful. To illustrate, imagine the cloth manufacturing industry (or a specific branch of it) to be in a state of stable equilibrium, in which position it is producing 10 million yards of cloth a year at the price of $2. Since a *condition* for equilibrium is that, at the prevailing price, the amount being bought (or consumed) is equal to the amount being produced by the industry, it follows that 10 million yards are being consumed annually in this equilibrium position.

Moreover, if we are talking about 'long period' equilibrium then, by definition of this term there can be no anticipation of further adjustment in the industry. The sum of payments to the factors employed in this industry – payments to labour, to land, to owners of the capital equipment – are such that there is no incentive for factors to move out of or into the industry. Apart from random movements due, say, to the weather, to occasional breakdown of machinery, or to temporary absence of workers, which causes some variation in outputs from one week to the next, the long period equilibrium is such that 10 million yards of cloth continue to be produced each year and sold at $2 a yard.

Now this long period equilibrium is one that we may wish to compare with another, one brought about as a result of some 'exogenous' change, for example (a) by a rightward shift of the demand schedule so that, say 15 million yards of this cloth are now demanded at the same price of $2. As a result, the new long period equilibrium once attained could be that 13 million yards of cloth are produced and sold each year at the higher price of $2.50 – allowing that, for one reason or another, the unit cost of cloth rises as more is produced. Another exogenous change (b) may be an improvement in technology that lowers unit costs of production, with no change in the demand schedule occurring. This new long period equilibrium when attained may show 12 million yards of cloth per annum produced and consumed at a price of $1.60. A third example of an exogenous change (c) might be the decision of the government to levy a tax of 50 cents a yard on this cloth. The resulting long period equilibrium, which is now conditional upon the maintenance of this tax, could be one in which, say 8 million yards of cloth per annum are produced and consumed at a price (including tax) of $2.20.

Whatever the type of exogenous change, however, it is tacitly understood that some time must pass before it is established. Labour has to be hired or laid off, additional machines have to be installed or old ones sold, the premises enlarged or reduced and so on. This period of adjustment is important for some problems, but in comparative economics the economist pays no heed to chronological time. He is concerned only with comparing the initial equilibrium position with the new one in a number of relevant respects, chiefly (though not exclusively) prices and quantities. And this equilibrium can be a long period equilibrium, as described above, or a 'short period' equilibrium defined as one in which some factor, say, capital equipment, remains unchanged, adjustment being made only through variations in some other factor, say, labour.

The normative economist is not able to say much about the resulting change in welfare from an exogenous change of the (a) type inasmuch as it arises from a change in tastes. He may be able to say that the redistribution of income associated with the change tends to greater equality, or the reverse – although, bearing in mind that in a partial economic context the segment of the economy under scrutiny is a tiny proportion of the total economy, the distributional change cannot be very significant. But inasmuch as the exogenous shift in the demand schedule is a consequence of a spontaneous or induced change in people's tastes, it is not possible to compare, and therefore to rank, the two equilibrium positions.

In contrast, normative economics is able to compare exogenous changes of the (b) and (c) type. Other things being equal, an innovation that reduces the unit cost of cloth manufacture is held to confer a benefit on society. Certainly there is a benefit to consumers of this cloth, one that can in principle be measured (as we shall see in Part Three). More interesting yet is (c), an exogenous change that is the result of a deliberate act of economic policy, since the economist hopes to discover policies that will promote the general welfare. In the excise tax mentioned, the new equilibrium resulting may be ranked as less efficient than the original equilibrium or, in other circumstances, as more efficient. In some cases, the normative economist may measure the welfare change; for example, he may come up with an estimate that the imposition of the excise tax on cloth incurs a net social loss equal to, say, $300,000 per annum. And, if tempted to impress the layman with his expertise, he may talk of a 'deadweight' loss of $300,000 – by which sombre adjective he implies merely that the loss attributable to the excise tax is in fact a *net* loss to the community.

Dynamics

Dynamics takes a number of different forms in economics. One is concerned with the time-path of adjustment – measured in terms of price change or quantity change – between two equilibrium positions. Another form is that of a stylized 'ideal' growth path over time of the economy as a whole, often measured in terms of per capita real income or consumption. The main features of the latter are changes in aggregate saving and investment, and sometimes changes also in technology and population, with auxiliary interest focusing on the broad division of the aggregate product between labour and capital.

Neither of these dynamic forms is of particular interest to normative economics. Much more pertinent for the normative economist is the method of assessing over a chronological period of time the stream of welfare effects which are the result of an act of policy either by economic entities in the private sector or, more commonly, by government departments.

The most familiar of these actions taken by governments, or the so-called government sector or public sector of the economy, is an investment project or a number of investment projects planned to be undertaken simultaneously or successively. For illustrative purposes, however, a single investment project will suffice. Thus, beginning at the time the project is initiated by some outlay of capital, the subsequent passage of time up to an (often arbitrary) terminal date is divided into equal periods, usually years. For each of these years an estimate is made of the value of the aggregate net benefits (or net losses) within a given area, often within the country as a whole. In order to make such an estimate, the economist will require the relevant price and quantity data, an understanding of the key concepts and their limitations, an economic criterion, some skill in evaluating effects that escape the price system and, last but not least, a good deal of audacity.

This appraisal of an investment project, or the ranking of alternative investment projects, is not surprisingly called project appraisal and follows a method of attack known as cost–benefit analysis. This latter term rightly suggests that for each project social costs (or losses) are to be compared with social benefits (or gains). If we were faced with the problem of introducing a single project, say, the building of a dam to provide both hydroelectric power and improved irrigation, our concern, broadly speaking, would be that the resources withdrawn from the rest of the economy in order to build the dam should yield society greater benefit than if, instead, the resources were not withdrawn but left to continue in their current uses.

For this single project, then, the alternative is not to undertake it. Therefore the real cost of actually undertaking it is, clearly, the benefits that would have to be forgone in withdrawing the necessary factors from their existing employment so as to build the dam. This real cost is spoken of as the 'opportunity cost', a term wholly appropriate inasmuch as its true cost to society is not so much the financial outlay itself, but the opportunities for benefits that have to be sacrificed in using this financial outlay to withdraw factors from their current uses. Since this term, opportunity cost, is one of the key concepts – possibly the most important concept – of the economist interested in the allocation of resources, I shall discuss it further in Chapter 8.

The economist using the methods of cost–benefit analysis, the most popular application today of normative economics, will usually want to rank several alternative investment projects or else to choose a number of investment projects subject to some financial limitation. If there are but two projects to consider, I and II, we shall suppose that the calculations made lead the economist to expect the following two streams of net social benefits (+) or net social costs (−) over a seven-year period:

I	−100	+40	+45	−10	+30	+30	+20
II	−100	+20	+30	+30	+40	+40	+40

In the first year, call it year zero or year nought, there is a net cost of $100 million for each project. There may, of course be some social benefits also during this year nought, but the costs exceed them by $100 million. Project I shows a net social benefit over cost of $40 million in year 1, a net social benefit over cost of $45 million in year 2, a net social cost over benefit of $10 million in year 3 (because, say, in that year heavy expenditures on additional plant have to be anticipated) and so on. The figures for project II show that in year 1 and all subsequent years there are net social benefits.

Of the number of issues pertinent to a cost–benefit analysis, three deserve passing mention. First, the comparison of two 'streams of net returns', such as I and II above, proceeds by reducing each of the streams to a single figure at a common point of time, generally at time naught. Thus, by use of a discount rate, each of the above streams may be reduced to a discounted present value. Obviously if II has a higher present value it is ranked above I. The only problem is what the discount rate should be, a topic about which there is still some division of opinion.

Second, there is the problem of uncertainty. The longer the period in question and the further, therefore, into the future we must peer, the less confident our calculations of net benefits or costs are likely to be. How to deal with different sorts of uncertainty is not altogether a settled question in economics. Third, and related to the problem of uncertainty, is the choice of the length of period.[1]

I shall say no more about cost–benefit analysis in this book simply because the core of normative economics can be made accessible to the general reader without reference to some of the auxiliary and controversial issues peculiar to that area of expertise.

Before ending this chapter I will mention some of the allocative problems which are frequently dealt with by the method of comparative statics within a partial economic context, a method addressed in the following chapters. We have already had an example of the imposition of a unit or excise tax on cloth. Similar arguments apply to the introduction of an excise subsidy or the removal of an excise tax or an excise subsidy. Other problems focus on the effects of rationing or price controls. The method may be used cautiously in comparing the economist's stylized version of a monopolist and a competitive industry. (I say 'cautiously' because the organization of other industries in the economy cannot reasonably be disregarded in such comparisons: the comparison has, therefore, to be made under restrictive assumptions.) Since the 1960s, as a result of the public's growing concern with pollution, noise and congestion, there has been a substantial literature on spillover effects, the greater part of which is treated as an exercise in comparative statics within a partial economic context.[2]

8 The key concepts of social value and social opportunity cost

The important question for the economist interested in allocation is not so much the price of the good, nor what a person actually pays for a good, but what its value is. More precisely it is the *social* value of that good, even though it is bought, possessed and used by only one person, that is important. If a person's use or possession of that good has no effect whatever on the welfare of other members of the community then the value to him, reckoned, say, as the most he is willing to pay for it, is also the social value. If, on the other hand, his possession or use of the good does affect the welfare of others, then the value of these effects on others also has to be calculated and (algebraically) added to his personal value in order to determine its social value.

In practice, value is measured in terms of money; dollars in America, pounds sterling in Britain, marks in Germany, and so on. In abstract treatises, it is thought to be an advantage in adopting within a general economic context some particular good as a unit of account – for example, a bushel of wheat or an ounce of gold – and refer to this good as the *numeraire*. One day, perhaps, the singular advantages of using a *numeraire* instead of money will be revealed to me, and I too shall be able to talk blithely of the wheat price of watches, the wheat price of nylon nighties and so on without feeling slightly foolish. Until the dawn of that day of enlightenment, however, I shall continue to talk of the value of a good in terms of money, preferably dollars – it being understood, I hope, that the dollar is deemed to remain stable in value.

Of course, we live in days of high inflation. The value of the dollar (in terms of the goods it can buy) depreciates over time. And the economist gets around the problem in an obvious way; for example, by using the price level of a particular year, say 1970, in comparing alternative situations occurring at different times. If the comparison being made is that of the collection of goods produced by the economy in 1970 and the collection of goods produced by the same economy in 1975, the economist may use the 1970 prices for both the collections being compared. Alternatively, and bearing in mind that the prices of some goods will change relative to others, he can price the two collections at the 1975 prices. Better still he can try using first the 1970 prices on each of the two collections and then the 1975 prices on each of the two collections. He probably hopes that the 1975 collection will be valued higher than the 1970 collection whether he uses the 1970 prices or the 1975 prices. But he would not be astonished, as we shall see, if he obtained different rankings by using the different prices.

This use of the set of the prices of all goods in a particular year (or, for that matter, a particular month) is reasonably satisfactory if we are trying to measure the 'real' change in value of goods for the economy as a whole (or for some specific region) over an interval of time. If, in contrast, we are concerned only with changes in one or two particular prices, as we are in a partial economic context, the real change in this one price, or these two prices, are their movements *relative* to other prices. For example, we might measure the change in one price relative to the average change of all prices. Thus, if the price of leather has risen from $100 a square yard in 1970 to $300 a square yard in 1975, and all other goods prices have risen between 1970 and 1975 by an average of 200 per cent, then the real price of leather is taken to remain unchanged relative to other prices. If, instead, all other prices have risen over that same period on the average by only 100 per cent – so that if leather *had* followed suit it would be priced at $200 in 1975 – then, compared with the average price rise, leather will be said to have risen 50 per cent in real terms ($300 being 50 per cent above $200).

A little more approximately, but more practically, we may measure a rise or fall in the 'real' price of leather over the period in question by comparing its percentage rise with that of the general index of all prices (including the price of leather). And although there are important distinctions to be made between various kinds of goods, say between 'final' goods (as bought in the shops) and 'intermediate' goods (components and materials used in final goods), or between finished manufactured goods as a whole and services as a whole and so on, and although, again, there are many ways of calculating price indices, there is nothing essential lost in the analysis to come if we walk around these distinctions simply by imagining that, in a partial economic context at any rate, all prices remain constant except those we are examining. Later on, in a general economic context, we shall talk of a change in the relative price of goods – or, in our simplified models, of two main groups of goods (usually reduced to a two-good economy) – without having to bother with the purchasing power of money. This is because the total amounts of the two goods that can be produced in each of the two situations being compared are assumed to be known to us.

Having decided to use money of constant value as our unit of account within a partial economic context, the next thing is to define the value of an object to a particular person A. If A is apparently willing to pay $12 for a waistcoat that catches his fancy, you might conclude that its value to him is $12. But if we observe A in the act of paying $12 for the waistcoat, all we may legitimately conclude is that it is wortth to him *at least* $12. For had the price been $15, or even $22, he might still have bought it.

It is a matter of some convenience, therefore, to define the worth of a good to a person not as the sum he actually pays for it, but as the *most* he is willing to pay for it. The problem of discovering just what is the most he is willing to pay we leave aside for the present. We shall come to this problem of calculating such values in the following chapter on consumer surplus and, again, in the chapters on spillover effects and public goods in Part Three.

Since the *removal* of a 'bad' – a bad being something that reduces well-being in contradistinction to a good – is equivalent to the acquisition of a good, we might as well define the value of a thing to a man more comprehensively as the maximum sum of money he is willing to pay for a particular good or for the removal of a particular bad.

An alternative definition of the value of a thing to a person – one which often makes little difference but which (as we shall see in Chapter 13) can sometimes make a critical difference – turns not on a willingness to pay principle but rather on the willingness to accept payment for going without it. This value of a thing to a person can therefore be defined as the minimum sum of money he is prepared to accept in order to forgo a particular good, or else to bear with a particular bad.

In order to impress upon your mind the distinction between these two definitions of the value of a good until such time as we can make good use of it (Chapter 13), imagine that you are afflicted with a heart disease that, if not operated on within the next three weeks, will certainly cost you your life. Assuming you are not already fed up with this fugacious life and that you want to go on living, you will certainly want the heart operation, especially if it has a good chance of being successful. The most, the very most, you are willing to pay for the operation is likely to be almost as much as, if not equal to, the largest amount of money you can raise by any means fair or foul. That sum could be $250,000. If you happen to be the scion of a wealthy family it could be as much as $25 million or more. But whatever this sum, it will certainly be a finite figure.

If now a group of well-meaning citizens came together, all of them members of RPAAC (Reduce the Population at All Costs), and earnestly inquired of you the least sum you would accept in order to forgo the operation, and so reduce the world population by one, it is most unlikely that you would accept the sum of $250,000 or $25 million, whichever it may be, or indeed, much more than either sum. It is not wholly impossible, of course. For you could be a devoted philanthropist and therefore plan to devote the proceeds to a number of your favourite charities or to some institution engaged in medical research to perfect a fertility pill. But the chances are that you are as unredeemingly selfish as the rest of us and that you would refuse to forgo the opportunity of undergoing the heart operation for any sum of money.

For the time being, however, let us think of only one value of a good, that being the most a person is willing to pay for it. If the person who obtains the good is the only person whose welfare is affected by his having it, then his personal valuation is also the social valuation. If, on the other hand, the welfare of other people are also affected in any way by his having this good, then the aggregate of the gains or losses each of these others experience enters along with his own valuation to result in the social valuation of that good.

If, for example, person A plants an apple tree which is worth to him annually $30 (that being the most he would pay for it), and the sight of it pleases two of his neighbours, B and C, but annoys another neighbour D because it obstructs his view somewhat, we have three additional valuations to take into account – assuming, always, that everyone else in the country has no reaction whatever to person A's tree-planting enterprise. Let person B's joy at beholding A's apple tree extend to $5 a year, and C's to $4 a year, while person D's annoyance is costed at $6 (the most he is willing to pay to have it removed); then the social value of A's apple tree is the algebraic sum of $30, the value to A himself, *plus* $5 for B, *plus* $4 for C, and *minus* $6 for D, yielding a net benefit therefore of $33.

Because of the economic data available from market studies it is much less difficult to estimate the value that a person himself places on the goods he buys, or on the factors he offers to the market, than to estimate their social valuation – the algebraic aggregate of the effects his purchases or sales have on everyone including himself. In some cases the effects on the welfare of other people of each particular person's purchase or sale is too slight to make any significant difference to the economic situation. But in many instances that have come to engage the attention of economists over the last two decades – those, say, in which investment projects have considerable impact on the environment – each unit of output produced is likely to affect quite a number of people other than the buyer of that unit and other than those who have contributed to its production. In some cases the estimate of the social value of a unit of a good or of a whole investment project may take the form of inspired guesswork. For all that, an understanding of the relevant economic concept at least ensures that we are guessing at the magnitudes of the right things.

Social cost

The concept of social cost follows immediately from an appreciation of the concept of social value inasmuch as social cost is interpreted as the social value that has to be sacrificed in undertaking to produce one thing rather than another. To illustrate, if a private business pays a particular worker $400 a week, the $400 a week is clearly the cost to that private business of the worker's labour. Let us call the $400 a week the private cost or the commercial cost of that labour. It is not necessarily *also* the social cost, or the social value that would be placed on his labour if, instead, it were used to produce goods *other* than those produced by this private business. Of course, his labour might be able to produce valuable goods of many different kinds in the economy. You might then conclude that there is a whole spectrum of opportunity costs of this particular worker's labour. But the context usually makes clear which social opportunity cost is the relevant one.

To continue with the above example, the private firm pays $400 a week for this additional worker's labour (all other costs being fixed costs over the period in question). The largest sum that consumers would pay for the additional product this newly hired worker creates during the week is, say, $750. This $750 is referred to by economists as the 'value of the marginal product of labour' – where 'marginal' is interpreted as a small increment. Inasmuch as only the welfare of the consumers of this marginal product of the work is affected, the value of the marginal product may be referred to as *private*. It is also the *social* value of the marginal product of labour if nobody else is affected. If, as indicated earlier, people other than the consumers of this marginal product of the worker are affected, then the social value is likely to differ from the private value. But, to make things simple for the moment, we suppose that the private and social value of the worker's marginal product are the same, or $750.

Now this looks very profitable, for we are hiring an additional worker at $400 when the product of his labour is worth as much as $750. But the normative economist is interested not in the profits of the firm but in the gain to society. He will therefore want to compare this $750 of social value not with the *private* cost of $400 but with social opportunity cost of bringing this workman into his business which, let us say, produces good X. This workman may have come from an industry that produced another good Y (where he was also paid $400 a week for the same labour, or even less). However, the social value of his marginal product in Y could have been $900. When he moves from Y to X, therefore, there is a loss to society of $900. This $900 of social value forgone in industry Y (in order that the worker may produce $750 worth of X) is the social opportunity cost of the amount of X that the worker produces in the X industry. Since we are dealing with small additional increments, however, we should say that $900 is the *marginal* social opportunity cost of producing the *marginal* output of X which, as mentioned, has a *marginal* social value of $750.

From the standpoint of society, therefore, the transfer of this worker from Y to X entails a net social loss of $150: the marginal social value forgone (when he removes his labour from Y) is $900 and the marginal social value gained (when he uses his labour in X) is $750. Or, put differently, the marginal social value of $750 in X is below its marginal social opportunity cost of $900.

But, you might interject, we could also have transferred to this X industry a worker from another industry, Z, in which the social value of his product was higher than $900, say $1100. Why should we not take this $1100 to be the marginal social opportunity cost to X of the worker's output there? And so we might continue.

I suggest, therefore, that we make a distinction within the opportunity cost concept between, on the one hand (a), the *actual* opportunity cost of a good in the X industry, this being the social value that has actually to be forgone when the necessary factor(s) are removed from a specific use, say Y, in order to enter X, and (b) on the other hand, the *potential* opportunity cost of a good, this being the social value that the necessary factor(s) might create were they to be placed in uses other than Y (from where they were actually taken).

This distinction is useful, however, only when labour (or other factors) is about to be transferred to the production of good X. If in undertaking a public investment project designed to produce good X in a particular region, labour entering the project can be counted on to move from industry Y, the actual opportunity cost can be easily estimated.[1] It is possible, moreover, that the labour moving into the public project comes from the regional unemployment pool. In so far as unemployed workers in this region place a value on their 'idleness' or 'non-market activities', they will not be willing to enter the project unless paid, say, at least \$200 a week. If this \$200 is the only value that has to be forgone when the worker moves into the project, it becomes the actual opportunity cost to the public project (even though the project pays \$400 per week, or more, to the worker). Again, if markets are so competitive that in all uses the marginal social value of this labour's product is the same in all uses, say \$750, then – provided always that a few workers only are attracted from any one use – the actual opportunity cost of labour to the public project will be \$750.

In contrast, if we begin with an equilibrium situation in the production of good X, the distinction cannot be implemented. Labour *already* employed in producing X cannot have an actual opportunity cost as distinct from a potential one since it can, in principle, be employed in the production of any other good, Y, Z, W, etc., in the economy. The potential opportunity cost is of an indefinite range, although in fact it may not be very wide. Indeed, if something like perfect competition prevails over the whole economy (and spillover effects are negligible) a unit of this labour will have the same marginal social value, say \$750, in all uses to which it can be put. In that case, its actual and potential marginal opportunity cost is also \$750. This perfect-competition assumption is often made by the normative economist in partial economic analysis.

A final and straightforward qualification in the calculation of the social opportunity cost has to be introduced once we remove the tacit assumption, inherent in the preceding discussion, of 'occupational indifference' – the assumption, that is, that the workman is equally content to work in any industry or project, X, Y, Z, W, etc., provided the pay is the same in each. This is by no means always the case, and where it is not we have to adjust the social opportunity cost accordingly.

If when ignoring the occupational preference of the workman we had calculated the social opportunity cost of his labour to the public project as $750 and then discovered that our worker preferred to continue working in Y rather than in the public project (for the same wage), the strength of this preference has to be measured. If it emerges that compelling him to work in the project X rather than Y is equivalent to imposing a loss of $100 on him, the social opportunity cost of his labour in X has to be revised upwards to $850 – that is, a loss of value of $750 to the rest of society when he moves from producing in the Y industry *plus* a loss to himself of $100.

Symmetrical reasoning applies if, instead, he prefers to work in the new X public project rather than in Y. If we discovered that he preferred working in X to the extent that he would be willing to accept as little as $300 to do so rather than to continue working in Y at $400 a week, we may reasonably infer his occupational preference for X over Y to be worth $100. The revised social opportunity cost of his labour in X is, therefore, $650 a week. For although, as consumers of Y, society loses an amount of good Y to the value of $750 when our workers moves from Y to X, the worker himself is better off to the extent of $100.

Comparing his social opportunity cost of $650 with the social value, say $700, that he produces in X, there is clearly a social net benefit of $50. Thus, transferring the worker from Y to X is an economic rearrangement that meets the Pareto criterion – 'everyone' can be made better off by the transfer since gains exceed losses by $50. And this will be true irrespective of the actual wage the worker will receive in the X project: the higher his wage there, the more of the $700 he creates accrues to him and the less to consumers of X – a distributional effect only.

9 Consumer surplus: a measure of welfare change

Let me remind you that we are to be concerned, within the book's first four parts which are treated within the traditional framework of assumptions, almost entirely with comparative statics; with the ranking, that is, of alternative equilibrium situations. Working within a partial economic context, as we are doing now in Part Two, it happens to be easier to measure differences in net social value or benefit. Thus we are able not only to rank alternative situations within this context, but we can put figures on them and on their differences. Yet this apparent facility in measurement is, in part, the result of a number of simplifications built into the method. In order to assess the validity of such measurements we have continually to bear in mind the simplifications frequently used and the likelihood of their being approximated in the particular instance.

By far the most popular measure used by economists working within the area of welfare economics is that broadly referred to as 'rent'. The word does, indeed, have some connection with the price paid for the use of land or buildings. But for the normative economist, rent is simply a measure of the change in welfare in a comparison between two equilibrium situations.

Moreover, it is traditional to split the rent concept into a *consumer* rent and a *factor* rent. The former, a measure of the welfare change experienced by members of society in their capacity as consumers, is more commonly spoken of as 'consumer surplus' (following the terminology introduced by the famous Cambridge economist, Alfred Marshall). The latter, a measure of the welfare change experienced by members of society in their capacity as suppliers of factors, historically preceded the concept of consumer surplus and is frequently referred to simply as 'rent'.

Consumer surplus lends itself more easily to measurement than rent, as we shall see, and is widely used in cost–benefit analysis and also in evaluation of cost-reducing innovations, spillovers and the effects of excise taxes and subsidies, rationing and price controls. This chapter is devoted to a leisurely elucidation of the consumer surplus concept and is followed by a shorter chapter on rent.

In *positive* economics, a single person's demand schedule, or demand curve, for a good x is defined as a schedule of the largest amounts of it he is willing to buy for each price over a continuous range. A picture is drawn in which the price of the good x, usually, is measured along the vertical axis of Figure 1, and the amount of x per week, say, is measured along the horizontal axis. The student's eye becomes accustomed to travel horizontally from left to right, as indicated by the arrowheads along the lines P_1D_1 and P_2D_2. Thus the largest number of x units this person would buy at a price P_2 (which is, say, \$2 per unit of x) is 10 units a week. The horizontal distance P_2D_2 therefore is equal to 10 units. At a lower price P_1, the corresponding horizontal distance P_1D_1 is equal to 15 units, indicative of a willingness to buy up to 15 units of x per week at this price, say \$1.

If, beginning with the price P_2 of \$2, the price fell to P_1, or \$1, per unit x, and the consumer expected the price to remain thereafter at \$1, he would eventually adjust his purchases to 15 units of x a week – assuming, always, that he is allowed to buy all he wants at the price.

By taking a range of different prices beginning at zero (x being then a free good) and raising it by increments of \$1 until at some

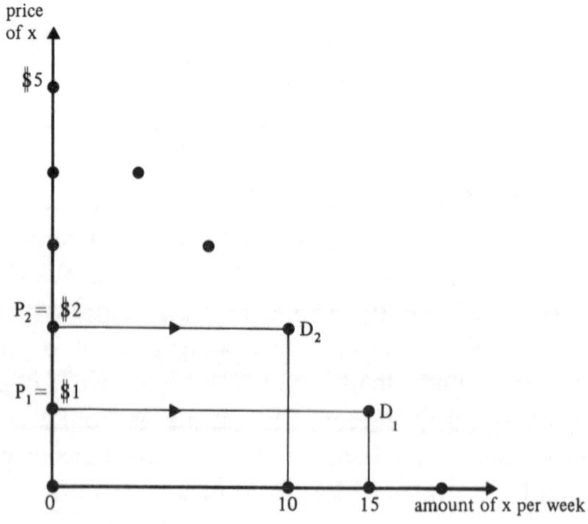

Figure 1

price, say \$5, this consumer decides not to buy any x, the resulting demand schedule (under the assumption of stable price expectations, as mentioned in the preceding paragraph) will be represented by six points sloping downwards from left to right – the highest point being on the vertical axis and the lowest on the horizontal axis. These six points are shown in Figure 1.

If we made the increments of price change much smaller, say of a cent instead of a dollar, and divided each unit of x into 100 units, the points of the resulting demand schedule would be so close as to appear virtually a continuous line rather like D′D in Figure 2 which is in fact drawn as a continuous line. At a price P_5 of \$5 (and any price above \$5) our consumer buys none of good x at all. The point P_5 along the vertical axis is also the point D′, the beginning of the demand curve. Along this continuous demand curve, points D_2 and D_1 show the amounts corresponding to prices P_2 and P_1 respectively. The end of the demand curve is at point D, indicating that at a zero price for good x, only a finite amount, OD, will be taken by the consumer.

This way of looking at a demand curve – horizontally from left to right – is sometimes called 'price-into-quantity' or 'p-q' for short. It is entirely appropriate to think in terms of p-q in positive economics. For *normative* economics, however, it makes better sense to conceive of the demand curve as 'quantity-into-price', or 'q-p' for short. Thus, in normative economics you are advised to begin with a point on the horizontal axis and let your eye travel vertically upward to the corresponding point on the D′D curve.

To illustrate with Figure 3, we may start along the horizontal of x-axis with some arbitrary point x_1. The distance Ox_1 could be, say,

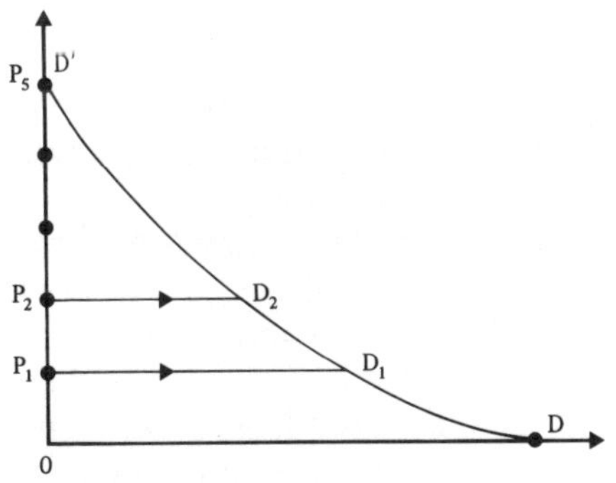

Figure 2

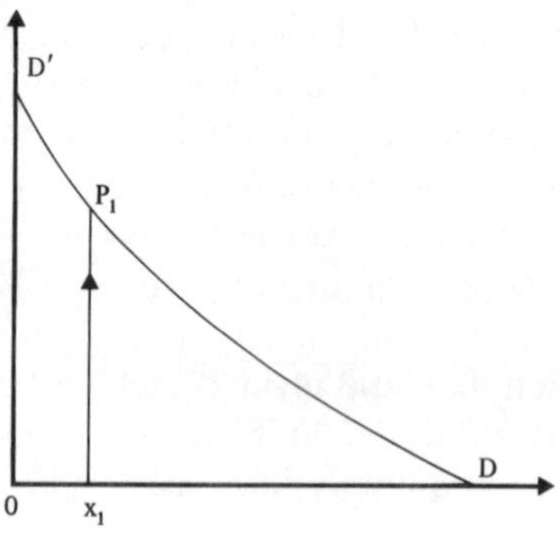

Figure 3

200 units of x per week. Following the vertical line upward from x_1 to P_1 we measure a distance corresponding to value (or price) to the individual. The distance is to be interpreted as the incremental, or *marginal* value conferred on the individual by the two-hundredth unit – or, if you like, the additional value the person enjoys from having 200 units of x per week rather than 199 units.

While the D′D curve in Figure 3, like that in Figure 2, is drawn continuously for diagrammatical convenience, and although we shall soon return to drawing curves as continuous lines, there is an initial advantage in visualizing the diagram as made up of a series of vertical strips as in Figure 4, the width of each successive strip measuring exactly one unit of the good x – a much larger unit now than in Figures 2 and 3.

If you like, think of units of x as being oranges of standard size and flavour, and begin with a situation in which oranges cannot be had for love or money. A particular person is chosen and 'put through a truth machine', the question being the absolute maximum sum he is willing to pay for a single orange each week. Let the answer be $4.50, and represent it by the vertical height of the first strip in Figure 4. For a second orange each week, the most he will pay is $4.20, this being the vertical height of the second strip.

You will notice that the vertical axis is no longer labelled 'price' but 'marginal valuation'. This change of label may seem a bit arbitrary and unnecessary, but it often helps in thinking about the problem. True, the sums $4.50 and $4.20 can properly be thought of as the largest prices that our chosen person is prepared to pay for the first and second orange respectively. But since the word

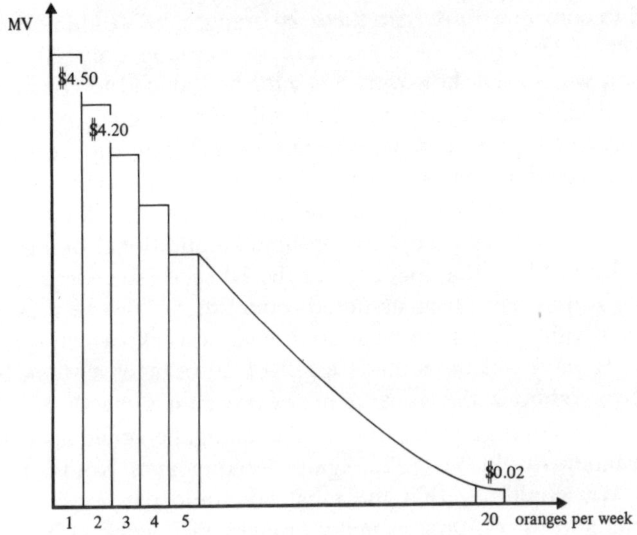

Figure 4

price tends to be associated with the price set by the market, or by the seller rather than the buyer, it is less ambiguous to visualize as money valuations the largest sums that a potential buyer is willing to pay, even in the absence of a market, for successive oranges.

As for the adjective 'marginal' which characterizes so many of the economist's comparisons, it is here used as a synonym for *incremental* inasmuch as we are measuring units – that is, oranges – as discrete units. More generally, the *addition* to the total value enjoyed by the person's consuming n units of any good (where n can be any positive number) as compared with (n − 1) units is said to be the marginal valuation of the nth unit of the good.

You will observe from Figure 4 that the marginal valuation of the twentieth orange – that is, of yet one more orange when the consumer has put a maximum value on having 19 oranges a week – is but two cents, this $0.02 being the height of the twentieth strip. For additional oranges above 20 a week, he will pay nothing.

Thus the most he will pay to have all the oranges he wants – 20 each week in this example – is given by adding together the areas of the successive strips from 1 to 20 inclusive. The total would, therefore, be $4.50 + $4.20 + $3.90 + . . . + $0.02, say, a total of exactly $32.00.

(You might correctly conclude, in passing, that if he were compelled to consume *more* than these 20 oranges, he would not be so well off as he would be if he were to consume only 20. If no coercion were used, however, he *could* be induced to consume a twenty-first, a twenty-second, and still more oranges only if he were paid enough to compensate him for his growing aversion to having to consume more oranges than 20. The marginal valuation to him of oranges beyond 20, therefore, takes the form of the *minimal* sum he will accept to consume an additional orange.)

Given that this area, made up of the 20 successive strips above the horizontal axis is, as assumed, equal to \$32 – the most the person is willing to pay to have 20 oranges a week (which is all he wants anyway) – if he is made a gift of 20 oranges a week by a friendly neighbour, the worth of his weekly gain is exactly \$32. Put differently, if oranges were free for the taking, he would also make a consumer surplus of \$32. Again, looking at it from another angle, you could say that the most he would pay for a licence allowing him to consume as many oranges each week as he wants without charge is \$32. If the licence comes to him for nothing, compliments of the Ministry of Fruit, he saves as much as \$32: it is therefore equivalent to a gift of \$32.

Figure 5 is the same as Figure 4 except for the addition of a horizontal line beginning from price P, which we assume is 50 cents per orange. This price P, we can suppose, is the market price per orange that any consumer now has to pay. Thus our particular consumer can be imagined reasoning as follows: the most I should be willing to pay for a single orange a week is \$4.50. Since in fact I can buy it for 50 cents, the purchase of a single orange leaves me with a net gain, or consumer surplus of \$4 (this \$4 being the excess of the amount I am willing to pay, \$4.50, over the price I have to pay, 50 cents). If I buy a second orange, this additional orange is worth to me at most \$4.20. Since I have to pay no more than 50 cents for this one also, I make an additional surplus equal to \$3.50. If I go on to buy a third orange, worth to me at most \$3.90, for the market price of 50 cents, my consumer surplus goes up by another \$3.40, and so on.

By reference to Figure 5, it should be clear that he will eventually choose to buy exactly 10 oranges and no more. For his marginal valuation of the tenth orange happens to be just over 50 cents, say 52 cents. His purchase of the tenth orange, therefore, adds to his consumer surplus but two cents. But he has no incentive to buy

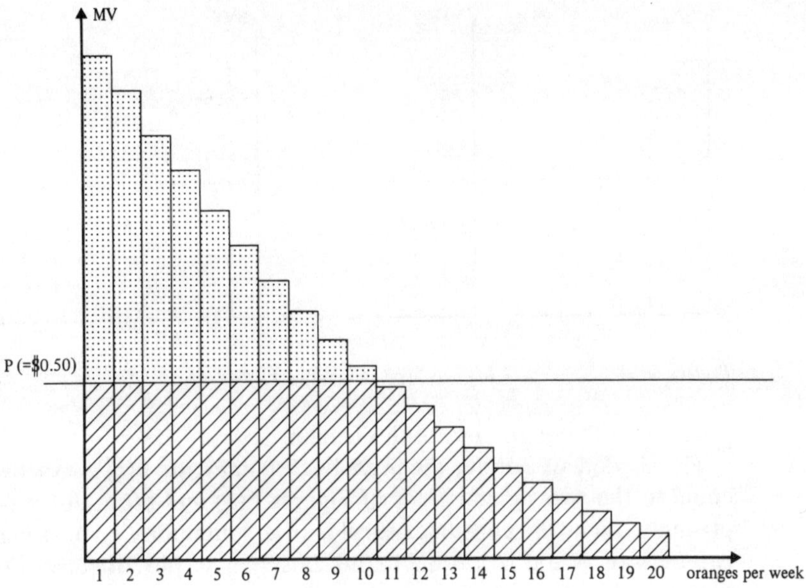

Figure 5

an eleventh orange at a price of 50 cents when the most he is willing to pay for it is 45 cents. So he settles for a purchase of 10 oranges a week when the market price is 50 cents an orange.

What is the consumer surplus of his chosen purchase of 10 oranges a week? You could, of course, work it out by adding together the consumer surplus on each successive orange, as on page 73. Diagrammatically, however, it is the area of the first ten strips *less* what he actually pays for ten oranges. Since he pays $5 for ten oranges, a sum that is indicated by the shaded rectangle in the figure – 50 cents height of each of the first ten strips – it follows that the consumer surplus he enjoys from being able to buy oranges at 50 cents is equal to the area of all those strips *above* the 50 cents price-line, the dotted area in the figure.

Figures 6(a) and 6(b) are abbreviated versions of Figure 5 and pertain to two persons, A and B respectively. MV obviously stands for marginal valuation as measured along the two vertical axes, with the strips or columns for person A in Figure 6(a) containing the letter A for identification, the letter B identifying the columns for person B in the Figure 6(b). The consumer surplus for each of these two persons is shown by the two shaded areas above the

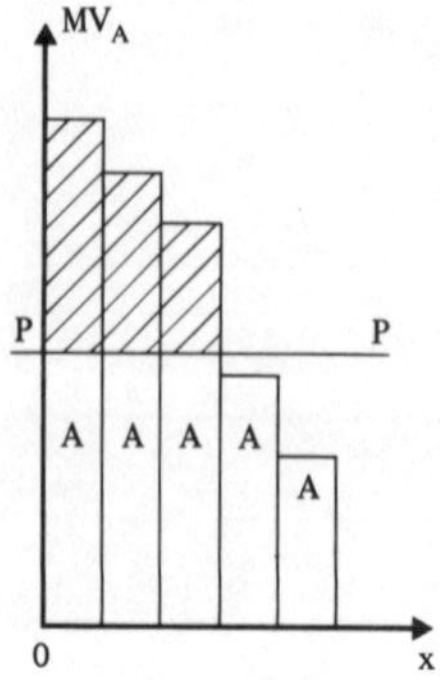

Figure 6(a)

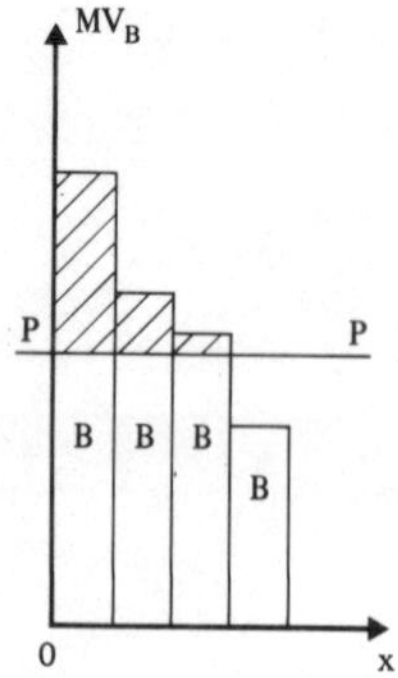

Figure 6(b)

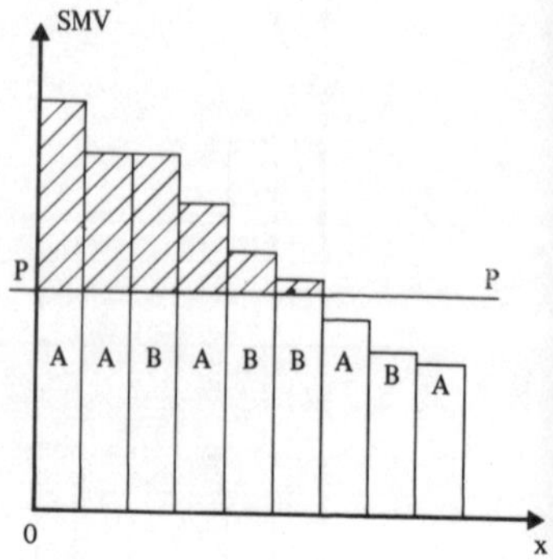

Figure 6(c)

price-line PP, common to both of them.

The shaded area above the price-line PP in Figure 6(c) is exactly equal to the two shaded areas of Figures 6(a) and 6(b). Not surprisingly, then, the consumer surplus of a community comprising two persons A and B is equal to the consumer surplus of person A *plus* the consumer surplus of person B.

You may think that I am labouring the obvious, and you are almost right. I say 'almost' because you are now to notice the order of the columns in Figure 6(c), a figure whose vertical axis is dignified with the title '*society's* marginal valuation' (SMV) even though, in this instance, society consists merely of two persons. The highest column, belonging to person A, comes first in Figure 6(c). The next two highest columns, one from A and one from B, are equal. The fourth highest column is that of A; the fifth that of B; and the sixth that of B also. All the remaining columns in Figure 6(a) are below the price-line PP.

By once again subdividing the units into ever smaller parts (we can forget about oranges since they are unlikely to be sold by segments), or by increasing the period to, say, a year, we should approach the continuous-line diagrams like those of Figures 2 and 3. We should then redraw the marginal valuation curves for persons A and B, as in Figures 7(a) and 7(b) respectively, and their summation into a marginal valuation for a society comprising persons A and B as in Figure 7(c).

Bear in mind that the manner in which we constructed Figure 6(c) from the Figures 6(a) and 6(b) is effectively reproduced in these continuous-line diagrams – the curve of marginal valuation for society in Figure 7(c) being the 'horizontal summation' of the

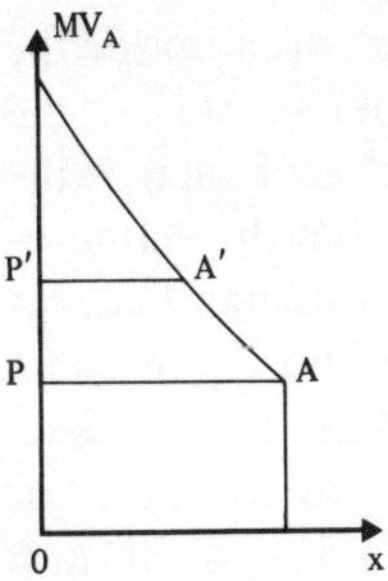

Figure 7(a)

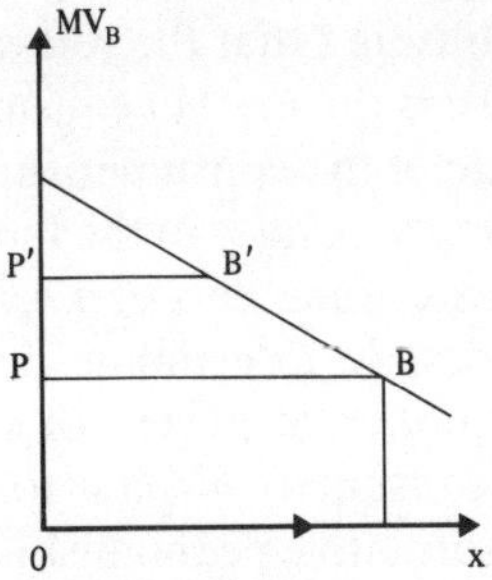

Figure 7(b)

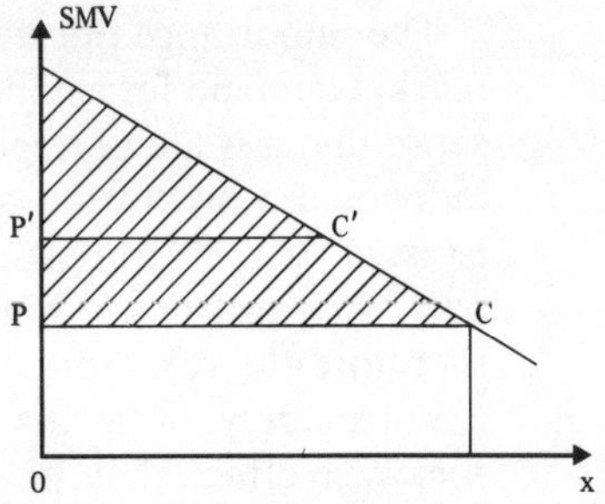

Figure 7(c)

two individual marginal valuation curves shown in Figures 7(a) and 7(b).

This 'horizontal summation' technique requires that in Figure 7(c) the horizontal distance from any point on the vertical axis to the corresponding curve is equal to the two corresponding horizontal distances in Figures 7(a) and 7(b). For example, the horizontal distance PC in Figure 7(c) is equal to horizontal distance PA in Figure 7(a) plus horizontal distance PB in Figure 7(b). Again, the horizontal distance P′C′ in Figure 7(c) is equal to P′A′ in Figure 7(a) plus P′B′ in Figure 7(b). It follows that once the market price is fixed, for example at P, and people allowed to buy all they want at the price P, each person chooses a quantity that results in his marginal valuation being equal to the price – and therefore equal also to the marginal valuation of every other person buying that good.

No matter how many consumers there are, the procedure is the same. And the purpose of this exercise becomes clear once we recall that these marginal valuation curves, although they suggest a different way of looking at the demand curve (q into p rather than p into q), are effectively demand curves themselves. Since the area under the *market* demand curve is the horizontal summation of the areas of all the individual demand curves, it follows that the area between the market demand curve and a given price line is to be interpreted as the sum of the consumer surpluses of all the individual buyers at that price. Thus, given price P in Figure 7(c), the shaded triangular area above the horizontal line PC is the aggregate or market consumer surplus resulting from that price P and, in this simple two-person example, is equal to the two shaded triangular areas in Figures 7(a) and 7(b) – the individual consumer surpluses of persons A and B respectively.

The importance of establishing that the relevant area under the market demand for a good x is the market consumer surplus, in the sense that it is the aggregate of the consumer surplus of each of the individuals who buy the good x, resides in the fact that the economist is, at best, able to estimate some part of *market* demand curves only. It is practically impossible to estimate demand curves, and therefore the relevant consumer surpluses, of single individuals.

Fortunately, it is the consumer surplus for the market, for society in effect, that the normative economist is trying to capture. Therefore estimates of the market demand curves for particular goods will admirably serve his purpose – which is not to say that there are not statistical difficulties in estimating many such demand curves owing to the paucity of data.

After this somewhat leisurely exposition, we can begin to romp along at a brisker pace. Figure 8 shows a market demand curve DD in which the price has fallen from P_2, say \$10 per unit x, at which price the amount OQ_2 was bought, to P_1, say \$8 per unit, at which price the amount OQ_1 is bought. A fall in the price of x by \$2 implies an increase in the welfare of buyers of x; at least, it does so if no other goods prices rise, which we may assume in a partial context. The measure of the gain in social welfare from this fall in price is the consumer surplus as measured by the shaded area between the two horizontal price-lines from P_2 and P_1 respectively.

If this is not evident at first, look at it thus: if the price P_2 were first established where previously the good x had been unobtainable, the improvement would have been measured as a consumer surplus equal to the triangular area DP_2E. If, instead, the lower price P_1 had first been established, the improvement would have

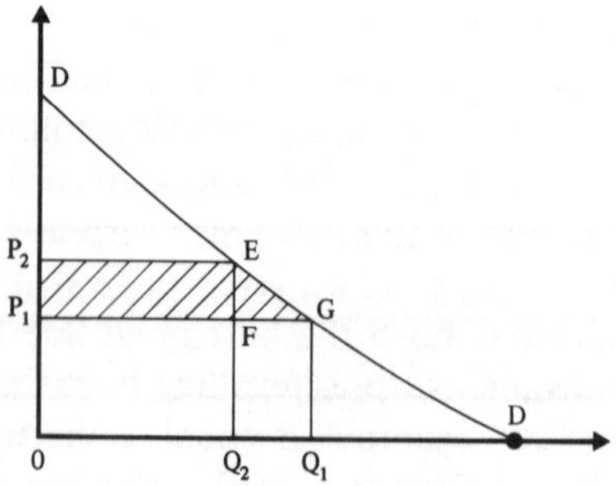

Figure 8

been a larger consumer surplus, one equal to the larger triangular area DP_1G. It follows that the difference to consumers of x from having the lower market price P_1 rather than P_2 is the difference between the two triangular areas, a difference that is measured by the shaded horizontal strip P_2P_1GE. This latter area then is the consumer surplus for a fall in price from P_2 to P_1.

Perhaps you would like to look at it another way, more intuitively obvious to some. The rectangular part of the shaded area P_2P_1FE is the price difference on the original amount of x, OQ_2, bought when the price was P_2. Were consumers restricted to buying this same amount OQ_2 of x (even though the price had fallen to P_1) they would have saved just that much money. For this shaded rectangle P_2P_1FE is equal to the price difference $(P_2 - P_1)$ times OQ_2 of x. Thus this area measures the most consumers would pay for this fall in price *provided* they were allowed to buy no more than OQ_2, this being the amount of x they bought at the old price P_2.

But in so far as they are *not* subjected to this restriction, they will choose to buy the larger amount OQ_1. In doing so, their consumer surplus increases beyond the area of the rectangle P_2P_1FE by the small triangular area EFG. This is easily explained. On the unit of x immediately after OQ_2, the consumer surplus to the particular buyer of that unit is just under FE. For the most that buyer would pay for that unit is just less than Q_2E, yet he can now buy it at P_1 (equal to vertical distance Q_2F). The next unit of x following that has a slightly lower marginal valuation for its buyer and the consumer surplus for that unit is correspondingly less. And so on until we reach the Q_1th unit of x which has a marginal valuation for its buyer exactly equal to the new price P_1, so conferring him no consumer surplus.

It follows that, in allowing the amount of x bought to increase from OQ_2 to OQ_1, in accordance with consumers' desires when price falls from P_2 to P_1, an additional bit of consumer surplus equal to the small triangular area EFG accrues to consumers of good x. And this EFG area *added to* the price-difference saving on the original amount OQ_2 (the rectangular area P_2P_1FE) gives a total consumer surplus P_2P_1GE conferred by the fall in price from P_2 to P_1.

Needless to remark, the exercise is symmetric. If, instead of a fall in price from P_2 to P_1, the price rose from P_1 to P_2, there would be a loss of consumer surplus equal to the shaded area P_2P_1GE.

I have deliberately omitted mention of several issues that often arise in connection with the analysis of consumer surplus. None of them, however, affects the broad picture of this concept as described above, or at least not sufficiently to prevent economists using consumer surplus as a measure of change in welfare.[1] I will note and discuss them briefly for the sake of the economics student who wishes to go further into the refinements of the subject. Readers who are chiefly concerned with the outline and essentials of subject can afford to pass them by with a cursory glance.

First, there is no difficulty in calculating the resultant consumer surplus of a simultaneous change in a number of goods prices. The method used is to calculate the consumer surplus of each price change in turn, bearing in mind that after the first price has changed (any price can be the first, second, and so on), the market demand curves of all other goods will have changed, similarly after calculating the consumer surplus of the second price change, and so on. The method is argued and illustrated in Hicks (1956), also in my *Introduction to Normative Economics* (1980).

Second, in partial economic analysis the *ceteris paribus* clause (the proviso that other things 'remain equal') has always to be borne in mind. In positive economics, the market demand curve for a good is drawn on the assumption that all other prices in the economy remain unchanged. If we include among these prices those of factors (and suppose also that the capacity and property of each person do not alter) then the real money earnings of each person remain the same.

Yet the larger the change in the price or prices of the particular goods being examined, the less likely is this *ceteris paribus* clause to obtain. The economic system is one of intimate interdependence. An alteration in any one price produces ripple effects throughout the system, effects that are deliberately neglected in partial economic analysis. Clearly this neglect is warranted only when it is reasonable to suppose that these incidental repercussions are slight relative to the exogenous price changes we are focusing on.

Third, in normative economics this *ceteris paribus* clause is extended to include the individual's welfare level. The marginal valuation curve of the individual, that is, has to be drawn so that, moving along it, his level of welfare remains unchanged. Thus if we are drawing this curve by reference to the most he is willing to pay for successive units of the good, it is necessary to assume that he does indeed pay the maximum sum for each and every amount –

for otherwise (if he pays *less* than the maximum) his welfare would rise as we move along the resultant curve.

To be more explicit, if the consumer has to pay for the first unit of a good a price that is less than the most he is willing to pay for it, then he makes a consumer surplus on that first unit. Consequently his welfare level rises. We might say that his 'real' income is now higher. And because of this higher 'real' income, the most he is willing to pay for all units of this good (in fact, for all units of all goods) is likely to be revised – generally upwards (although in some cases it can be downwards). In brief, a consumer surplus on the first unit bought shifts this and all other marginal valuation curves; so does a consumer surplus on the second unit of the good, and on the third and on all subsequent units. This means that by the time the final revised marginal valuation curve is established – when, at the amount bought, the individual's marginal valuation is equal to the price – such marginal valuation curve corresponds to a higher level of welfare than does the original marginal valuation curve. It is sometimes useful to identify the original marginal valuation curve as MV_1 and the final marginal valuation curve as MV_2.[2]

Carrying this argument further, you will recall that in Chapter 4 a distinction was made between two measures of the worth of a thing to a person: the most he is willing to pay for a good (which we have decided to adopt for the time being) and, as an alternative, the smallest sum he will accept in order to go without it.

The consumer surplus that is measured as the area under the MV_1 curve corresponds to the first measure, the maximum the consumer will pay to be able to buy all he wants at that price (or the maximum he will pay for a fall in the price). In contrast, once he has had the benefit of that price, or the price change, and he is therefore that much better off, the relevant area under the MV_2 curve corresponds to the minimum sum he would accept rather than go without the price, or the price change, in question.

I have ignored the so-called 'aggregation problem' which happens to be closely related to the second point above. In fact it is a problem arising out of a particular aspect of the second point. For as we move downwards along the market demand curve and the particular good therefore becomes available to all buyers at a lower price, the ripple effects, or repercussions, throughout the system will – though possibly in small degree – make some persons better off and others worse off and so alter the shape of their individual demand curves for the good x.

We have, therefore, to conclude that the resultant demand curve is not so much a horizontal summation of given individual demand curves as the locus traced by continuously shifting individual demand curves. This is obviously more difficult to interpret, and to this extent the area under the market demand curve is a less reliable measure of consumer surplus.

Apparently this is a subject which fascinates some theorists. Yet the normative economist who is also engaged in the actual task of estimating a consumer surplus is not unduly perturbed. Bearing in mind the limitations of partial analysis, he will regard the area under the market demand curve as a good approximation wherever the segment of the economy he is investigating is a small proportion of the total economy. After all, there will also be some unavoidable statistical error in measuring the market demand curve, and this error, it is surmised, is likely to be larger than that caused by the shifting individual marginal valuation curves.

Finally, students of welfare economics are frequently misled by the literature into believing that a correct measure of consumer surplus requires a constant marginal utility of money income (with respect to price changes), and also into believing that the particular sequence in which a number of simultaneously occurring price changes is taken can make a difference to the theoretically exact measure of consumer surplus for any particular individual. These beliefs are shown to be erroneous in my *Introduction to Normative Economics* (1980).

10 The difficulty of measuring rent

There is no more difficulty in defining rent than there is in defining consumer surplus. Both are measures of a change in the level of welfare, and it is only for convenience of measurement that we separate them. In the preceding chapter, the consumer surplus of a single person was conceived as a measure of the change in his welfare following some alteration in the prices of goods – or, possibly, following some rationing or price-control schemes – given that his money income remains constant. For a community of individuals, an ideal measure of consumer surplus for a change in goods prices would require all factor prices to remain constant – an ideal requirement approached within a partial economic context which presupposes that any resulting factor price changes are negligible.

In contrast to consumer surplus, the rent of an individual is conceived as a measure of the change in his welfare following a movement in factor prices only – or following some restriction on his supply of factors – when all goods prices instead are assumed to remain constant. For the community of the relevant factor-owners, an ideal measure of rent for a change in their factor price would, therefore, require that all goods prices remain constant, a condition that is approached within the context of partial economic analysis.

Thus, although there are advantages for the purpose of measurement in separating consumer surplus and rent, it is as well to bear in mind that, in general, the individual's welfare can be affected simultaneously by changes in the prices of both goods and factors. To any such change there corresponds a distinct measure of gain or loss. This measure is, as always, in terms of money where, it is often alleged that the value of money can be determined unambiguously only by reference to all those other prices that have *not* changed. (If, for example, the prices of eggs and cheese only have fallen, the individual consumer surplus, it is said, has to be measured in terms of a 'money' in which the prices of all goods other than eggs and cheese are held constant.) But the definition of consumer surplus (and rent) does not require a constant real value of money. Thus, if an individual with an income of $100 a week buys only eggs and cheese, both of which fall to half their previous prices, his consumer surplus is in fact $50, this sum being the most he would pay for having these lower prices of the only two goods he buys.

The difficulty in measuring rent is simply that the individual's supply curve of the factor – conceived, in normative economics, as the value he places on successive units of the factor, say, labour hours, that he offers to an industry – does not approximate the relevant upward-sloping marginal valuation curve as closely as the demand curve approximates the individual's downward-sloping marginal valuation curve. Why is this?

You will recall that at the close of the last chapter I included as a 'refinement' the distinction between two possible marginal valuation curves which I labelled MV_1 and MV_2. The MV_1 was calculated by reference to the individual's initial level of welfare, prior to the change, whereas the MV_2 was calculated by reference to the level of welfare resulting from the change in the price of the good. However, since the difference in the individual's welfare from the change in the price of a single good, or even in the prices of several goods, is likely to have a small effect on his welfare, inasmuch as the individual spends his income on a wide range of goods, the difference between MV_1 and MV_2 may be taken to be small. Consequently, the ordinary demand curve of the individual, which traces a path between the MV_1 and MV_2 curves, is accepted as a good approximation to either curve for the purpose of calculating the individual's consumer surplus.

For consumer surplus, then, we may ignore the refinement just indicated, and accept the relevant area under the market demand curve – as, indeed, the normative economist does – as a pretty good measure of the change in welfare arising from a change in the price of a good or arising from its introduction. For the measure of rent, in contrast, the difference between MV_1 and MV_2 is far from being a refinement. For a person usually works at a single job, even if some manage to run two jobs and also, perhaps, to receive income from properties and securities. Nevertheless, for most workers, a change in their wage or salary makes a substantial difference to their welfare. As a result the curves MV_1 and MV_2 represent respectively considerable differences in welfare and therefore may be widely separated. You might think that this means only that the individual supply curve of labour, say, is a far less accurate approximation to either of the two upward-sloping marginal valuation curves, MV_1 and MV_2. While this is true, it is true to an extent that can be wholly misleading, as we shall see presently.

Interesting though this difference is between the demand curve measure of consumer surplus and the supply curve measure of rent to the more specialized reader, I do not want to dwell on it long here. It has little bearing on the more crucial issues in normative economics, some of which are treated in the chapters on spillovers in Part Three, but more of which are treated in Parts Four and Five. Readers who want to go further into the rent issue may consult Part 5 of my *Introduction to Normative Economics.* My immediate concern is with those readers who seek a quick route to the central issues of the subject yet who are not averse to pausing now and again to take in a view of the landscape. With them in mind, I shall follow the plan of the argument in the preceding chapter on consumer surplus, but moving more rapidly.

Imagine first an individual doing a specific job. We put him through our handy truth machine and discover that the smallest wage that will induce him to work just one hour a week is $5. Hence the figure 5 in the first column of Figure 9. Assuming he is paid this $5, we then discover that for a second hour a week, the smallest sum he will accept is $6. Again, assuming he is paid the $6, for the third hour the smallest sum he will accept is $8, and so on until we reach the fortieth hour which he will not work unless he is paid $28. Adding up the heights of the successive columns gives a total of, say, $670. We conclude then that in order to induce him to work 40 hours a week he must be paid not less than $670. In other words, there would be no difference for him between working 40 hours for a sum of $670 and not working at all.

If the actual wage is less than $5 an hour, he will obviously not work even an hour a week. If the wage is just over $8, he will work three hours a week only. If it happens to be $28 an hour, or slightly more, then he will certainly work more hours in the week. His surplus on the first hour (the excess of the wage of $28 over the minimum he would accept, $5) is $23. His surplus on the second

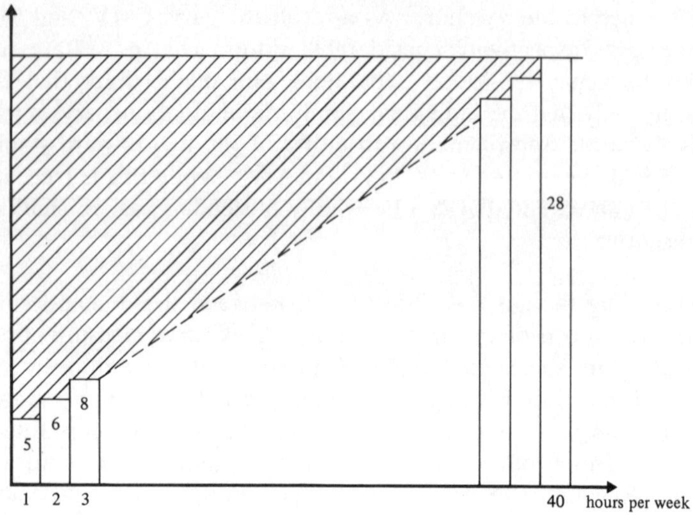

Figure 9

hour is, likewise, \$28 less \$8, or \$20; and so on. The rent he makes working the 40 hours at a wage of \$28 an hour is given by the shaded area above the columns and beneath the wage line W. Thus of his wage of \$1120 a week, we may suppose that \$450 of it is rent.

We can interpret this rent of \$450 as the excess of what he receives in pay above that sum necessary to induce him to labour at this particular occupation for 40 hours a week. Inasmuch as this rent is in the nature of a bonus or surplus, it was common to believe that a tax up to the amount of this rent can be levied without affecting the amount of labour forthcoming on the market. This is true, however, only if the work provided by the individual is invariant to the level of his welfare – a special case, which is made explicit in the following section. As you would expect, this sort of reasoning applies equally to the supply of any factor of production, and not only labour.

Following our earlier procedure, let us now draw a smooth curve instead of the sequence of columns as in the preceding figure. Label this curve MV_1, and let it cut the horizontal wage line W at a point above 40 hours as in Figure 9. But this MV_1 curve is not the worker's supply curve. He moves along MV_1 *only* if his initial welfare remains unchanged. And this would be the case only if he were actually paid no more than \$5 for the first hour, no more than \$6 for the second, no more than \$8 for the third and so on, a total of only \$670 (equal to the area between the MV_1 curve and the horizontal axis up to 40 hours).

However, if he were offered the wage W of \$28 per hour – for which, as we said, he would be willing to pay at most \$450 – but now receives this option for nothing, his welfare rises. Being considerably better off, he would, normally, demand more for each successive hour's work. Thus the minimum sum he would now accept for one hour's work might be \$8, for another hour's work \$9 and so on. The resulting marginal valuation curve MV_2 corresponding to this substantial increase in his welfare would be everywhere above the initial MV_1 curve, as shown in Figure 10. The point S_2 on the W wage line, just above 35 hours, denotes the number of hours he would in fact choose to work at the wage rate of W.

It may clarify things a little if you look at the point on the MV_2 curve that is vertically above the 40 hours point on the horizontal axis. This point on the MV_2 curve is the minimum he would accept if he had to work the fortieth hour. Since the wage W is below this sum, he chooses to work only 35 hours.

Before the wage rate W was introduced, the individual's position was at S_1 on the vertical axis. For at a wage equal to height OS_1, or \$5, he would be indifferent whether to put in an hour's work or not. When the wage is raised to W, he chooses 35 hours and is therefore at point S_2 along the W line, where his MV_2 curve

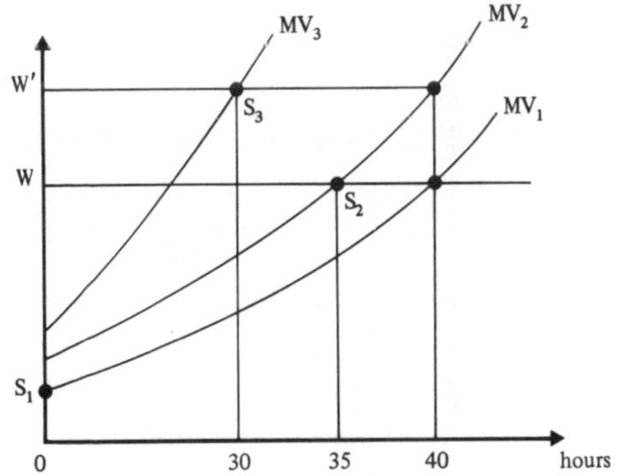

Figure 10

cuts it. Now raise the wage further to W′, and in so doing raise the individual's welfare level so that this resulting marginal valuation curve is now MV_3. This cuts the W′ line at S_3.

It is altogether possible, though not necessary, that S_3 is to the left of S_2. In the figure S_3 is in fact to the left of S_2, vertically above 30 hours' work. Since S_3 is also a point on the worker's resultant supply curve, we infer that at some point between S_2 and S_3 the locus of choices that generate the worker's supply curve in response to a continuing range of wage levels is 'backward-bending'. Over that region, a higher wage rate induces workers to labour fewer hours – not at all an unusual economic phenomenon.

This backward-sloping supply curve passing through points S_1, S_2 and S_3 is depicted in Figure 11 (which is much the same as Figure 10 except that the three marginal valuation curves have been removed to eliminate clutter). The area above this backward-bending supply curve and the W′ wage line is shaded. The question is: does this shaded area give a good approximation to the measure of rent? True, as we are drawing the diagram arbitrarily and without the benefit of actual empiric data we cannot say with confidence that the shaded area is a very poor measure of rent. Perhaps, for very small increases in the wage, it would be a fair approximation. But since accurate measures involve the areas above the MV curves, the larger the change and, therefore, the further apart are the MV curves, the less adequate is the area above the supply curve.

However, should we want to draw the supply curve of labour to *an industry* or to a *government project*, we can slip around this difficulty, at least conceptually, if we suppose that each worker is

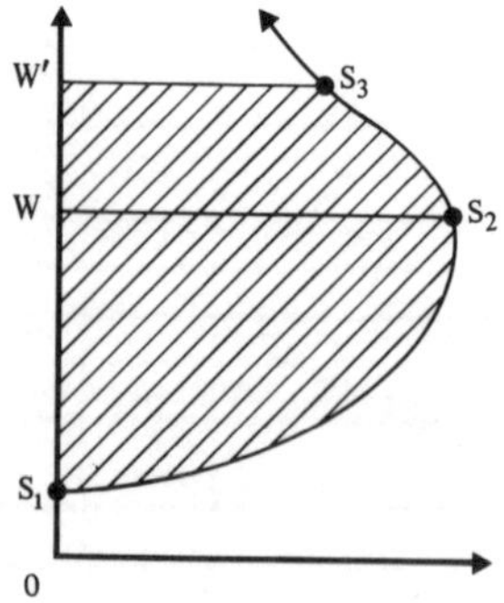

Figure 11

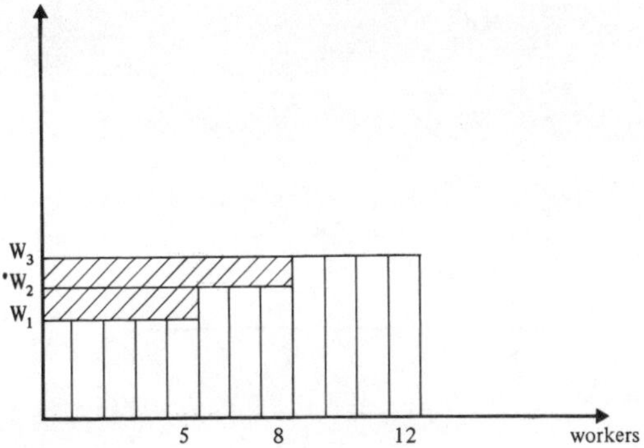

Figure 12

to be employed for the same number of hours, say, 40 per week, and that all workers are equally efficient. (Nothing astonishing takes place if we modify these assumptions, however.)

At a wage of W_1 we can suppose that exactly 5 workers offer themselves, although none of them makes a rent by so doing. They are on the 'margin of indifference'. At the higher wage W_2, 3 more workers decide to enter the industry as depicted in Figure 12. Each of the first 5 workers, whom we may now call the 'intra-marginal' workers, make a rent equal to the difference between W_2 and W_1 per week. At a yet higher wage W_3 we suppose 4 more workers are just induced to enter the industry, a total now of 12 workers. Of the 8 intra-marginal workers, the first 5 make a rent each of $W_3 - W_1$, and the remaining 3 (who just entered at the wage W_2) make a rent of $W_3 - W_2$. The 4 marginal workers, of course, make no rent.

The total rent when 12 workers are employed in the industry is given by the shaded area above the columns in Figure 12.

We could, of course, continue in this way, but it is once again more convenient to draw instead a smooth supply curve of labour to the industry or project as shown in Figure 13. At the prevailing wage rate equal to OW, the number of workers choosing to enter the industry is equal to ON, and the aggregate of their weekly rents in that industry is equal to the shaded area between the supply curve of labour and the wage line.

So much for rent. (Perhaps it is too much for an introduction after all. If students and reviewers let me know that this chapter is troublesome, or that the insight gained is not worth the effort, I

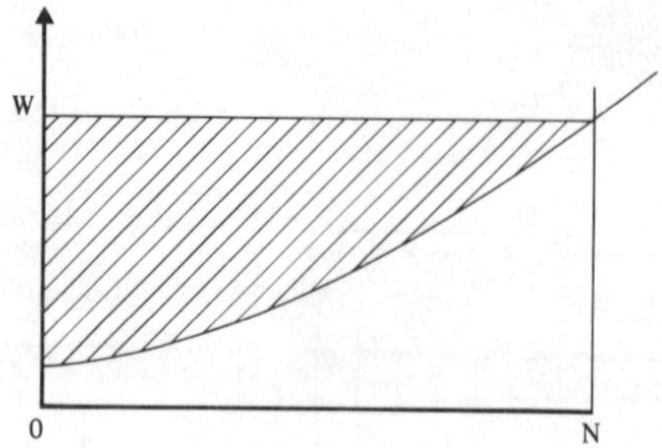

Figure 13

shall take note and simplify in the next edition.)

None the less, I have omitted some rather evident extensions of the analysis which, if included, would have resulted in some subtraction of potential rent wherever, as is common in modern industry, individual workers are not freely permitted to choose their hours at the going wage, but have to abide by the hours decided by the management whether or not in consultation with the representatives of labour. Also omitted is the depiction of a positive rent accruing to a worker who moves to a lower-paid but preferred occupation, although this possibility was mentioned earlier in Chapter 8.

11 The allocative virtues of a competitive economy

The word 'allocative' in the title is to be emphasized, since virtues of a competitive economy other than allocative ones are also frequently elaborated, particularly in debates about the respective merits of centralized planning, commonly associated with a communist regime, and decentralized planning through competitive markets, associated with idealized private enterprise or capitalism. At the mention of a market, the non-economist tends to visualize some arrangements of stalls in a small town selling fresh produce and trinkets – perhaps an extended mart of a Petticoat Lane or an oriental bazaar. They are indeed markets, but the word 'market' has a range of meanings readily confirmed by any good dictionary. For the economist, however, it is primarily an institution through which the economic life of the country can be regulated. In its most reduced form, a market is formed when two or more persons come together for business purposes. In its most expanded form, it can be a world market dealing with any one of a variety of commodities such as coffee, wheat, sugar, cotton, cocoa, coal, steel, oil, wood, etc., or with a wide range of securities or with foreign currencies. Of course, costs are incurred in operating a market – costs of capital and maintenance, communication, keeping records and enforcing contracts.

I mention these obvious things only to draw your attention to the fact that 'the market' – the words often used to signify a system of interconnected markets used to regulate economic activity – is far from being a free good. Its day-to-day operations use up scarce resources, as does a planning bureau's. In fact, the costs of establishing and maintaining markets may be such that for a variety of goods having certain features the alternative of producing and distributing them through government machinery or through informal arrangements is the less expensive.

However, in a comparison between a market economy and a centrally planned economy, the Western liberal economist is prone to find in favour of the former. He believes that, in general, a market economy is less costly to run; that, despite advances in computer technology, it is more efficient in responding to the changing pattern of overall demand; that it is more productive of innovation; that, especially where it is competitive, it is less prone to corruption; and, not least, that it acts as a counterweight to the political power of governments.[1]

These are powerful considerations in any assessment of the respective merits of alternative economic systems. Some might go so far as to assert that they are the essence of political economy. And so long as we are agreed that the term political economy should be extended to encompass personal judgements of value and fact, we need not dispute such an assertion. However, since we also agreed in the first chapter to restrict our exposition of the subject to the literature on normative economics, conceived as being based on an ethical consensus, we shall proceed to examine the allocative implications of a competitive market ecomomy.

The features of a good textbook definition of a *perfectly* competitive industry – where the industry is frequently thought of as comprising a large number of firms all producing a standard good, at least so far as the consumer is concerned – is that entry into the industry is free, and that so many firms produce the standard good that no single firm can influence either the price of the good or the prices of the factors required to produce it. The notion of free entry, if not exact, is fairly clear. Entry into the industry by a firm may be regarded as free if the attempt to do so meets with no legal impediment or discriminatory commercial treatment. Ideally, capital and expertise are available to any incoming firm on the same terms as to the firms already in the industry. (It is tacitly understood – unless a theory of location is specifically being treated – that none of the firms of the industry has any differential advantage of locality; that transport costs from sources of supply and to distribution centres are the same for each firm.)

Bearing in mind that the unit cost of the standard good produced by these firms includes a return to capital, and that profit is defined as a return on capital in excess of the return that is normal for the economy as a whole (ignoring, or making allowance for, risk), a corollary of this definition of perfect competition is that in long-run equilibrium there is zero profit. This corollary follows from the notion that an industry's long-run equilibrium is the state in which there is no tendency for firms either to enter or leave the industry. For if there were, instead, a positive profit being made by firms in the competitive industry – a return on capital above that normal in the rest of the economy – additional firms would be attracted into the industry. Output would expand and the price of the good decline until profits were again zero and the industry, therefore, in equilibrium. On the other hand, if profit were negative firms would move out of the industry until equilibrium was restored at zero profit.

True, this notion of perfect competition is highly stylized. But it will serve. It is the conventional model used in positive economics in the context of comparative statics. It is also useful for studying the allocative implications in so far as such a model is an approximation to the more competitive sectors of the economy.

To get down to cases quickly, we shall first suppose that the unit factor cost of this standardized good, x, is the same for all firms and is invariant to the amount of x produced by the industry. And there is nothing to stop us going further and supposing also that all firms are equally efficient and of the same size. This constant unit cost of x, which implies constant marginal and average cost, is measured in Figure 14 as height OS. The supply curve for the industry is therefore the horizontal line SS′. The demand curve DD′ cuts this horizontal supply curve at point R. Since SS′ traces the long-run average inclusive cost curve to the industry, the amount OQ of x per annum is the long-run equilibrium output. At output OQ, the demand price, or marginal valuation, RQ, is

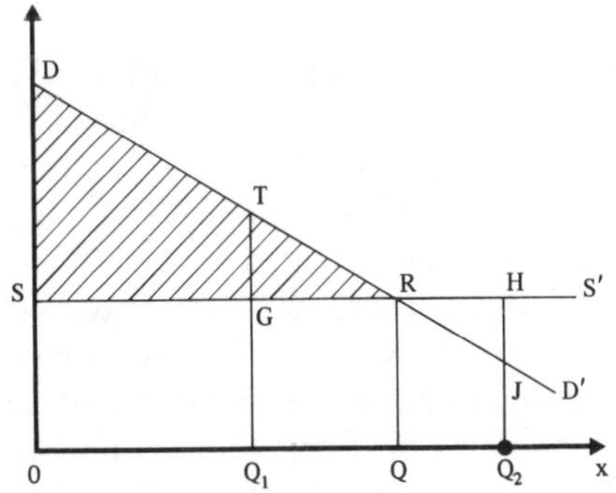

Figure 14

exactly equal to the unit cost RQ at that output. Each firm is making zero profit.

The consumer surplus for the community of being able to buy all the x it wants at price OS (equal to RQ in this constant cost case) is represented by the area of the shaded triangle DSR. If, somehow, we compel the community to consume an amount of OQ_1 that is less than the amount of OQ that it would choose to consume at price OS, its now-reduced welfare is measured by *subtracting* from the aforementioned area of consumer surplus, SDR, the area of smaller triangle TGR. In other words, since the community can no longer buy the additional Q_1Q amount that it would otherwise choose, it forgoes the amount of consumer surplus (area of triangle TGR) associated with the consumption of the last Q_1Q units of x.

If, on the other hand, the community were compelled to consume more than the amount OQ, say OQ_2, the resulting loss of welfare, measured by the area of triangle RHJ, has to be subtracted from the consumer surplus of the community (area of triangle SDR) when it is allowed to consume the chosen amount of OQ. As shown in Figure 14 the community is still, on balance, better off having to buy OQ_2 units of x at the price OS than not having the opportunity to buy any x at all at that price. But when constrained to move beyond OQ units of x to OQ_2, the additional Q_2 units of x involves it in a loss of consumer surplus equal to the small triangle RHJ; for it has to buy these additional units at the same price OS even though its marginal valuation of successive units of x, from Q to Q_2, declines continuously from QR to Q_2J.

Clearly the points Q_1 and Q_2 can be placed as close to Q as we wish without changing the argument. It follows, therefore, that any deviation – to the right or to the left – from output OQ entails some loss to the consumers. As a result, we are bound to infer that the output OQ is the best attainable output for the consumer.

Let us now consider the more typical case of a unit tax or excise tax levied on good x. To fix our ideas, we begin in the pre-tax equilibrium with a constant cost and price of OS, equal say to $5 per unit of x, and with an output of OQ of x per annum being consumed. Let the excise tax of $1 per unit x be represented by vertical distance SF in Figure 15. For every unit of x sold the industry now has to pay $5 plus $1, or $6 altogether, as measured by vertical distance OF. The effective supply curve of the industry is therefore

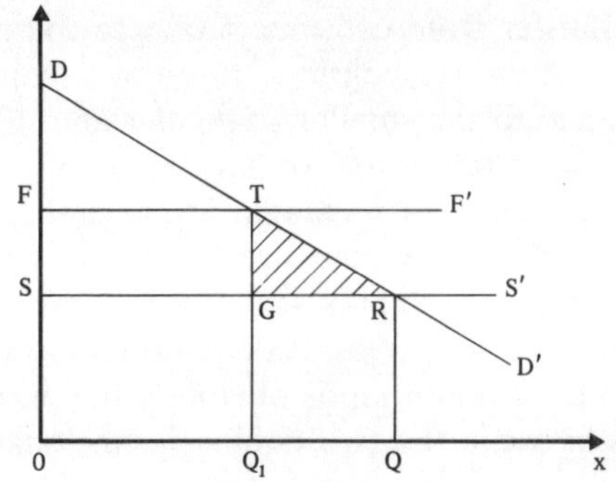

Figure 15

now raised to FF′, a horizontal line that is $1 above the original SS′ supply curve.

Since the demand curve DD′ cuts this cum-tax supply curve FF′ at point T, the resulting equilibrium output is equal to OQ_1. At this output OQ_1 – reached after a number of firms have moved out of the industry – the price of good x is $6, this being equal to the inclusive unit cost to each firm, leaving zero profit which is the condition for long-run equilibrium.

Notice the shaded triangular area GTR in the figure: there is no virtue in it. The sum of money this area represents has been damned many a time and is called a 'deadweight loss' by economists. It is not hard to understand why.

The consumer surplus remaining to society once the excise tax of $1 per unit x is levied (the consumers then buying OQ_1 of x at a price of $6, equal to Q_1T) is represented by the area of the triangle FDT. The tax revenue collected by the government (being equal to $1 per unit of the amount OQ_1 of x that is sold at $6) is equal to the area of rectangle SFTG. This latter sum, however, is not lost to society: it is the amount transferred from the consumers of OQ_1 of x to the government. The government could use that sum for building museums or post offices, or it could dole it out to the poor. You can therefore think of this sum as being transferred from one segment of society, the consumers of x, to another segment of society, through the good offices of the government.

At all events, we may record the following facts. In the initial no-tax equilibrium, the consumer surplus was measured as the area equal to triangle SDR. In the equilibrium following the $1 tax, the tax collected is equal to area of rectangle SFTG, this being effectively a transfer from consumers of x to the rest of society. Consumers of x, however continue to enjoy a consumer surplus *after* the tax equal to the smaller triangular area FDT. It follows that in the new tax equilibrium we have accounted only for a sum equal to the areas both of rectangle SFTG and triangle FDT, a total area of SDTG. Now compare that area with the original consumer surplus before the tax was imposed, the area of triangle SDR. What has been lost in the tax equilibrium as compared with the original no-tax equilibrium is obviously the difference in consumer surplus between the two equilibria, the shaded triangular area GTR.

And it is called a deadweight loss simply because it is a net social loss. In the transition from the pre-tax to the post-tax equilibrium, society as a whole is thought to be worse off by an amount equal to that shaded triangle.

The nature of this loss may perhaps be better appreciated if you imagine the government, after collecting the tax on the new output OQ_1 of x that is bought, allowing consumers to buy additional units of x free of tax and, therefore, at the old price of $5 per unit. Consumers would then buy Q_1Q additional x units, and make a consumer surplus on them equal to the shaded triangle GTR. The fact that such a pleasing arrangement would be administratively too difficult and costly to undertake is what prevents consumers from recapturing the shaded triangle of consumer surplus once the tax is imposed. Hence the inevitable sacrifice or deadweight loss arising from the excise tax.

How valid is this demonstration? Recall that we are considering the problem within a partial economic context, a context that is justified only in so far as all other prices can be assumed to remain constant, or almost so. Thus the method employed is reasonable when we are concentrating on some policy affecting the price of only one good. If, however, it happens that as a result, say, of lowering the price of a single good x, the equilibrium price of a closely related good, say y, also falls, then a gain of consumer surplus from the fall in the price of y has to be added to that from the reduced price of x. If, instead, the equilibrium price of good y rises, which is also possible, the resulting loss of consumer surplus has to be set against the gain in consumer surplus arising from the initial fall in the price of x. These adjustments for closely related goods pose no difficulty in principle, and we need not pursue them here.[2] Thus, unless otherwise stated, we shall continue to suppose that the price of no good other than the one under investigation is affected.

We now come to a more serious point. If we are concerned only with measuring the consumer surplus from a change in the price of a good x, we are addressing ourselves only to the welfare of consumers of x as consumers of x and not to their welfare as consumers or producers of other things, nor again to the welfare of any other group in society. In the above exercise we did indeed confine ourselves to the effect of the $1 excise tax on good x on the welfare of consumers of x, and concluded that they would be worse off in the post-tax equilibrium by an amount equal to area SFTR.

However, if we now go on to talk of the deadweight loss to *society* inflicted by the excise tax on x (the shaded triangle GTR in Figure 15) the welfares involved go beyond the consumers of x; for we are extending the argument to society as a whole. On reflection, then, we find we are unable to assert that society as whole is worse off by this deadweight loss without knowing more about the rest of the economy – for example, without knowing whether other goods also are being taxed, or whether other goods are being produced under conditions of perfect competition or under monopolistic conditions. Put differently, our demonstration of a deadweight loss resulting from an excise tax on good x is, strictly speaking, valid only if particular, and indeed unlikely, assumptions are made about conditions in the rest of the economy.

Thus the student who looks only at Figure 15 and bears in mind only that when consumers are free to choose how much x to buy at price OS, where OS is also equal in this example to marginal cost, they will together buy OQ of x and therefore enjoy a consumer surplus shown by the area of triangle SDR, might conclude that the ideal output is that for which price is equal to marginal cost. If this is so in x, he might then want to extend this rule to the economy at large and so conclude that the ideal collection of goods is produced if in the production of each good this marginal-cost pricing rule is realized.[3]

This conclusion, or rather the way he would reach it, is sure to exasperate the good academic since the student will be right for the wrong reasons. As we shall see (Chapter 12), only when for all goods simultaneously price is equal to (social) marginal cost have we met the necessary condition for an ideal output pattern of goods. This ideal output pattern is today commonly called 'Pareto optimality' for the economy at large. In view of our definition of the Pareto criterion in Chapter 4, this term is obviously appropriate inasmuch as it indicates a position in the economy where it is *not* possible to make 'everyone' better off – or, more precisely, a position from which it is not possible to make anyone better off without making at least one person worse off.

We have just mentioned that the necessary condition for Pareto optimality in the economy is that price everywhere is equal to marginal (social) cost. This is intuitively reasonable, for if this condition is met in production of all goods save good x (where, of course, any one good could substitute for x) then by choosing an output for x at which price is made equal to marginal (social) cost, the Pareto criterion is met; there is, in other words, an allocative improvement. And once this allocative improvement is effected, we can do no better – at least on the Pareto criterion.

Before we go on in the following chapter to show why we cannot draw conclusions for the economy as a whole – which is what the concept of a 'deadweight loss' to society implies – by attention only to a part of the economy, as in our example about the effect of an excise tax on good x, a parenthetical remark is in order. In saying above that a price equal to social marginal cost for all goods is a necessary condition for Pareto optimality, I am going along provisionally with current doctrine. I shall examine this condition more critically in Part Four. But, one thing at a time. We shall accept for the time being that, by an unwarranted generalization of Figure 15, which is a partial economic construct, the innocent student has stumbled upon an allocation rule which, when applied universally, transpires to be a necessary condition for an overall Pareto optimum.

12 Marginal cost pricing

By assuming that no economic effects escape the pricing system, we may omit the word 'social' before marginal cost, and think of marginal cost in this and the following chapter solely in terms of the costs of factors employed in producing a good. This simplification is convenient since Part Three will be devoted to these 'external' effects, commonly associated with environmental spillovers, which escape the price system but ought not to be excluded from the economic calculus.

Now in order to show how the extension of the marginal cost pricing rule to a particular good x is not necessarily an allocative improvement *when that rule has not been met in the remainder of the economy*, we need only bear in mind the production of one other good, say y. Thus, we are simplifying matters to the extent of assuming the existence of an economy that produces only two goods x and y. It simplifies matters still further to assume labour and other factors are fully employed and that factor prices are the same to both industries x and y. (I need hardly add that none of these simplifications is necessary to the conclusions which follow.)

Let us return to good x, as before an untaxed good produced in a competitive industry at price OS equal to its constant marginal cost of $5, already shown in Figure 15 and now also in Figure 16 as QR. In contrast, good y is not produced by a competitive industry. The constant marginal cost of y is $1. But it sells at $1.40 – at a price, therefore, that is 40 per cent above its marginal cost. I put it to you: is the output of good x ideal, in the Pareto sense, in these circumstances? You know I wouldn't ask you if the answer were yes. Let us find out why it is no.

In Chapter 8 it was argued that the true cost of a good x was its *opportunity* cost, which is equal to the value of some other good, say – as measured by the price of y – that has to be forgone elsewhere in the economy in order to produce more of that good x.

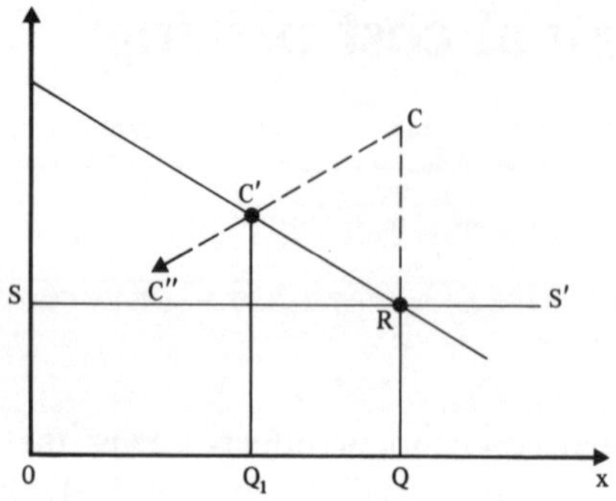

Figure 16

Instead of marginal *factor* cost (which is the cost to the firm producing good x) we shall therefore go over to the concept of marginal *opportunity* cost and apply it to good x.

Figure 16 reproduces much of Figure 15. The industry is in competitive equilibrium producing OQ of x where price is equal to marginal *factor* cost. Above R there is a vertical (dotted line) extension, RC. And from point C a broken line CC′C″ slopes downwards from right to left as indicated by the arrowhead.

What is the marginal opportunity cost of the Qth unit of x? Since in order to produce an additional unit of x we require $5 worth of factors and since (assuming full employment) we can acquire the $5 of factors only by reducing output of good y by 5 units the marginal opportunity cost of the additional unit of x is $7. For this is the value of the 5 units of y, priced at $1.40 each, which have to be forgone if an additional unit of x is to be produced. (Actually, it will be a little more than $7 since the price of y would rise a little if 5 units of good y were withdrawn from the market – but we can ignore this refinement.)

It follows that with OQ of x being produced in the competitive equilibrium, the price of x, being equal to $5 (although equal to its marginal factor cost), is well below its marginal opportunity cost of $7 as measured by QC in Figure 16. And if so, we may infer that we are producing too much x. Since it is a two-good, full-employment economy we infer also that if we are producing too much of good x we must be producing too little of good y. Clearly some reallocation of the factors is called for if optimality is to be reached in this economy.

Acting on the belief, then, that the equilibrium output of x, OQ is too much, let us imagine ourselves reducing this output one unit of x at a time. What happens to the marginal opportunity cost of x if we do this? Granted that the demand curve, regarded as a marginal valuation curve, for y slopes downwards to the right in the usual way, any *expansion* of the y output implies that successive marginal valuations of y (which could be produced by transferring factors from producing x to producing y) become smaller. Thus, in terms of the value of y forgone, the marginal opportunity cost of x declines as the output of x is reduced (and that of y expanded). And this declining marginal opportunity cost of x, as the output of x is reduced, is indicated by the broken line curve CC′C″ in the figure.

You will note that this segment of the marginal opportunity cost of x, CC′C″, cuts the demand or marginal valuation curve[1] for x at point C′. A vertical line joins C′ to Q_1. At the output OQ_1, then, the marginal valuation or price of x is equal to the marginal opportunity cost of x, Q_1C'.

A cursory reflection should convince us that when the price of x is equal to its marginal opportunity cost, the price of y is also equal to its opportunity cost and the economy is at an optimum: we cannot, then, increase aggregate value by producing more of x at the expense of y or *vice versa*. Why? Because the marginal valuation of x, Q_1C' in Figure 16, produced with $5 worth of factors, being equal to its marginal opportunity cost, is, by definition, also equal to the marginal valuation that this same $5 worth of factors will fetch in the y industry.

To illustrate, if Q_1C' were equal to $6 then the statement that $5 worth of factors produces in x a marginal valuation of $6, this being equal to its marginal opportunity cost, is equivalent to the statement that this $5 worth of factors produces $6 of value whether it is used either in x or y. This is an optimal position as can be realized from the fact that the demand curves for each good slopes downwards to the right. If, therefore, we continued to move factors from good y to x, so reducing the output of x to less than OQ_1, the price of x would exceed its marginal opportunity cost, the reverse being true in good y (its price being below its marginal opportunity cost). From this non-optimal position a restoration of the output of x to less than OQ_1, accompanied by a corresponding contraction of the y output, would increase aggregate value inasmuch as less value is being forgone in the contraction of y than is being gained by the expansion of x – until output of x is again OQ_1 and the marginal valuation of $5 of factors is the same in both goods x and y.

Thus, in view of the assumptions we have made about the y industry, it follows that an excise tax of $1 on good x will *not* produce a 'deadweight loss'. Quite the contrary, under these conditions the excise tax of $1 on good x improves things since it results in optimal outputs of x and y being produced.

Hence we can revise the rule and require now that outputs be chosen so that everywhere price be equal to marginal *opportunity* cost. In the preceding examples, where given amounts of factors are employed producing one good or another, the fulfilment of this condition leaves prices in both goods 20 per cent above their corresponding marginal *factor* costs – inasmuch as in x the price is $6 and marginal factor cost $5, whereas in y the price is $1.20 and the corresponding marginal factor cost is $1. This revised rule can also be expressed in the alternative form, that the ratio of the prices be set equal to the ratio of their corresponding marginal factor costs. Strict equality everywhere of price and marginal factor cost is, therefore, just a special case of the revised rule.

However, this special case of the rule – requiring price to be set exactly equal to marginal cost – happens to be the only correct rule wherever (contrary to our previous assumption) the factors available to the economy are not fixed in supply. In other words, the price-equals-marginal cost rule is the uniquely optimal rule wherever suplies of the factors available to the economy vary with their market prices.

This conclusion is intuitively evident when we suppose, as a limiting case, that labour is the only factor of production. In this case, let us assume that one hour of work fetches exactly $1 on the labour market. If now the supply curve of labour is upward-sloping, the worker can only be induced to give up an additional hour's leisure (in order to provide an additional hour's work) if the wage is set at something more than $1.

With this in mind, let us imagine that the price of good x or the price of good y (or both) happens to be below its corresponding marginal cost, which (following our supposition above) is made up wholly of labour. This implies that the marginal valuation of that good to the consumer is above the marginal valuation of the labour involved in producing it. In consequence the excess of the consumer's valuation of the good over the worker's valuation in producing it (the value, that is, of the leisure he has to sacrifice in order to produce it) is a measure of the net gain to society from producing another unit of the good – whether good x or good y or both. And this opportunity for net gains to society will continue until such additional amounts of good x and/or good y are produced that the prices of x and y are made equal to their corresponding marginal (labour) costs. We conclude, then, that in the variable factor case, optimality requires that outputs be produced so that the price of each good is exactly equal to its corresponding marginal cost.

In the remainder of this chapter I shall remove one or two simplifications and touch on matters of interest arising therefrom.

The assumption that the supply curve of the industry is one of constant marginal factor cost is, of course, easiest to work with, while the conclusions are usually quite general. Increasing marginal factor cost is the more popular assumption made in textbooks, with decreasing marginal factor cost treated as a possible though troublesome case. A few remarks on each case will not be amiss.

A rising supply curve of the industry SS′ in Figure 17 may be interpreted as increasing marginal factor cost in an economy in which factor supplies can be increased by paying them accordingly. This increasing marginal cost to the industry can arise for either or both of two reasons.

First, in a competitive industry the firms (contrary to our previous assumption) differ in efficiency. Each firm produces at constant marginal costs, but the first firms to enter, when demand is low, are firms with the lowest constant marginal costs. As demand expands, firms with higher constant marginal costs enter, and so on, until when demand has ceased growing the industry's upward-

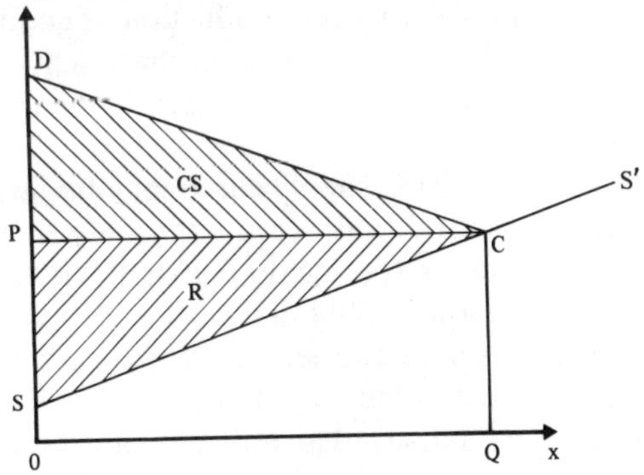

Figure 17

sloping supply curve can be interpreted as being made up of successive firms, each firm having a higher constant cost than the preceding one. The most efficient or lowest-cost firm clearly makes the largest 'profit' – the difference between its unit cost and the price, multiplied by the output it produces. The next most efficient firm makes a somewhat smaller 'profit' per unit, and so on until the marginal firm, being one whose unit cost is just equal to price, makes no 'profit' at all, The 'profit' which varies with the efficiency and size of the firm is properly a rent inasmuch as, in equilibrium, it does not accrue to the owners of the firms but is attributed to some advantageous feature of the factors employed by the firms. It may be unusually skilled labour, exceptional management, or highly fertile land. And, in a competitive market, the factors having more of such advantages will fetch a higher price than factors having less of them.

The aggregate of these rents can be shown as the shaded area R above the SS′ curve in Figure 17. In full equilibrium, when output OQ is produced and all rents are paid to those factors, the inclusive costs to all firms in the industry is equal to the area of rectangle OPCQ – notwithstanding which SS′ is to be regarded as the industry's supply curve since any point along it indicates the marginal factor cost corresponding to that output.

As for the shaded triangular area PDC, this is our old friend consumer surplus and is appropriately designated CS in Figure 17. On a strictly partial view then the equilibrium output of x, equal to OQ, reveals gains both for consumers of x and for the factors of production contributing to the production of OQ of x. Their sum, the total shaded area SDC is sometimes referred to as the *social surplus* conferred on society by the production of good x – a term which can mislead unless it is understood that such a net benefit accrues only to those people actually engaged in the production or consumption of x.

The second reason a rising supply curve may be interpreted as increasing marginal factor cost is because it is the result of 'diminishing returns' to a factor (or factors). If there is, say, a fixed amount of land of uniform fertility that can be used only for growing wheat, there comes a point after which applications of successive hours of labour to this land yield ever smaller increments of wheat. Economists would say that this is a case of (eventually) diminishing returns to labour owing to the fact that the total amount of land is fixed. If, as we suppose, the price of labour remains unchanged and (eventually) more and more labour has to be used to produce a bushel of wheat, the marginal labour cost of a bushel of wheat (eventually) rises. This rising marginal cost curve may also be depicted as SS′ in Figure 17, the rent R now being attributable to the owners of this fixed amount of wheat land.

This SS′ curve may rise for both these reasons. The first reason (different qualities of a factor, often land) used to be referred to as the 'extensive margin'. The second reason (the inaugmentability of a factor, often land) used to be referred to as the 'intensive margin'.

Needless to say, there may be other reasons. And, what is more, the rising SS′ curve is *not* always a marginal cost curve. It may be an average cost curve rising, chiefly, because the various factors are being used in different proportions as output expands and, in consequence, their relative prices change also. In that case the area above the supply curve marked R in Figure 17 cannot be taken as a measure of rent generated in the production of x.[2]

Turning to the case of a downward sloping supply curve, it may be helpful to the beginner to illustrate, first, the general relation between an average curve and its corresponding marginal curve. Bear in mind that the allocation economist is primarily interested in marginal curves whereas the private firm habitually thinks in terms of average cost. If a firm is to survive the price of its product must not be less than the average cost of its manufacture.

In Figure 18(a) we have three successive columns to represent increasing increments of cost. The first unit of x costs $4, the second unit $6, the third unit $11. The heights of the corresponding columns are, therefore, in the ratio 4 to 6 to 11. It follows that the average cost of the first two units is the average of $4 and $6, which is $5, as shown by the height of the short dotted line in the second column. The average cost of the first three units, being the average of $4, $6 and $11, or $7, is shown by the height of the short dotted line in the third column. Evidently the average cost of the first two units of x is below the incremental cost of the second unit and the average cost of the first three units of x is below the incremental cost of the third unit, and so we could continue.

If, as we have done before, we subdivide these discrete units of x so finely as to end up with smooth curves rather than a stepped line tracing the column tops, we have a picture like that in Figure 18(b), CM being the marginal cost curve of x, with CA the corresponding average cost curve. Clearly for rising curves the average is always below the marginal. If you like, you can think of the rising

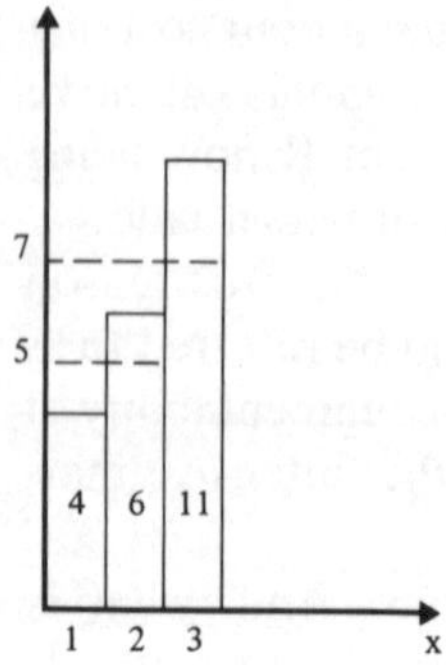

Figure 18(a)

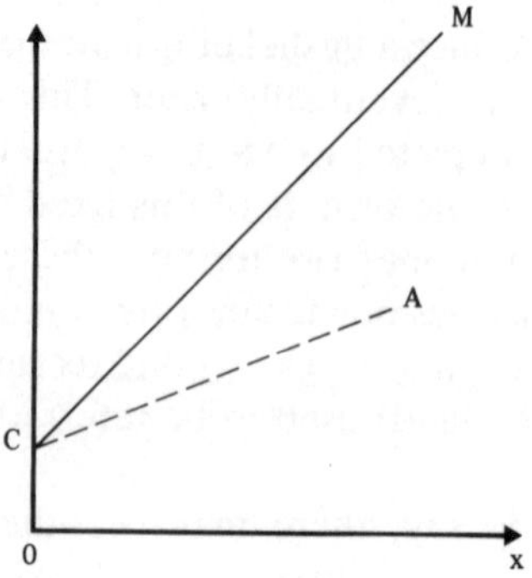

Figure 18(b)

marginal cost curve 'dragging up' the average cost curve after it.

Figure 19(a) illustrates the case of downward sloping curves, with \$8, \$6 and \$1 being the incremental costs of the first three units of x. The average cost of the first two units, being an average of \$8 and \$6, is \$7, as indicated by the dotted line above the second column. The average cost of the first three units of x, being an average of \$8, \$6, and \$1, is \$5, as indicated by the dotted line above the third column.

Figure 19(b) translates these results into continuous line curves, the average cost curve CA being always above the declining marginal cost curve CM. (Again, you can think of the more energetic declining marginal cost curve dragging down after it a reluctant average cost curve.)

In Chapter 14 on environmental spillovers, this relationship between rising average and marginal cost curves becomes important.

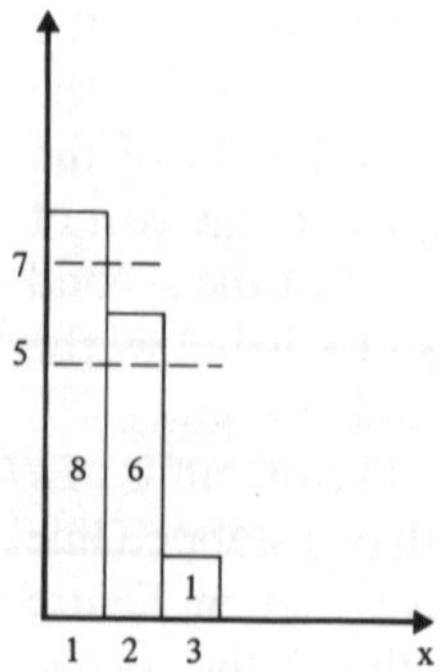

Figure 19(a)

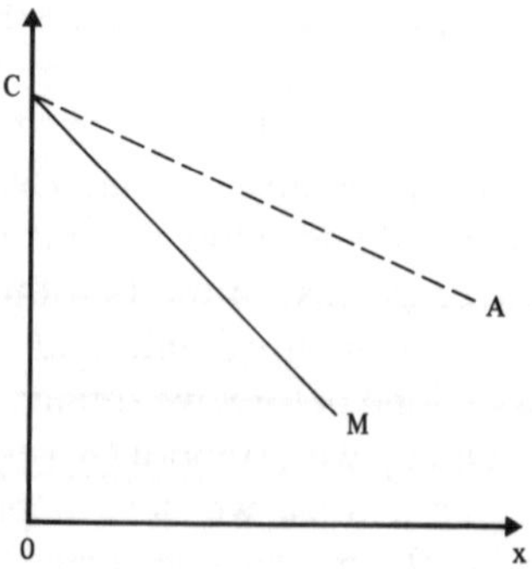

Figure 19(b)

For the present, however, if the downward sloping supply curve is regarded as an average cost curve, then the corresponding marginal cost curve will, as indicated above, slope downward more steeply. (It does not matter at this point whether the industry is a competitive one comprising a large number of firms or instead consists of just a single firm.)

If at the equilibrium output the industry just covers its costs, it sells output ON at the market price of P in Figure 20, ON being the output at which average cost SS′ cuts the demand curve DD′. The average cost of the ON output of good x is given by the vertical distance NR, which is exactly equal to vertical distance OP. Thus, the industry's total *cost*, as given by the area of rectangle ONRP, is exactly equal to its total *revenue*, also given by the area of the rectangle OPRN. But, within a partial economic context, this equilibrium output ON appears to be too small. The ideal, or optimal, output of good x is OQ, the point at which the marginal cost SM is equal to the demand price – at least if we assume, as we shall, that this marginal factor cost is also the marginal opportunity cost.

The proposition that the equilibrium output ON is too small is intuitively evident. For at output ON the corresponding demand price, or marginal valuation, of x is shown by the vertical distance NR which is clearly much greater than the marginal cost, as shown by the vertical distance NC. A surplus of marginal value to society over marginal cost to society is apparent. And this excess of marginal value to society continues, albeit at a decreasing rate, until output OQ is reached. Since the sum of marginal costs over a given output is the total cost of that output, the excess of total

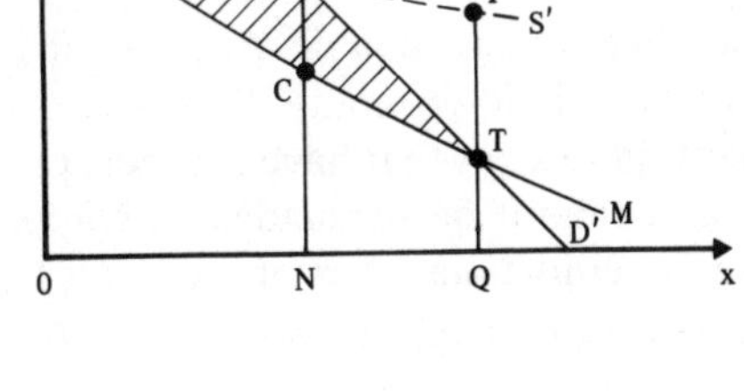

Figure 20

valuation over total cost is at a maximum at output OQ and is represented by the shaded area in the figure.

If the analysis is accepted, the question arises: how can we induce the industry to expand its equilibrium output beyond ON to the ideal output OQ? One common suggestion is to offer an excise subsidy to the industry equal to TF. Since at output OQ the residual average cost per unit x (after it receives a subsidy of TF on each unit) is QT, the industry will expand to OQ, at which its residual average cost QT is exactly equal to the demand price.

Another method, if the industry is a single firm, is to compel it to price the good at QT, so producing OQ output, and to let it cover its costs by charging each of its customers a fixed quarterly or annual sum in addition to the price QT per unit x. Alteratively, the government may compel the industry to produce OQ of x, and defray the resulting loss by direct grants to the firms.

Problems arising from these decreasing-costs industries used to feature prominently in the allocative literature before the second world war and for a little while after. They have receded in importance since then, being overtaken by the interest in spillover effects, which reflects the general public's deepening concern over the post-war growth in pollution and environmental degradation.

Finally, the two-good economy – referred to in connection with Figure 16 in order to illustrate the meaning and the importance of marginal opportunity cost in formulating the allocative rule – is also an introduction to the many-good economy. In such an economy it is possible that the ratio of price to marginal cost varies from one good to another. Such a situation is not optimal Generalizing from our two-good economy we can state the necessary optimality rule as follows: if all factors are fully employed in the production of goods, then prices everywhere must be equal to their marginal opportunity costs. Again, a special case of this is where prices everywhere are equal to marginal *factor* costs which, in such a situation, implies that they are equal also to their marginal opportunity costs.

Now suppose that we are unable to apply the marginal cost pricing rule over the whole economy. Suppose, that is, that there are some 'deviant' industries that have set their prices above their marginal costs and cannot be persuaded to conform to the rule. Accepting this as an unfortunate fact of economic life, the question then is: is there a correct allocative rule for the goods in the remaining or 'free' sector of the economy – or do we have to seek other pricing rules?

This problem is known as the problem of Second Best, and we may as well come to grips with it in the following chapter before turning to the environmental problems of Part Three and to the paradoxes associated with a 'first best' position in Part Four.

13 Second best and third best

Although among the conventional goals of economic policy that of securing a good allocation of resources ranks high, it is unlikely that an ideal allocation of resources – a Pareto optimum, in fact – will ever be attained. And if by some fluke it were attained, in consequence of continuing changes in technology and in the overall pattern of demand, it would not be maintained for very long.

Nevertheless there is a good case for prescribing allocative rules – in the absence of deviant sectors, the marginal cost pricing rule. For even though we cannot reasonably hope to reach an optimal position, by prompt adjustment to changes in economic conditions the economy need never be very far from a Pareto optimum.

As mentioned at the end of Chapter 12, however, a problem arises once we recognize the existence of a deviant sector, one in which industries cannot be persuaded to alter their outputs so as to meet the marginal cost pricing rule.

One example of a deviant sector is a monopolist who maintains his prices well above their marginal costs. Bear in mind, however, that the state itself fosters monopolies, even though the prices it sets may not be above (and, indeed, may be below) their marginal costs. For example, individual goods that are furnished free by the state are – provided they are not rationed – effectively priced and valued at zero. In that case their prices are certainly below their marginal costs. If then, for political reasons, such deviant industries have to be accepted by the economist as unavoidably violating the necessary conditions for an optimum, the 'first best' position is necessarily excluded. Again the question arises: how should the economist prescribe for the remaining or 'free' sector of the economy?

You might think that if the marginal cost rule is to be unavoidably violated in a number of industries, the best thing to do is to see that the rule is met in all the remaining industries. And it is not altogether implausible to believe that the greater the number of industries which follow the marginal cost pricing rule, the closer to a Pareto optimum the economy must be.

The simplest case that would vindicate this inspiration is one in which there is no relation, either on the demand side or on the supply side, between the industries of the deviant sector and the remaining free sector of the economy. If there is no relation on the supply side, we may think of a fixed endowment of factors available to the deviant sector of the economy irrespective of what takes place in the free sector. Since factors neither move into or out of the deviant sector, we may concentrate wholly on the amounts of factors that remain for the rest of the economy and achieve a Pareto optimum there by enforcing within it the marginal cost pricing rule.

The next simplest case is that in which there is only one deviant industry, or else a group of such industries all having prices, say, 50 per cent above their marginal costs. Clearly we should then prescribe that each of the remaining industries in the free sector of the economy choose outputs so that their prices also are 50 per cent above their marginal costs. For if every good in the economy is priced 50 per cent above its marginal cost, we have effectively realized the second-best rule. Indeed, if the amounts of factors available to industry are fixed in supply, this second best solution is as good as a first best or optimal position. As illustrated in the two-good economy case in Chapter 12, such a solution implies that everywhere prices are equal to their marginal *opportunity* costs. Any deviation from this solution entails some loss of aggregate value.

These are the simpler cases, and each offers a quantitatively exact rule for the free sector. But where neither of these conditions holds – where there are the usual economic connections between the deviant and the free sectors of the economy, and where at least two industries in the deviant sector have different marginal cost price ratios – the exact second best rule is difficult to calculate. In fact the information required makes the appropriate second best rule virtually impossible to calculate.

This observation might at first seem to suggest that, so far as we can tell, any allocation is as good as any other once some awkward deviant industries are introduced into the economy. But economists do not – or should not – really believe this. After all, just imagine producing a collection of goods (with all of society's resources) consisting only of pliers, pins and frozen peas!

Let us admit that the second best theorem (originally advanced by Lipsey and Lancaster 1957) does indeed establish a presumption against a policy of slap-dash marginal cost pricing wherever possible in the belief that it is bound to raise social welfare. Yet one should be able to contemplate this theorem without being paralysed by its conclusion that – save for exceptional circumstances – it is all but impossible to calculate a second best rule. Allowing that we cannot calculate the required second best rule and that, therefore, we cannot squeeze the utmost welfare from the free sector of the economy under our control, we can still do a lot better than shrugging our shoulders and doing nothing at all. By adopting rough and ready rules, say 'third best' rules, we can do much better than passively accepting the misallocation that results from the existence of deviant industries.

In order to have some idea about third best rules we divide our economy into two sectors, a deviant sector Y producing goods y_1, y_2 and y_3, and a free sector X producing goods x_1, x_2, x_3, x_4 and x_5. And to reduce repetitive terms let p/c denote the price/marginal cost ratio of the good in question. Thus a p/c of 1 for good x_1 indicates that the output of good x_1 is such that its price is exactly equal to its marginal cost. On the other hand, p/cs of 1.5 or of 0.8 indicate respectively a price that is 50 per cent *above* its marginal cost or a price that is only 80 per cent *of* its marginal cost. Nothing essential is lost in the argument which follows if you visualize the marginal cost of each good as remaining constant over the relevant range.

The following two propositions are intuitively plausible besides being mathematically demonstrable.[1]

1 The smaller the deviant sector Y (as measured by value added) is than the free sector X the more likely we are to improve matters – which means to add to the aggregate value produced by the economy – by continuing to adopt marginal cost pricing in all the industries of the X sector. Certainly if the deviant sector Y is a tiny proportion of the total economy we cannot be far from a Pareto optimum if we apply the marginal cost pricing rule to all industries in sector X, which is now the overwhelming part of the economy. For that reason, neither can we be very far from the

hypothetical second best optimum that is virtually impossible to calculate.

2 Reflecting a moment on the above proposition suggests a possible refinement. We can do a little better than merely applying the unqualified marginal cost pricing rule to all goods in the X sector, particularly if the Y sector is not so small. The third best rule to apply to the goods in the X sector, is not a p/c of unity, as in proposition (1) above. It is a p/c that lies somewhere between the highest and the lowest p/c in the Y sector. If, for example, good y_1 had the lowest p/c of 1.5 and good y_3 had the highest p/c of 2.5, then the p/c to adopt for all goods in the X sector is one between 1.5 and 2.5, say 2.0.

This proposition should strike you as sensible. For if, contrary to it, you set the p/c for the X sector goods outside these limits – either below 1.5 or above 2.5 – then the variations of the p/cs over the economy as a whole becomes wider. This is suggestive of greater misallocation as compared with a narrower range of p/cs over the economy. And clearly the narrower the range of p/cs over the economy the closer it must be to a Pareto optimal position. Had you been so perverse as to have chosen a p/c of, say, 4.0 as the third best rule in the above example, the p/cs would have varied from 1.5 for good y_1 at one extreme to 4.0 for all the X goods. On the other hand, adopting a p/c of 2.0 as suggested as our third best rule, the p/c range over the whole economy would have been narrower – between 1.5 and 2.5. Similarly, had you chosen a p/c equal to unity for goods of the X sector, the p/c range over the economy would have extended from 1.0 to 2.5.[2]

A cautionary remark, however. In the standard exposition of the second best theorem the costs of factor movements – the costs, that is, of transporting and re-installing specific pieces of capital equipment, and the pecuniary and psychic costs incurred in moving labour from one part of a country to another – are ignored. Once allowance is made for the costs of such factor movements, the proposed third best solution, even when it is relatively easy to calculate, may have to be qualified.

If, for example, a new project is expected to recruit all its labour from a free sector competitive industry x_1 which is close by and not from the competitive industry x_2 which is located far from the project, a third best rule that has established a common p/c for the X sector of the economy could be allocatively inefficient.

Since it is *less* costly for labour to move from the x_1 industry than from the x_2 industry, the consequent contraction of the x_1 industry implies a rise in its price, and therefore a rise in its p/c, compared with that of industry x_2. This higher p/c in x_1 is justified on allocative grounds. For if we were to follow the rule of maintaining the same p/c in both x_1 and x_2, labour would be obliged to move from x_2 also. We should then be incurring unnecessary movement costs. In other words, if the costs of moving labour (and other factors) to the project have to be minimized – which, in this example, implies that it must come from the nearer source, industry x_1 – the p/c of x_1 will have to be above that of x_2, though by no more than is necessary to reflect the extra costs of labour movement from x_2.

We need go no further in elaborating third best rules in an introductory text. Admittedly these exercises are still somewhat removed from the real world in which marginal cost price ratios are continuously changing and in which, over time, deviant industries may become less deviant and 'flexible' industries in the free sector less flexible. In the circumstances it may be seriously argued that the third best rule to be adopted for all industries currently in the free sector should be none other than the marginal cost pricing rule itself irrespective of the extent of deviances. After all, the costs of continually revising third best rules could be considerable, quite apart from administrative resistance and political unpopularity. Moreover, the more consistently marginal cost pricing is promoted as a norm of public policy the better are the prospects of its eventually being accepted by all industries in the economy.

It is not possible to end on a more definite note. The second best problem is simple enough to understand, and the ways of calculating third best rules simple to illustrate. But the welfare significance of a policy of continually recalculating appropriate third best rules, as against the alternative policy of always using marginal cost pricing in the free sector of the economy, does not lend itself easily to assessment. If the magnitudes of the p/c discrepancies in the deviant sector are not large, while allocative changes over time are rapid, a policy of third best rules is unlikely to be viable.

Bearing in mind the difficulties of calculating a continuing series of third best rules for a modern economy from masses of changing price–quantity data, the proposal that marginal cost pricing should remain the standard guide within the economy, irrespective of an altering pattern of deviant industries, is far from being an untenable one.

Further reading for Part Two

The opportunity cost concept, so essential in normative economics, is continually employed in cost–benefit analysis. I have discussed it at some length in my *Cost–Benefit Analysis* (1981). A general introduction to the consumer surplus concept, in which the distinction between alternative compensating demand curves is brought out, can be found in my *Survey* article of 1960. For definitions of rent that are on all fours with those proposed by Hicks (1944), the student is referred to my 1959 paper, where it is also shown that the classical definition of rent, associated with Ricardo, is a special case of these definitions. The relation between the supply curve of labour of an individual worker and the 'compensated supply curve' is brought out in Chapter 28 of my *Normative Economics* (1980).

Part Three

Collective goods and bads

14 Can the market cope with externalities?

Goods and 'bads' that go unpriced and are therefore external to the price-system are referred to as 'external effects' or, more briefly, as 'externalities' or 'spillovers', especially when – as in the example of traffic noise or of smoke emitted by a factory – they are not deliberately produced but are simply an incidental side effect of the productive process or of economic activity in general. The question posed by the chapter title can be rephrased: If all goods were produced under conditions of perfect competition (let us say that everywhere price is equal to marginal factor cost) would the resulting allocation be ideal in the presence of externalities?

You might well think that if the answer were yes, I should not have troubled to write this chapter. But the answer may be that under certain conditions or institutions the market can in fact cope very well. If so, the task I set myself is to reveal these conditions and institutions.

Let us take the simplest possible case in which, seemingly, the market cannot cope. To simplify further we shall assume an economy in which the outputs of all goods are such that their market prices are equal to their corresponding marginal factor costs and then consider only one externality or spillover in the entire economy; namely, the smoke that is incidentally emitted in the production of good x. The industry's supply curve of x, SS′ in Figure 21 is of constant unit cost and therefore also of constant marginal cost. The demand or marginal valuation curve is shown by DD′ which cuts the SS′ supply curve at E, the resulting equilibrium output being ON.

We can, of course, suppose that the smoke created varies directly with the output of x – say one puff of smoke emitted for each unit of x produced. Yet the harm that the smoke does, and the discomforts it causes, need not vary directly with the amount of smoke produced at the x industry's location. It is possible that the

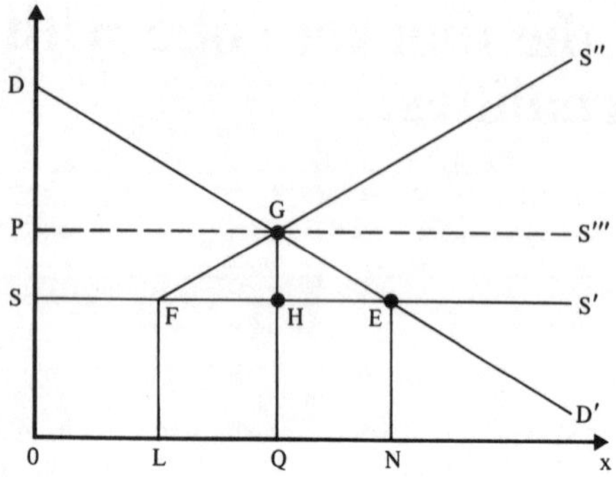

Figure 21

first 100 puffs of smoke (from producing the first 100 units of x) go unnoticed. But once the 100th critical puff of smoke is passed, damage and discomfort is experienced which rises rapidly as successive smoke puffs are emitted. Assuming we are able to evaluate the smoke damage, let us suppose that, after output OL has been reached, the marginal cost of smoke increases. Thus, in Figure 21 the *social* marginal cost of x, which is the sum of the marginal factor cost of x and the marginal smoke-damage cost of producing x, is given by the 'curve' SFS″, where F is vertically above point L. This social marginal cost curve of x intersects the demand curve DD′ at point G.

The optimal output, that at which the price OP is equal to social marginal cost QG, is therefore OQ. (If we produced less than OQ, marginal valuation would be above social marginal cost, and expansion to OQ would confer some extra net benefit on society. *Per contra*, if we produced more than OQ, social marginal cost would exceed marginal valuation and contraction of output to OQ would *reduce* extra net *loss* to society – and, therefore, confer extra net benefit.)

You will notice that optimal output OQ is one for which some smoke damage continues to take place: in fact, on our assumption of one puff of smoke for each unit of x, LQ damaging puffs of smoke are included in the optimal output of x. However, from L to Q the marginal value to society of x exceeds its social marginal cost, so that in spite of smoke damage there is a net social gain in producing x up to output Q.

Nothing very interesting occurs if, instead of the horizontal factor supply curve SS′ in Figure 21, which is the industry supply curve (interpreted as a marginal factor cost curve), were either upward or downward sloping. The marginal cost of smoke curve is simply measured vertically at each point of the rising or falling marginal factor cost curve respectively.

Allowing that whatever the shape of the supply curve of x, optimal output OQ entails a reduction compared with the equilibrium output ON, the marginal smoke damage at the optimal output may be measured as GH as in Figure 21. An excise tax on good x equal to GH will cause the equilibrium output to establish itself at OQ, the optimal output. This is because the excise tax GH has now to be added to the unit cost of x by each firm in the industry. The new industry supply curve is, therefore, effectively shifted from SS′ in Figure 21 to PS″ ′, and this new industry supply curve cuts the demand curve DD′ at point G. As a result the new post-tax equilibrium output for industry x is OQ which is, as we know, the desired optimal output.

The way this example has been cooked up suggests that the production of an undesirable spillover such as smoke results in a competitive output of x, equal to ON, that exceeds the optimal output OQ; that accordingly some means has to be found of reducing the competitive x equilibrium from ON to OQ. The demonstration is useful in illustrating the possibility that the market may need correction. The extent of the correction, however, even the direction of the correction, will depend upon the considerations we introduce once we move away from our initial simplification of universal perfect competition with no good other than x generating an externality.

It is possible, for example, that perfect competition prevails everywhere except in the externality-generating x industry which is a monopoly having an output ON at which its price is already well above its marginal factor cost. The addition of the marginal cost of smoke to the marginal factor cost yields a social marginal cost which, though obviously higher than the marginal factor cost, may yet be well below the price of x. Optimality would then require an expansion of the output of x to the point at which price is just equal to its social marginal cost. On the other hand, if there were monopolies in all industries other than the spillover industry x, which alone was competitive, then the condition that price should everywhere be above marginal social cost by the same proportion might require contraction of the x industry to an output smaller than OQ.

Thus, the externality problem, as we have presented it in Figure 21 cannot be satisfactorily expounded within a partial economic context. The conclusions reached within such a context are warranted only in special cases, one case being that in which the remainder of the economy is already 'optimally organized', say price being equal to social marginal cost in all goods save the spillover-generating good x. Only as a heuristic device can such an assumption be justified, since it enables us to focus on at least one important issue: the divergence of marginal *social* cost from marginal *factor* cost in the production of x. But we should never forget that whenever we talk of an ideal or a better allocation of resources we are, in the last resort, concerned with the economy as a whole. Of course, if the damaging spillovers generated in producing x are really very large, then it is almost certain that the equilibrium market output will exceed the optimal output and, though we may not know by exactly how much (in view of the second-best problem broached in the preceding chapter), some reduction of the spillovers is called for.

Having slipped in this cautionary remark about the limitations of a partial economic context, let us now look at a competitive industry, say sea fishing, in which the rising supply curve is one of *average*, not of marginal cost.

Each firm comprises an identical fishing boat along with a crew of 12 equally efficient men. To appreciate the genesis of this upward-sloping supply curve, imagine first a small number of fishing vessels all of them fishing within given waters and all making splendid profits. As additional boats are launched into the area, however, the price of fish, and therefore of profits per firm, begin to decline. Yet long before equilibrium is reached, with zero profits being made by each firm, the average cost of fish begins to increase. For as more fishing boats exploit these particular fishing grounds, the catch of fish per boat declines whereas factor costs per fishing boat remains unchanged.

To illustrate, if there are 100 boats each catching one ton of fish per day, the cost per ton of the 100 tons of fish caught by the fleet is, let us say, $200. Profits are high enough, though, to attract additional boats. Introduce another boat and the fleet is now 101 strong. But this additional boat crowds the fishing grounds a wee bit; to the extent, at any rate, of reducing the average catch of each boat. As a result the cost per ton of fish rises for each of the 101 fishing boats. It is usual to suppose that the owner of the additional fishing boat, before entering the fleet, is aware of these facts, but that he is concerned only with his own profits. He therefore compares his own expected cost over the future with the expected market price. If the price per ton of fish is expected to be higher than the cost per ton to him – say, the price is expected to remain at $250 per ton – he has no hesitation in adding his boat to the existing fleet.

But should this additional fishing boat be allowed to fish on those fishing grounds? (Obviously we are asking an economic question, not a political one!) Prior to the entry of this additional boat, the cost per ton for each of the 100 boats was $200. The total cost of the 100 tons of fish per day was therefore $20,000. Once the new boat joins them, the catch for each is less as described. If each boat insists on catching (on average) one ton per day, it has to stay on the sea a bit longer and so incur additional costs. We suppose the cost per ton rises to $205 for each boat. The addition of this new boat can therefore be said to inflict an additional cost per ton of fish of $5 on each of the 100 boats of the original fleet; an addition of $500 of cost for the 100 boats.

If we ask the question: What is the cost of the ton of fish caught by this one additional boat? The answer is *not* the $205 which it itself has to pay. For to this $205 cost incurred by the additional boat we have to *add* the $500 cost that its presence on the fishing grounds inflicts, in total, on the original 100 vessels. The resulting figure of $705 is, therefore, the true cost to the fishing industry as a whole of the additional ton of fish caught. Clearly, it is far above the price per ton of $250. On the Pareto criterion, then, it is *not* economic to allow an additional boat to enter the fishing grounds. In other words, it is not economic to increase the daily output of fish from 100 tons to 101 tons.[1]

Nevertheless, this additional boat will indeed choose to fish in these waters since it does not have to concern itself with the costs it imposes on all the other boats. And the matter does not stop there. For new boats continue to be attracted to these fishing grounds until an equlibrium is reached – one for which, let us say, the average cost per ton caught by each boat is $230 at the same time as the market price has declined to $230 per ton.

Let us translate this illustration into the appropriate jargon. The additional boat we made such a fuss over is, of course, the *marginal* boat or, more generally, the marginal firm. The original fleet of 100 boats are, in such an exposition, the *intra-marginal* firms. And the true cost to the industry incurred by the marginal firm is, as mentioned above, the industry's *marginal* cost of that firm's output.

Resorting to our continuous curves, and simplifying the construct by assuming that the average cost curve rises along its entire length, the relationship between the fishing industry's average cost curve OA and its marginal cost curve OM is shown in Figure 22. (This relationship between average and marginal curves has, you will recall, already been explained in Chapter 12.)

If the upward sloping supply curve of the competitive industry is an *average* curve such as CA in the figure, the competitive market equilibrium will be at output ON. The optimal output, in contrast, is OQ, which is the output for which the price is equal to the industry's marginal cost. As in the preceding example, optimal output OQ is below the competitive equilibrium output ON.

Observe, however, that the externality is not diffused over society at large as in the smoke example where citizens outside the industry suffered from the smoke damage. In the fishing example, the externality in question falls only on those within the industry. To use the words of Alfred Marshall (1930), who first conceived of such problems, the externality is *internal* to the industry (though external to the firm).[2]

However, you will be glad to know that an excise tax equal in Figure 22 to GH – equal, that is, to the marginal externality at the

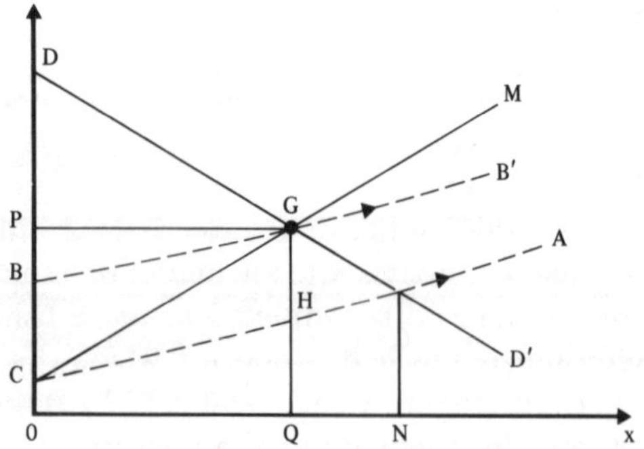

Figure 22

optimal output OQ – will again-do the trick. For this excise tax of GH raises the effective supply curve CA to the industry to BB′. This resulting cum-tax industry supply curve BB′ cuts the demand curve DD′ at output OQ which becomes the new equilibrium output, equal to optimal output, at a price equal to OP.

Another example of externalities that are internal to the industry or, more generally to the economic activity in question, is that of traffic congestion. If we assume that all other costs of motoring remain constant at OC (which assumption of constancy makes no material difference to our conclusions) we can use Figure 22 to illustrate this case also.

Thus, you are to visualize the traffic flow on a given stretch of highway. After a given number of vehicles is exceeded, each additional motorist has to bear with some congestion, a cost which we may assume is recognized by this additional motorist. What he does not recognize, or rather what does not matter to him, is the congestion costs that he necessarily imposes on all the other traffic, on the 'intra-marginal motorist'. Thus, in the decision whether or not to undertake the journey each motorist compares the value of the journey only with the costs of the congestion he himself has to bear; he ignores the congestion costs that he inflicts on the intra-marginal vehicles.

The cost of the journey as seen by each successive motorist is depicted by the average curve CA in Figure 22. The corresponding marginal cost curve, which includes the congestion costs borne by *all* motorists on the road, is shown by the curve CM. Thus CM is the true or marginal cost of the activity, motoring, along this stretch of highway.

The marginal valuation curve DD′ can be taken to represent the value successive motorists place on the journey beginning with the one who places the highest value on it. Consequently, the equilibrium volume of traffic (or number of journeys per day) is given by ON, the value of the journey to the Nth motorist being just equal to the congestion cost he himself experiences. The optimal volume of traffic is, however, given by OQ at which the value of the journey to the Qth motorist is just equal to the marginal congestion cost he incurs with respect to the motoring activity as a whole. A toll per vehicle equal to GH raises the average cost experienced by successive motorists from CA to BB′ and therefore produces an equilibrium volume of traffic OQ, equal to the optimal volume.

Prompted to think along the lines suggested by these three simple examples, you may be tempted to conclude that the answer to the question posed by the chapter title is No.

Let me persuade you to resist this temptation even if you imagine that these examples are typical. At all events, you ought not to conclude that only an excise tax can direct the industry to produce an optimal output. What is more, even if it were the case that only an excise tax could alter the amount of pollution generated it would *not* follow that government intervention of this sort would necessarily bring about a net social gain. For I have deliberately omitted from the foregoing exposition any reference to a crucial consideration; namely, the costs that are unavoidably incurred in making all the arrangements needed to reduce the initial equilibrium output to that output we have designated as optimal. Such costs can well exceed the otherwise anticipated social benefit from moving to the optimal output – a possibility to be mentioned again toward the close of the following chapter, and to be explored more fully in Chapter 16.

15 Diminishing returns to agriculture as an instance of externalities

Two examples of externalities internal to an activity is surely enough. And were I restricted to two examples I should have left out one of the two given in the last chapter and insisted in bringing, in its stead, that of agriculture. Familiarity of economists with the case of agriculture makes it the more illuminating example, in particular as it is not usually recognized as being an instance of externalities that are internal to the activity. For the competitive equilibrium turns out, after all, to be equal to the optimal output, in contrast to the preceding two cases. And the reason is that in agriculture there is (implicit) acknowledgement of the existence of property rights in the factor land, as a result of which land also has a competitive price on the market, one that enters into the cost of the agricultural product. In the preceding two examples, nobody had property rights, respectively, in the fishing grounds or in the road. Neither factor therefore had a market price. Each was treated as a free factor, a defect in the system that caused overproduction of the good using that factor.

So let us go to work with a farmer who owns a piece of land of 100 acres which can be used only for corn-growing. We may imagine that he cultivates it himself but separates the cost of the labour he puts into land from any return he receives as a landlord. A simpler expositional device, however, would dissociate the two factors, labour and the services of land, by supposing him to hire labour at a fixed market price. His object would then be to maximise his 'profit' or, rather, the return on his land.

Since he has only 100 acres of corn land, there is obviously a limit to the total amount of corn that can be grown on it. But long before that absolute limit is reached, diminishing returns to labour set in. After some point, that is, the *average product* (in terms, say, of bushels of corn) per labourer declines as labour is added to that piece of land. Since the wage is assumed fixed, this means that (eventually) the *average labour cost* per bushel of corn increases. This increasing average cost curve is shown as the broken line curve c a in Figure 23, and we shall assume that our farmer knows the shape of this average cost curve exactly. (For the time being you and he are to ignore the cm curve.)

Our small farmer may be the most amiable of men with his friends and family, but as an economic man he is held to be the embodiment of self interest. He therefore wants to squeeze the largest 'profit' or return from his land. Since he knows the shape of his average cost curve c a and knows also the price of corn P, his task is to discover that output of corn which will yield him the largest rent – rent being measured here as the excess of his total revenue (price of corn *times* the quantity he produces) over his total cost (average cost of corn *times* the quantity he produces). We can picture the farmer seeking this output in Figure 23. His eye moves along the average cost curve c a in search of that point for which the excess of price over average cost *times* corn output yields him a maximum sum.

Obviously he will not produce an output equal to On, where price is exactly equal to average cost, since his 'profit' will then be zero. If he produced a little less than On such that the excess of price over average cost is equal to eb in the figure, his 'profit' is equal to eb *times* the corresponding output of corn Or, a sum that could therefore be measured as a rectangle eb *times* Or. But he can do better by producing a somewhat smaller output, one that results in the largest rectangle area that can be fitted between the ca curve and price-line PP′. It transpires that the maximum 'profit', equal to the largest rectangle Pdhg, accrues to him if he produces output Oq.

Now to discover this maximum 'profit', which we shall now call rent, you do not really have to compare the area of all possible

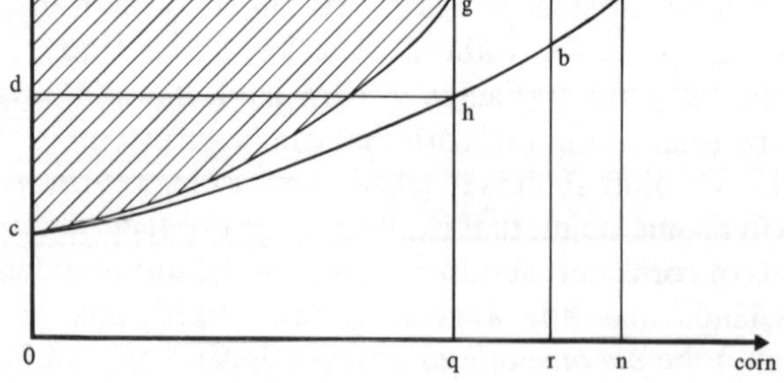

Figure 23

rectangles that can be fitted between the curve ca and the price-line PP′. You can draw a curve cm that is *marginal* to the average cost curve ca. The point g at which this marginal curve cm cuts the price-line PP′ also determines the maximum rent output Oq. You know this to be the maximum rent because – as we have already observed in measuring the worker's rent in Figure 9 and workers' rents in Figure 13 of Chapter 10 – rent is also measured as the area between the marginal cost curve and the price up to any output. And this measure of rent, shown by the striped area Pcg in Figure 23, is at a maximum at output Oq.

It follows from the above two paragraphs that we can measure rent at any output either as the excess of price over average cost *times* that output or else as the area between the marginal cost curve and the price up to that output. Thus, in Figure 23, the maximum rent is measured either as the area of the rectangle Pghd or else as the striped triangular area cgP. It is convenient, however, for the economist to suppose that the farmer is, after all, guided by his marginal labour cost curve cm in choosing his maximum rent.

The above analysis should be familiar enough to first-year economics students – though I admit that I am sometimes pleasantly surprised to discover that it is not. But first-year students and non-economists may have to concentrate a little in this present section. It is worth their while re-reading it if necessary since the conclusions we are to draw have been of the utmost importance in influencing a powerful school of libertarian economists (often associated with the Chicago School of economists) to regard the institution of private property within a competitive economy as an essential feature of an allocatively good economic system.

One more simple diagram, however, before drawing these conclusions. Just as Figures 7(a), 7(b) and 7(c) in Chapter 9 suggested the validity of a horizontal summation of all individual demand curves for a good x in order to construct the market demand curve for x, so can we horizontally sum the marginal cost curves of all corn farmers to yield the market marginal cost curve for corn which, in Figure 24, appears as the supply curve of corn SS′. We may also, of course, sum the average cost curves of all farmers so as to produce an average cost curve SA for the market output of corn (or else we can derive SA as an average curve from the original SS′ supply curve).

The intersection at point G of the market demand curve for corn

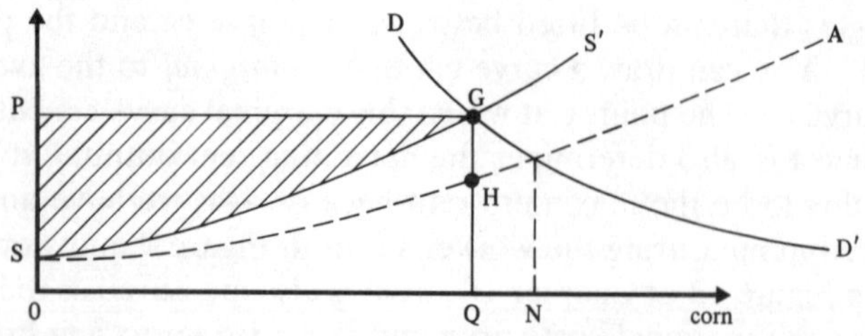

Figure 24

DD′ with the supply curve SS′ determines the equilibrium corn output OQ with price equal to OP. The equilibrium output OQ is here the optimal output since SS′ is a marginal cost curve to the corn-growing industry. The aggregate of the rents accruing to all corn land is given by the striped triangular area PSG – or, by analogy with Figure 23, is equal to the area of the rectangle of side GH and width PG.

Note also that the marginal cost supply curve SS′ is a marginal *labour* cost. Labour being in fact the only variable factor in this simple agricultural model it is also the relevant marginal opportunity cost – at least if we assume that in the production of all other goods the marginal cost of labour used is equal to its marginal social value. We can therefore generalize within this partial economic context to the extent of concluding that competitive agriculture tends to produce optimal outputs.

But, you may well ask, what has agricultural production to do with externalities? And just where does private property tie in?

It ought not to try your mind too much to conceive of the average cost curve for a single farmer ca in Figure 23, or the average cost curve SA in Figure 24 for the economy's entire corn output, as rising because of externalities that are *internal* to the corn-producing activity. After all, the production of an additional bushel of corn does raise the average (labour) cost of all the intra-marginal bushels of corn. The nature of the externality involved can indeed be thought of as a form of congestion – much like 'too many boats' on the fishing grounds or 'too many cars' in the preceding two examples. In the case of corn there are eventually 'too many labourers' working on a given acreage of corn land.

In the production of corn, however, the equilibrium output is *not*, as distinct from the equilibrium output of fish or the equilibrium flow of traffic, determined by the point at which the average cost is equal to the demand price. It is, as we have shown, determined by the point at which the marginal cost is equal to the demand curve. At this optimal output OQ, Figure 24 reveals that the *average* rent per *bushel* of corn – the difference between the price of corn and the *average* cost of labour QH – is equal to GH. (Remember, a total rent accruing to corn land is equal to GH times PG.)

Suppose now that there is a competitive market in corn land, so that the total corn land fetches a price equal to the total rent. The farmer who has to buy land at the market price can make no profit. At the equilibrium output OQ, the *average* cost of a bushel *inclusive* of rent is QG, of which QH is the average labour cost per bushel and HG is the average rent cost per bushel. And, of course, in equilibrium this average cost including rent, equal to QG, is for each farmer in the corn-growing industry exactly equal to the market price OP.

But you will recall that QG is the *marginal* labour cost or, if you like, the marginal cost of corn *excluding* rent. It follows that the *marginal* cost of corn *excluding* rent is equal to the *average* cost of corn *including* rent. Thus the industry supply curve SS′ in Figure 24 is, after all, an average curve also, but one that includes rent, this being the price of the factor land. And the price of land is included because we have assumed, implicitly or explicitly, that land, being privately owned, has to be bid for by farmers who seek to buy land[1] as well as labour in order to grow corn.

If, instead, this corn land were *not* privately owned – if it were held in common by all aspiring corn farmers as a free factor of production – farmers would continue to grow corn on the given acreage of corn land, by hiring labour at the market price, until again profits were zero. Only now equilibrium output would be at ON, at which output there would be no excess of price over the average labour cost alone. There is, in that case, no rent to consider since land is treated as a free asset. Thus, when land is treated as a free asset, we reach the same result that we reached in the fishing example and in the traffic example since in these two cases it was (tacitly) understood that the fishing grounds and the road were being treated as free assets.

In the case, then, where all the corn land is held in common and the equilibrium output is ON, an excise tax on corn equal to GH would raise the average supply curve SA so that it cuts the demand curve at point G. With this excise tax GH, the equilibrium output becomes OQ, the required optimal output.

From the above arguments, the rationale of private ownership, and the maximizing of rents by landowners finally emerges. For this tax GH per bushel of corn, which is necessary to induce an optimal output OQ when the land is treated as a free resource, is, of course, exactly equal to the *average rent* per bushel of corn when, with private ownership of land, it enters along with wages into the average cost per bushel of corn. In consequence the equilibrium output is OQ, the optimal output, since the resulting average cost *including* rent QG, is exactly equal to the price OP at output OQ.

These three examples can now be considered to have illustrated a common principle: wherever there is a limited amount of a scarce resource – be it an area of fishing grounds, a stretch of road, or an area of corn-growing land – the average cost curve of the good that uses it along with other (variable) factors will eventually rise in consequences of externalities that are internal to the activity in question. If this scarce resource is properly priced – and it is, by definition, properly priced if the rent accruing to it is a maximum – then the equilibrium output is also the optimal output. If, on the other hand, the scarce resource goes unpriced, the equilibrium output of the good is too large, being that at which average cost *excluding* rent is equal to the price of the good.

We conclude that the equilibrium output of any such goods can be optimal whether the relevant limited resource is put into private ownership and priced in a competitive market or whether, instead, it is treated as a free resource by producers with the government then intervening to the extent of levying an optimal excise tax on the good. The maximum rent collected by the private owners of land, or of other limited resources, is exactly equal to the maximum revenue that is collected by the government – as a glance at Figure 24 makes evident, since average rent per bushel, GH, when the industry supply curve is at SS′ is also equal to the excise tax levied by the government when the industry supply curve is SA. Thus the difference between using the institution of private property or the institution of government in order to achieve optimality is, formally speaking, one of distribution only. In the former case the rent, or revenue, accrues to the private owners of the limited resource; in the latter case, it accrues to society as a whole via the government.

For those people who are averse to bureaucratic control and

who believe that the dispersion of wealth among society acts as a check to the economic power of the government, the extension of the institution of property to cover private ownership of limited resources is seen as the best means of enabling the ordinary operation of competitive markets to produce an efficient economy.

It has been acknowledged, however, that the institution of property rights in scarce resources within a competitive economy acts easily to promote optimal outputs only in the case of externalities that (like the above examples) are *internal* to the activity in question. Where, on the other hand, the externalities are *external* to the activity, as in our smoky factor example depicted in Figure 21 (page 120) the introduction of property rights would work only in a hypothetical world in which each person owned property rights in some part of the limited volume of clean air over the area. In such a world no person would agree to give up their portion of clean air for factory use (that is, allowing factory smoke to be placed in it) unless he were paid a satisfactory price. A competitive market in units of clean air would determine the price industry had to pay to acquire space in which to dispose of its smoke. All smoke-generating industries would then have to include the rents or payments made to the owners of available air space in their average costs along with factor payments. The resulting average cost curve *including* rent, which would be the supply curve of such an industry, would also be the marginal cost curve *excluding* rent, and so the competitive equilibrium output would again be the optimal output.

However, this hypothetical world does not correspond with the world we inhabit. Externalities that are external to the industry are in fact excluded from the supply curve of that industry. For such cases there would seem to be a *prima facie* case for government intervention either in the form of excise taxes or of direct controls or regulation. On the other hand, if the damage created by the externality that is currently external to the industry is not widely diffused, the creation of property rights may be able to 'internalize' them into the industry. An instance that comes to mind is the pouring of industrial effluent into an otherwise clean body of water, say a lake. If this lake were sold by the government to a group of people, industries would not be permitted to pour effluent into it unless they paid an effluent charge, which charge would then be included in the average cost of the goods produced by such industries.

Since the second world war there would, I think, be broad agreement that externalities that are *external* to the economic activities creating them have been growing faster than externalities that are *internal* to such economic activities. Most of those in the former category include a wide range of new spillovers and pollutants, the outcome of technological innovation in industrial processes and products. It is doubtful whether any of these new spillovers and pollutants can be internalized into the industries generating them through the creation of property rights.

Important though these conclusions are, we must now be explicit about simplifications that were surreptitiously inserted into the arguments in order to reach the conclusions as painlessly as possible. I hasten to point out, however, that (as an approximation at least) such conclusions are, in the main, valid. But we shall improve our understanding of the analysis and its limitations by brief consideration of a number of points which, for pedagogic reasons, I have left to the end of this chapter.

1 A tacit assumption in this and the preceding chapter has been that a particular externality or spillover damage varies with the output of the good responsible for it. But it is sometimes just possible, for technical reasons, that the spillovers are in effect 'overheads'; which is to say that spillover damage occurs even when no output is actually being produced simply because the machinery or part of it is still active. If the losses so incurred are such as outweigh the benefits otherwise conferred at *any* output, the optimal output is clearly zero. The plant should be scrapped.

2 I have ignored the question of variation in spillover damage with respect to time and location. Smoke damage, noise, traffic congestion, and industrial effluent, for example, all vary with time of the day and with change of season, and the damage inflicted on the population at large varies both with the location of the industry and of the population. Although the principles discussed are unaffected by this consideration, the resulting pattern of efficient taxes is more complex and becomes more costly to calculate and implement.

3 The assumption of a given cost of spillover damage, whether total or marginal, ignores the difference between the maximum sum a person will pay to avoid the damage and the minimum sum he will accept to bear with it. This distinction can be important

where the spillover effects make a large difference to people's welfare. We discuss the issue in the following chapter.

4 I have also deliberately disregarded all the cost associated with the calculation and implementation of a system of taxes or tolls, also any negotiation costs as between the parties concerned with different forms of pollution. We also introduce all such costs under the umbrella term 'transactions costs' in the next chapter.

5 So far we have restricted the analysis and the examples to spillovers generated by one industry and falling either on the population at large or on another industry or other industries. Although the essential ideas are more easily grasped by focusing on 'one-way' spillovers of this sort, economists sometimes invoke examples of two industries or two firms, each bombarding the other with spillovers. Such examples make the optimal system of excise taxes slightly less simple (though it requires only a solution of simultaneous equations). They also suggest the possibility of a merger of two such firms since, in that event, the reciprocal externalities would be internalized into the merger. Once internalized, the externalities are properly costed by the merger, its equilibrium outputs will be optimal – at least, if the merger cannot influence the prices of the goods it produces.

6 We have been tacitly assuming that the only way of reducing unwanted spillovers is by reducing the outputs of relevant goods. This assumption helps us to cut through to the core of the matter. It should be evident on reflection, however, that spillovers may be reduced by a number of alternative methods, of which the reduction of the output of the spillover-creating goods is only one. For example, a particular spillover or, more generally, the damage cost of a particular spillover, can also be reduced by a change in the location of industry, by the dispersal of the affected population to other areas, by the installation of antipollution devices, or by recycling the waste products that pollute the air or water. Incidentally, the levying of an effluent tax – a tax on a firm that varies directly with the total damage created by its spillover or effluent – provides the firm with an incentive to discover the cheapest way of reducing the spillover or effluent in question. This cheapest way may well involve a combination of different methods of reducing the spillover.

7 The fact has to be faced that the actual estimating of an ideal effluent tax is fraught with difficulties in a dynamic economy. In view of this, a number of economists have proposed that a *political*

decision be reached about a 'tolerable level' of effluent, and that this tolerable level be implemented by means of an effluent tax. The required effluent tax may be difficult to calculate *a priori*. But by experimenting with size of this tax over time, something close to this politically-determined tolerable level of effluent would eventually be realized. Even so, the tax would have to be changed from time to time as population and real income grew, as new technologies were introduced, and as changes occurred in the patterns of demand and available resource endowments.

16 Environmental spillovers: what difference does the law make?

The answer to the question in the chapter title may seem stunningly obvious. Inasmuch as the law can prohibit or regulate the emission of pollutants in a number of ways, it can make an enormous difference – the difference between an effluent and garbage-littered community and a clean and tidy one. True, but the economist interested in allocative efficiency is asking a different question. Recall that in the preceding chapter we made frequent reference to optimal outputs. By extension, we could also have spoken of optimal levels of pollution; meaning those pollution levels corresponding to the optimal outputs of the goods giving rise to them. In the simple models we used the optimal outputs were assumed exact, being determined uniquely by the intersection of the demand curve and the social marginal cost curve. Toward the end of the preceding chapter, however, I indicated that a unique solution depended, among other things, on two assumptions: first, that the marginal valuation of the spillover damage is effectively independent of the 'property rights' assignment – independent, that is, of whether the victim of the spillover damage has to pay the pollutor to reduce the damage or whether, instead, the pollutor has to pay the victim for putting up with spillover damage; and second that the transactions costs involved in reaching and maintaining an agreed solution are zero.

What we have now to think through is the difference made when we remove these two assumptions, which we now proceed to do.

The easiest way to grasp the implications of removing the first assumption is to forget about *variations* in output and effluent for the time being and to think, instead, of an all-or-nothing environmental change. If, say, the environmental change in question is an improvement we can (as already mentioned more than once) ask the beneficiary either one of two questions: (a) what is the most he is willing to pay for the environmental improvement, or (b) what is the smallest sum he will accept to forgo it.

If, on the other hand, the environmental change is a bad one for him, we can again ask either one of two questions (a)′ what is the most he is willing to pay for the removal of this environmental degradation, or (b)′ what is the smallest sum he will accept to put up with it.

If you ponder on it for a moment you will perceive that (a) and (a)′ effectively ask the same question since an *improvement* of the individual's welfare can take the form either of having a good thing or of removing a bad thing. Similarly, you will perceive that (b) and (b)′ effectively ask the same question since a *reduction* of the individual's welfare can take the form either of forgoing a good thing or of bearing with a bad thing. Consequently, whether the environmental change is one that raises or lowers the welfare of the individual, we still have but two ways of calculating its value to him: (a) a truthful answer to the question, what is the most he will pay (either for a good or for the removal of a bad), and (b) a truthful answer to the question, what is the least sum he will accept (either for forgoing a good or for bearing with a bad). From a reading of Chapter 4 you may have already convinced yourself that there can be a big difference in the answers to questions (a) and (b).

Let us apply these alternative methods of calculating the cost or value of an environmental change to a conflict between two groups; on the one hand, a group of speedboat enthusiasts, group S, seeking to build a boat house along a quiet stretch of coast and, on the other hand, group C, the citizens already living along the coast who cherish peace and quiet above all.

Now the Pareto criterion is met if the gainers from a project can more than compensate the losers. If, however the losses from implementing the project exceed the gains, introducing it violates the Pareto criterion. What we now demonstrate is that the outcome of the Pareto criterion can depend upon the assignment of the property rights since such assignment determines the questions to be asked of the two groups.

Hypothetical (though not implausible) figures for the situation described above are summed up in the table below, where a + sign before the figure indicates willingness to *pay* the sum and a − sign before the figure indicates willingness to *receive* the sum.

	Value to C	*Value to S*	*Social net gain*
1 Rights assigned to S	+ 60,000	−100,000	− 40,000
2 Rights assigned to C	−250,000	+ 80,000	−170,000

The first line tells us that if the S group has a legal right to build a boat house on this strip of coast, and so introduce speed boats there, a motion by group C to prevent this innovation would be defeated financially, and therefore, in this instance, also on the Pareto criterion. For the most that group C is willing to pay to group S to desist is $60,000, whereas the minimum sum acceptable to the S group is $100,000. If, notwithstanding, the speedboat enthusiasts were banned, there would apparently be a net social loss of $40,000 (equal to a net social gain of *minus* $40,000 as in the table). Since the proposal to ban the boat house has been *rejected* on the Pareto criterion, allocative efficiency effectively comes down in favour of the introduction of speedboats.

The second line tells us that group C has a legal right to prevent speedboats along the strip of coast, consequently the intitiative has to come from the S group with its proposal to build the necessary boat house. But in this case the minimum sum that will reconcile group C to the eventual disruption of its peace and quiet is $250,000, whereas the most the S group is willing to pay is $80,000. Clearly the expected gains from group S's proposal falls short of the expected losses it would inflict on the C group by $170,000. The proposal to build a boat house is, therfore, *rejected* on the Pareto criterion. Allocative efficiency now comes down against the introduction of speed boats.

The outcome of the Pareto criterion clearly alters with the state of the law with respect to property rights. If the law favours the S group, as in line 1, then the Pareto criterion favours the boat house proposal. If, instead the law favours the C group, as in line 2 of the table, the Pareto criterion rejects the boat house proposal.

We may, each of us, have different ideas of how to proceed when such awkward cases arise. But it is important that we should at least recognize the possibilities.

The above example may now be extended to a situation in which the environmental change being contemplated can be varied. We shall assume, therefore, that the boat house has already been built and negotiations are taking place in order to determine the number of speedboating hours to be allowed each week. If property rights are assigned to the S group (as in case 1 above), the marginal damage curve to the C group is S_1S_1 in Figure 25. Thus, the vertical distance from any point on that curve to the horizontal axis measures the aggregate damage inflicted by the marginal unit of speedboating time on the members of the C group, the damage being valued as the largest sum they would collectively pay to avoid it. The marginal benefit curve of the S group is given by the D_1D_1 curve, the vertical distance from any point on that curve to the horizontal axis measuring the aggregate benefit enjoyed from the marginal unit of speedboating time by its members, such benefit being valued as the smallest sum they would collectively accept to forgo it.

These two curves, S_1S_1 and D_1D_1, are those pertinent to the assignment of property rights to the S group. The optimal number of speedboating hours, OQ_1 is given by the intersection of the two curves, where the marginal benefit is exactly equal to the marginal cost.

Where, however, the law assigns property rights to the C group, the pertinent curves are S_2S_2 and D_2D_2. Any point on the curve S_2S_2 measures the value of the marginal speedboat damage as the minimal sum collectively acceptable to the C group for putting up with it. Any point on the D_2D_2 curve measures the value of the

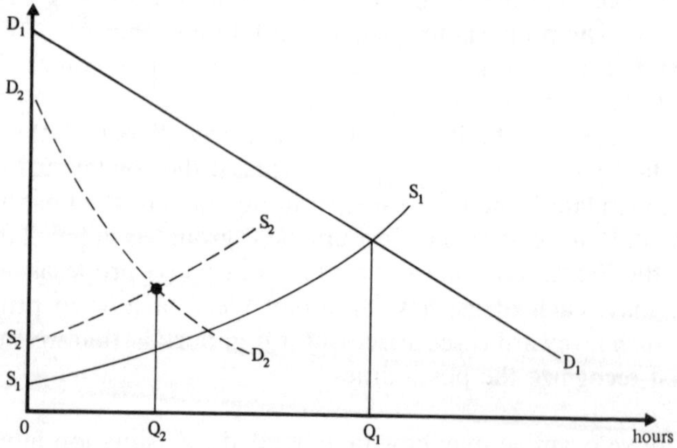

Figure 25

marginal speedboat benefit as the largest sum the members of the S group would pay for it. Under this law, one assigning property rights to the C group, the optimal number of speedboat hours that emerges is equal to OQ_2.

We conclude that the optimal amount of spillover is generally smaller under a law that assigns property rights to the spillover victims than one that assigns them to the creators of the spillovers – which is easy to remember since it accords with common sense.

We have now to switch our thoughts to the difference made by the assignment of property rights when transactions costs are brought into the picture. To avoid unnecessary elaboration in the discussion that follows, we shall assume that the marginal benefit and marginal damage curves are again uniquely determined.

The term transactions costs is broadly defined in the economic literature to encompass costs incurred both through government intervention and as between groups negotiating an agreement. The former would include administrative and legal costs involved in determining and enforcing government controls. The latter would include the bargaining costs of the opposing groups, the costs of maintaining and revising agreements, and capital expenditures necessary to implement the agreements. Concerning the latter, the more important are likely to be the bargaining costs of the opposing groups, which costs can be broken down into a number of elements; the costs of identifying the members of one's own group, the costs of persuading them to make or accept an offer, the costs of reaching agreement among members of one's group on all matters incidental to negotiation with the opposite group, and the actual costs of negotiating with the opposite group.

One cannot, however, assume that the transactions costs of direct agreement between the two groups are necessarily greater under a law conferring property rights on the spillover-creating group. All that can be said in general is that transactions costs increase with the numbers in each group and with their geographical dispersion: the more widespread and pervasive the spillover, the larger the magnitude of the transactions costs.

The voluntary-agreement transactions costs will be treated here as a form of overhead costs with respect to a given situation (and will be regarded, therefore, as independent of the magnitudes of optimal amount of spillovers and of the respective gains of the two groups should agreement be reached). Such transactions costs are real enough inasmuch as they involve time and effort that might otherwise be employed in producing goods. Let us designate the size of these transactions costs by the letter T, and that of the social net benefits that would accrue at the (assumed uniquely determined) optimal output *in the complete absence of transactions costs* by the letters NB. The exercise consists simply in comparing T with NB. And it stands to reason that if the magnitude T exceeds that of NB in a particular instance the movement to the relevant 'optimal' position would, in fact, result in a *residual loss* to society and would not, therefore, be undertaken. (The word 'optimal' is placed in quotation marks since, in this context, it will be truly optimal – in the sense of producing a *residual gain* – only if T is smaller than NB.)

The curve DM in Figure 26 is that of the marginal net benefits accruing to the 'pollutors' – which term covers all those who benefit from the production or consumption of the goods associated with the spillovers in question.[1] The SS′ curve is the marginal net damage curve. Since it cuts the DM curve at G, the optimal output is OQ. Prior to any bargaining between the two groups, 'pollutors' and victims, the market output will be equal to OM.

At market output OM, however, marginal net benefit to the 'pollutors' from producing the good x is zero, whereas the marginal net damage to the victims is MS′. Ignoring transactions costs for the moment, a marginal reduction in x clearly results in a social

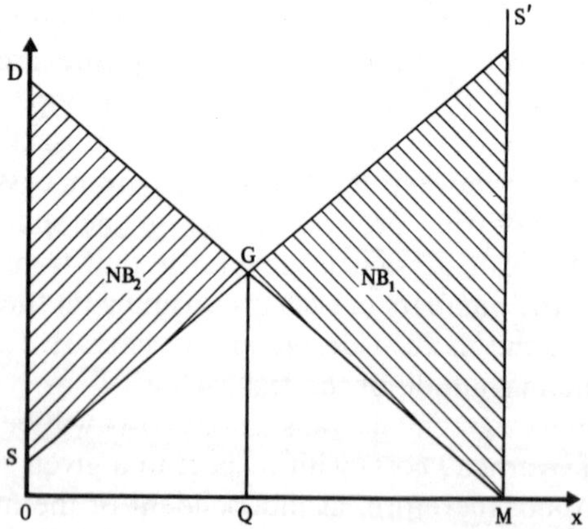

Figure 26

net benefit. And so we could continue to augment this social net benefit by reducing the output of x to OQ, at which output the resulting social net benefit will be equal to the shaded triangular area NB_1. (Put differently, to induce 'pollutors' to reduce output by MQ, they would have to receive at least an amount equal to the triangular area QGM, since this sum is equal to the net benefit they would forgo by reducing output from OM to OQ. On the other hand, the victims would pay at most a sum equal to the area QGS′M to reduce output of x by MQ, since this is value of the damage that would be removed thereby. Therefore the excess of the sum the victims are willing to pay for the reduction of output by MQ above the minimum compensation required by 'pollutors' is equal to this shaded triangle NB_1.)

Now bring in the transactions costs by supposing that they are known to the parties concerned who are contemplating the negotiation of a movement from the existing market equilibrium output OM to the 'optimal' output OQ. If it is then observed that, in fact, the parties do not agree to reduce output from OM to OQ, or thereabouts, it may be inferred that T does indeed exceed NB_1; that, consequently, market output OM is the socially preferred output since there would be a *residual loss* to society in moving to OQ once account is taken of the magnitude of T.

This conclusion is one that lends itself admirably to a conservative doctrine; stated loosely, one that says 'the market knows best'. For if the parties agree to reduce output from market equilibrium OM to output OQ, one must infer a residual gain to society – that is, NB_1 must exceed T. If, on the other hand, output continues at market equilibrium OM, one is to infer instead that T exceeds NB_1 and that, therefore, it is better that OM continue being produced.

Let us go over this argument more carefully with the aid of Figure 26. We spoke above of the market equilibrium output OM. But this is strictly true only if the property rights – the right to pollute in fact – are vested with the 'pollutors'. There is nothing to prevent our assuming these property rights to be assigned instead to the victims. Nor are we restricted to consider transactions costs that arise only in voluntary negotiations between 'pollutors' and victims. We may also consider transactions costs that arise from various forms of government regulation.

First, however, let us reverse the assignment of property rights. They are now conferred on the victims of pollution. If you like, we can refer to them as 'amenity rights' and regard them as part of the constitution of a civilized society.[2]

The initial market output resulting from such amenity rights has to be taken as zero output or very little output inasmuch as the potential victims of the pollution in question will exercise these rights and prohibit any polluting output unless they are fully compensated for the damage they suffer. Again, ignoring transactions costs for the moment, a first unit of output produces a marginal net benefit OD in excess of marginal net damage OS. And this net social benefit can be augmented by extending output to OQ at which point the net social benefit, equal to the shaded triangular area NB_2, is realized.

Now bring in the transactions cost. If NB_2 exceeds T, then negotiation will be successful and output OQ will in fact result. This output OQ may properly be called the market output also since it is the outcome of voluntary financial agreement, one that confers a *residual gain* on society. If, on the other hand, T exceeds NB_2, the production of output OQ would inflict a *residual loss* on society. But, of course, it would *not* be produced since the transactions costs involved would be greater than the net social benefits. Thus 'the market knows best' also when property rights are assigned to the victims. For if T is greater than NB_2 the market output (at least in the situation depicted in Figure 26) is zero. Good x could not be produced efficiently.

Clearly it can make a whale of a difference to the resulting pattern of outputs in the economy if property rights are conferred on 'pollutors', deliberately or by default, or if, instead, they are conferred in the form, say, of amenity rights to all potential victims of pollution.

Broadly interpreted, the guiding doctrine of the courts over the last two centuries has been that, in the interests of industrial progress, it is not unreasonable for the public to have to bear with occasional inconveniences. So expressed, the doctrine seems to sound a note of good common sense, its being implicitly understood that, on balance, the public interest is promoted thereby. But in view of the extraordinary proliferation of new forms of spillover over the last generation, there is at least an arguable case for shifting the right to compensation from industry (or the users of industrial products) to the citizen wherever it is feasible to do so.

The second point to be made about transactions costs is that initiatives by the government might go far toward reducing the costs of voluntary agreement between the two groups, so that the 'optimal' outputs become more likely to confer *residual gains* on society. Again, the transactions costs of *direct* government intervention – either through regulation or effluent taxes – may well be considerably lower in many cases than voluntary transactions costs between the opposing parties. Thus, even where the community accepts a law conferring property rights on polluting industries, the observation that the opportunity for *voluntary* agreement between the 'pollutors' and their victims appears to have no effect on the outputs of the polluting industries is far from being conclusive evidence that there is no residual gain to society from contracting the size of such industries. For it is altogether possible that although the net social benefit (ignoring transactions costs) of moving from the existing market output of an industry toward an 'optimal' output falls far short of the magnitude of the *voluntary* transactions costs, it will be in excess of *government* transactions costs.

None the less, antagonism to the extension of government powers does, admittedly, act to militate in such cases against acceptance of government intervention.

A final word. The arguments above used in connection with Figure 26 might strike you as being a little restrictive since it is output of good x that is being measured along the horizontal axis. The argument looks more general if, instead, we measure units of pollution along the horizontal axis. This is perfectly possible and, indeed, necessary whenever the pollution in question is more economically reduced by a combination of different methods, among which the reduction in the output of good x is merely one.[3]

17 Non-environmental spillovers: some ethical questions

If the subject of welfare economics were the study of the welfare actually experienced by members of society (which it is not) then whatever confidence is reposed by economists in the pricing system of competitive markets as an institution for the promotion of society's wellbeing is likely to be diminished once serious account is taken of the incidence of those spillovers that are often referred to as 'interdependent welfare effects' or ' interdependent utility effects'. As this terminology suggests, the spillovers in question are the effects on some people's welfare of the welfare of other people, the latter being measured by their income, wealth, expenditure or status. Scepticism about the allocative virtues of competitive markets may be further provoked when non-environmental spillovers are extended to encompass the response of some people to the consumption of particular goods by others, to the particular activities of others, or to their group characteristics, whether ethnic or religious. For these preferences and prejudices which enter into the determination of a person's welfare do not, in general, register on market prices or outputs – except, perhaps, very indirectly. As a result, any movement toward an apparent overall optimal position for the economy (say that for which there is universal marginal cost pricing) may, in fact, be a movement away from a true optimum, even when there are no environmental spillovers.

Let us consider two examples of non-environmental spillovers commonly mentioned in the literature.

First, there is the possibility that a transfer of income from a rich person A to a poor person B is one that makes both actually better off, so realizing an actual Pareto improvement. In this case it is imagined that \$1 received by the poor person, B, is valued by him at exactly \$1, whereas person A who donates the \$1 derives more than \$1's worth of satisfaction by donating it to B than by spending it on goods for himself. The market, as commonly understood, does not bring this about. But there is nothing to prevent persons such as A transferring sums of money to poor persons – always assuming that transactions costs are, or can be made to be, low enough.

There can, however, be variations on this theme that tend to raise the transactions costs of such transfers. For example, it may be that person A derives satisfaction not only from his giving money to B, but also from the knowledge that other donors also give money to B. In consequence, the amount of A's donation to B may be made conditional upon the contribution of other donors. Raising the community's welfare through transfers of this sort now becomes a little more complicated, though not wholly impracticable if we are content to effect *some* improvement without striving always for the uttermost – for the elusive optimal combination of transfers.

Government coercion in transferring dollars from rich to poor might also be justified on the Pareto criterion (one that meets a *potential* Pareto improvement). For the satisfaction from donating $1 to B experienced by our person A, although now valued by him at less than $1 of expenditure on himself is yet positive (say it is worth 15 cents to him). And allowing once more that the $1 received by person B is valued by him at exactly $1, the transfer of this $1 from A to B produces a net satisfaction equal to 15 cents.[1]

Second, there is the possibility that person A's welfare depends, among other things, upon the amounts of some *specific* goods consumed by others. If, for example, person A wanted to help the poor, he might get much greater satisfaction if his money transfer were used to present the poor with certain kinds of food and clothing than if, instead, his money were transferred direct to them (person A suspects that some of the poor would use money transferred directly to them to buy liquor or to gamble with).

Let us go a step further by starting from a position in which A has already raised his own welfare by transferring some money direct to a poor man B. Person A has gone as far as he can go in raising his welfare by this means. Nonetheless, by transferring additional money to B *conditional upon* B's spending it on only specific goods designated by A (say goat milk and wholemeal bread) person A's welfare can be raised yet more. Indeed, it is possible, given A's welfare responses to B's consumption, for A to augment his welfare further by bribing B to consume less of tobacco and liquor in favour of other things.

Such operations bring about an actual Pareto improvement inasmuch as both A and B benefit from them. They are obviously not market operations as commonly understood, although they are feasible enough in a small community. The larger the community, however, the more institutionalized become the means of effecting such charitable operations and the larger, therefore, are the transactions costs. And the larger the transaction costs the smaller the residual gains to the community from such operations.

For all that, a case may be conceived for transfers in kind rather than in cash, especially if the differences in transaction costs are small and if the donors would donate substantially less were they forbidden to specify the sort of goods to be given to the poor. Thus, despite the stigma of paternalism associated with the idea of transfers in kind to the poor, the level of both donors and recipients may be made higher than if only cash transfers are permitted. (For although the poor prefer, say, $100 cash to goods of the same value, they may much prefer $200 of specific goods. And a transfer of $200 from the rich used to buy these specific goods for the poor may also afford the rich more satisfaction than a cash transfer of $100.)

Although – as I say at the beginning of the preceding paragraph – a case may be conceived for tranfers in kind rather than in cash, the matter does not end there. Inasmuch as welfare economics is raised upon an ethical consensus, these interdependent welfare effects do not automatically qualify for inclusion in the welfare calculus. The citizens of a civilized community may reasonably affirm that, in respect of market goods at least, it is right and proper that all adults, even the poorest, be treated as responsible beings; on a par, that is, with other adult members of the community. Only exceptional circumstances would then warrant the indignity implied by treating them as less responsible.

Again, although the existence of a positive relation between person A's welfare and that of person B's income (or expenditure) would meet with society's considered approval, the reverse relationship might not. Thus, if knowledge of an improvement in B's welfare caused person A's welfare to decline, society in its ethical capacity may agree to disregard A's reaction: it may lay it down generally that reactions arising from envy or resentment should not be respected and, therefore, should not be counted.

A more general form of this envy or resentment is that described by the phrase 'keeping up with the Joneses', abbreviated here to the 'Jones Effect', and originally dignified by the term ' the relative income hypothesis'. Formally this hypothesis states that what matters to a person in a high consumption society is not only his absolute real income, or his command over market goods, but his position in the income structure of society. In an extreme case, the citizen would choose, for example, a 10 per cent increase in his real income provided that the average real income of society remained unchanged rather than a 50 per cent increase in his real income accompanied by a 50 per cent increase in the real income of every one else in society.

The evidence in favour of this hypothesis in this extreme form is not conclusive, although it is not implausible to believe it holds among wealthier groups. However, in its more general form – the view that in the affluent society a person's *relative* income also affects his welfare – it is hardly to be controverted. After all, the satisfaction we derive from many objects depends, in varying degrees, both on the extent of their scarcity and on the prestige associated with our ownership of them. So why not, also, our income relative to those of others, regarded as an index of our success or merit?

Recognition of this Jones Effect, and the belief that it can only grow with the general rise in living standards, does put a damper on the hopes of growthmen. People – singly or in groups – will, we may suppose, continue to try to improve their income position. But in the limiting case in which a person's welfare depends *only* on his income relative to others, it is no longer possible to meet the Pareto criterion: by costless transfers, that is, to make some people better off without making any one else worse off. For the fact of making some people better off will always, of itself, make others feel worse off. In short, allocative improvements would be impossible if the Jones Effect were paramount.

In the name of social justice, of course, policies that redistribute income in favour of the relatively poorer members of society may continue. But if ever real income were always equally distributed among members of the community, an impasse would be reached: no rise in welfare would ever be experienced by *anyone* even though per capital real income continued to climb.

If we are considering the welfare response of people to the goods or activities of others, mention must be made of the notion of a 'merit good' – and, by extension, a 'demerit good'. The term merit good has been used rather loosely by economists to indicate a good that is socially desirable independently of the valuation placed on it by beneficiaries. The task of designating which goods are merit goods has been assigned to a group called 'the decision makers' by a number of writers on methods of project appraisal.[2] This powerful group of 'decision-makers' is a somewhat nebulous conception that seems to be invoked by writers in the last resort whenever the economic calculation of some effect or other begins to look sticky. A critical issue is fudged by such writers whenever they assure the reader that such decision makers are responsible for the nation's economic objectives. Since decisions about the economic objectives of the nation, if they are deliberately formulated at all, are formulated independently of the norms of allocative economics, they must be the outcome of political decisions. But the question of whether economic magnitudes ought in an economic evaluation to be determined by political decisions is a controversial one, perhaps too controversial to be broached in an introductory text.[3]

In order to bring the concept of a merit good within the ambit of allocative economics, it has to be viewed as an externality, one arising, again, from the dependence of a person's welfare on the particular sorts of goods consumed by others. For the merit good, however, the 'others' who are consuming the particular sorts of goods are not the poor but the public at large. Thus, if I and others who affect a concern for high culture approve of concerts of classical music, of art galleries, of opera and ballet, then quite apart from our personal enjoyment of any of these art forms, the economist may properly translate our approval of them into a willingness to pay in order to promote their popularity. Put more formally, a good x becomes a merit good for me in so far as the consumption of good x by others adds something to my welfare – its being understood that the addition to my welfare arises only from my approval of their action in consuming good x.

Note particularly that the sum I am willing to pay to see more of these merit goods in the community is quite distinct from the sum I am willing to contribute toward the building of a project (say a railway or a recreational area) simply because I may one day have beneficial recourse to it even though I cannot say when or if I shall ever make use of it. The latter sum would be referred to in economic parlance as 'optional demand' for the obvious reason that the sum I pay is for the option of making use of the good (at its prevailing price, if any) at some future date, even though I may never exercise the option. This option-value sum is effectively an insurance premium against not having the use of the good in a possible emergency or in altered circumstances in which it would be valuable to me.

In contrast to option value, the value I attach to a merit good is 'disinterested', in the sense that this value is wholly independent of the extent, or even hope, of my participating in the consumption of the merit good or activity. According, then, as people generally regard an operatic performance as a merit good, the *social* marginal valuation curve lies above the private marginal valuation curve (or market demand curve) – the vertical difference between the two curves at any point being a measure of the aggregate sums which people approving of opera are willing to pay for 'marginal extension' of it (the 'marginal extension' should, perhaps, be thought of in terms of number of performances, given the number of opera houses; in the longer run, in terms of number of opera houses themselves in the country).[4] The optimal output of the merit good, that at which its social marginal valuation is equal to its marginal cost, is larger than the market equilibrium output. Consequently, there exists an optimal excise subsidy which would expand market output so as to equal the optimal output. At all events, this economic concept of a merit good would rationalize the case of subsidies to the arts.

The concept of a merit good can, moreover, be extended to justify preservation of the blue whale, the redwood tree, and other endangered species of fauna and flora despite the importunities of the market. In general, if the preservation of an old building, of an area of natural beauty, or of the living conditions of any animal species, matters to members of the public independently of their material advantage as consumers or producers, the market solution cannot be vindicated on grounds of economic efficiency. The merit good aspect has to be entered into the calculus as an important and, perhaps, decisive datum.

Figuratively speaking, there is an invisible collective valuation for each merit good, be it a symphony orchestra, the Indian tiger, or the Amazon forest (or portion of it) that is ignored by the market. What is more, the magnitude turns again on the implied ownership of property rights: on who is to pay whom. Is it to be assumed that the concerned public should pay the timber companies to forbear from sawing down redwood trees and big game hunters to forbear from killing tigers? Or is it to be assumed that commercial ventures and sportsmen should bribe the concerned public to permit them to continue their activities. As suggested in the preceding chapter, the economic solution could be critically different according as the property rights were (implicitly) assigned to one group or the other.

The economic concept of a demerit good is, of course, perfectly symmetric with that of a merit good, and may be construed to provide the rationale of a tax on liquor, gambling or pornographic material. In a pluralistic society, however, it is not altogether impossible that something which would be regarded as a demerit good by one group may be regarded as a merit good by another. In that case, the algebraic sum of the two groups would determine whether on balance, the good is more of a merit than a demerit good or *vice versa* and whether, therefore, allocative consideration calls for a subsidy or a tax. This last possibility, however, gives rise to critical reflections which will be taken up towards the end of Chapter 28 (Part Five).

Finally, in this connection, the economic calculation of the merit or demerit good might be difficult to make whatever the legal or moral position in respect of property rights. Yet, for practical purposes, rough estimates or even 'guesstimates' may be sufficient to indicate clearly that current policies being pursued are far from being economically efficient. Certainly, consideration of the allocative importance of the concept of merit goods, suggests that there can be no presumption in favour of the market in any activity that causes widespread misgiving among segments of the public.

To coin a phrase, then, sentiment carries as much 'clout' in normative economics as material self-interest. But if so, where does normative economics end? Where do we draw the line?

If everything that matters to a person can, in principle, be translated into a money value (the most he would pay for it, or the minimum he would accept to go without) then, assuming there is no ethical objection to its inclusion in the welfare calculus, there is no formal limit to the application of normative economics. If measurement were always practicable, the economic calculus would be all-embracing and would be properly regarded as socially decisive in that no relevant aspect would be omitted. Thus, it would no longer be a question of an economic calculation being but a *contribution* to the decision-making process, for the economic calculation would encompass all matters of concern to society.

Against a decision resulting from the all-embracing economic calculation we could always place a decision based on some constitutional procedure, say majority rule based on adult suffrage. This latter method of decision-reaching may often produce solutions that are contrary to those reached by the economic calculation. What is more, the political decision would always prevail on constitutional grounds. Yet even so, if people were allowed (at small cost) to trade their votes for money the political decision would be revised to accord with the economic one in the process of which 'every one' would be made better off – as required by the Pareto criterion.

But though *in concept* everything can be reduced to economic measurement (How much would compensate you for your lover's death? An infinite sum, since no finite sum is large enough? Possibly. But this too might produce a clear economic solution to the problem.), a deterrent is the cost and practicability of reliable measurement. 'In practice', all that can be actually measured is often a small part of the change in welfare wrought by the project or policy in question. This measurable part may grow over the future. Yet it is doubtful whether those components of welfare that turn on sentiment, loyalty, religious conviction, social cohesion and other intangible but powerful considerations will ever become amenable to the economist's measuring rod.

True, such limitations may not signify in simple problems; such as whether to build one large bridge or two smaller ones. But the sort of decisions we have to make today in a complex and high-technology society have far reaching repercussions on our lives which, even if we could know and understand them, would elude economic measurement. Since, then, the economist's evaluation of a contemplated change cannot be more than a part of some hypothetical all-embracing evaluation, his actual evaluation has to be seen, in a pragmatic sense, as no more than a contribution to a social decision that is reached through the political process. The economist offers an estimate (of varying reliability) of the algebraic result only of a number of effects on the welfare of that society, *the particular effects being made clear in his report*. It is up to society in its political capacity to attach what significance it deems proper to such a report.

18 Favourable spillovers and collective goods

That which I call a collective good is more commonly spoken of by economists as a 'public good', a term that misleads the beginner and has also misled economists.[1] Public goods bring to mind the goods provided by the state, such as courts of law, highways, police protection, and often education, public utilities, and medical services. In a thoroughgoing socialist state all goods produced would be public on this conception, whereas it is not wholly impossible to provide every good in the economy, including the armed forces, within a private enterprise economy. The distinction between the category of collective goods and all other goods has to be a functional one. It must hold irrespective of ownership or management. This means that, either within a thorough-going socialist state or else within a thorough-going private enterprise economy, the economist should still be able to distinguish between *collective* goods and all remaining goods, which may be called *private* goods.

The interesting fact to me personally is that so very little analysis has gone into the literature on collective goods. The bulk of the literature on the subject can in fact be boiled down to semantics and the confusions arising therefrom. But if this is interesting, it is not also surprising. For the analysis of collective goods is formally symmetric with that of externalities as treated in Chapters 14 and 15. Indeed, adverse spillovers may be spoken of as collective bads wherever the damaging effects fall on the public at large. As distinct from collective goods, however, these collective bads are (as mentioned earlier) assumed *incidental* to the process of production or use of an item – an assumption which, possibly, accounts for the relative leniency with which they have been regarded by the law. Collective goods, in contrast, can either be, again, incidental to the production or use of an item, or else they can be deliberately produced.

The incidental collective goods, or favourable spillovers (especially environmental spillovers) warrant only the briefest mention, being the opposite of adverse environmental spillovers. Thus, instead of being added to the costs of production as are adverse spillovers, the value of favourable spillovers are subtracted from costs of production. If, for example, my keeping of honey bees has the effect of increasing my neighbour's apple harvest, there is a positive connection between the amount of honey I produce and the amount of apples that he produces. Let the bees required to yield each pound of honey result in an additional yield of apples worth $1.50, and the *social* cost of each pound of honey I produce has to be reckoned as $1.50 less than its private cost to me. (If there were an enforceable law, I should collect the whole of the $1.50 conferred on my neighbouring apple-grower for each pound of honey I produce. In this way I would have 'internalized' the externality, and reduced my private marginal cost of honey to equal the social marginal cost.)

Drawing a continuous marginal cost curve for my honey, s′s′ in Figure 27, the social marginal cost curve s″s″ is parallel to it and below it. Given the price p, the optimal output of my honey is Oq (at which price is equal to social marginal cost) which is larger than my chosen output Om – always assuming, realistically, that I cannot persuade my neighbour to pay me for the incidental benefits my honey bees confer on his apple harvest. An excise subsidy on honey, equal to hg has the effect of making s″s″ my effective marginal cost curve, in consequence of which I will expand my output of honey from Om to Oq.

Figure 28 represents the market situation where large numbers of bee-keepers confer benefits on all neighbouring apple-growers. The supply curve S′S′ represents the horizontal summation of all

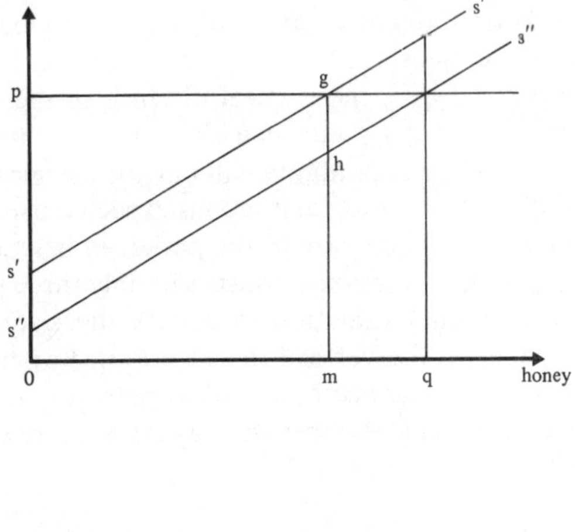

Figure 27

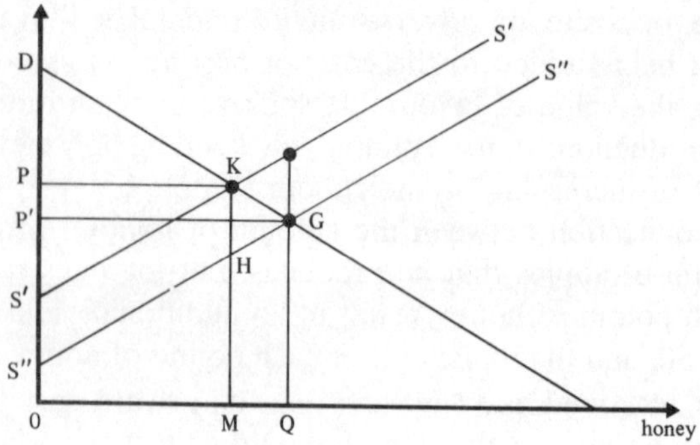

Figure 28

the individual cost curves of the bee-keepers (assuming all variable factor prices do not change).[2] Once optimal output OQ is established as a result of an excise subsidy HK, the price of honey falls from OP, corresponding to the original market output OM, to OP′ corresponding to the optimal output OQ. For good measure, consumer surplus in Figure 28 increases from the triangular area DPK in the pre-subsidy position to the larger area DP′G in the optimal position. Likewise, the rent accruing to bee-keepers' land increases from area PS′K to P′S″G.

Although the above example is one of beneficial externalities that are *external*, it is possible also to have cases in which the beneficial externalities are *internal* to the activity.[3]

If we now turn to the deliberate creation of a capital *asset*, say a park, designed to produce a collective *good* – the service yielded by the park – the demand curve for the collective good, DD′ in Figure 29 is to be thought of as a collective marginal valuation curve. Thus, if we measure, first, the size of the park to be built along the horizontal axis, the vertical distance of the curve from the horizontal axis at any point measures the maximum amounts that each person in the community will pay for marginal increases in the size of the park, bearing in mind his expected use of the park over the future. Thus, if the size of the park is to be equal to OM_1 in the figure, and the community consists of only three persons, A, B and C, the marginal valuation of a park the size of OM_1 to person A is equal to the vertical distance a_1b_1, to person B it is equal to the vertical distance b_1c_1, and to person C it is equal to c_1M_1. The maximum sum all three will pay is therefore equal to the

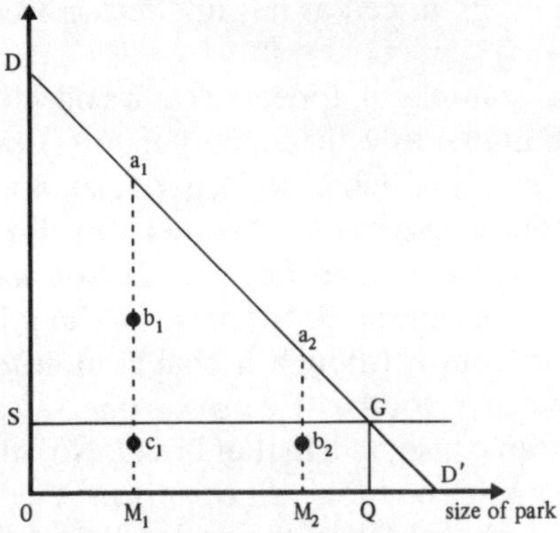

Figure 29

vertical distance a_1M_1. For the larger size OM_2, the marginal valuation for person A is equal to a_2b_2, for person B it is equal to b_2M_2, and for person C it is zero.

We can suppose that we have this information that enables us to draw the Collective Marginal Valuation curve DD′ prior to building the park, also the marginal cost curve SS, which for simplicity is assumed constant. The optimal size of the park is therefore equal to OQ, since with a park of that size the collective marginal benefit expected from the park is just equal to the marginal cost of its construction. The consumer surplus of this park is clearly equal to the area SDG.

Once a park of given size is built, however, we can measure park service along the horizontal axis and determine the optimal amount of it in exactly the same way. Provided that OQ park service (per week) is rendered, optimality is achieved whether the costs are covered wholly, partly, or not at all. For the covering of costs by beneficiaries under any system of prices or taxes is no more than a transfer of income within the community – a distributional and *not* an allocative effect.

In the shortest period over which the weekly park service cannot be changed, variations in the use of the park by persons, A, B and C does not incur any variations in cost. Neither does the use of the park by additional people (ignoring externalities such as overcrowding) incur any additional cost in this period. Marginal cost is nil and therefore use of the park should be priced at nil for the joint beneficiaries. It follows that for each beneficiary also the use of the park should be priced at nil; in effect, a free good.

From the above example, it appears that a collective good is one that confers simultaneously the same benefit(s) on a number of people. Since a marginal increase in park size does not confer a benefit on any one person *alone*, neither can the corresponding marginal cost be attributed to any one person alone: it can be attributed only to the community of persons who jointly and simultaneously benefit from it (though probably in different degrees). Contrast this collective good with a *private* one, say a loaf of bread. Person A alone can consume a loaf of bread. No others simultaneously can consume this one loaf. Since person A's demand for this loaf incurs a cost, the whole of the cost can be attributed to him alone.

The marginal cost of artificial rain – to change the example of a collective good – cannot be attributed to any one out of the many beneficiaries who, simultaneously (though in different degrees) receive it. A few such examples are enough to suggest that we define a collective good as one whose marginal cost of production cannot be attributed except collectively to the members affected by it.

So far we have abstracted from adverse externalities, particularly those that are internal to the use of the collective asset. A highway is a collective good on the above definition if the costs of wear and tear of a single vehicle cannot be identified. But once the traffic increases beyond a point, each additional vehicle can be said to inflict marginal congestion costs (equal to the sum of additional delay costs imposed on all the intra-marginal traffic) by reference to which an optimal amount of traffic may be determined as indicated toward the end of Chapter 14. Similarly with our previous park example: if too many people enter the park as to get in each other's way and reduce the enjoyment of the park, the social marginal cost is no longer zero but equal to the resulting marginal congestion cost. The optimal use indicated is then smaller than that resulting from free entry, and may be implemented either by direct rationing or by an entrance fee.

Bear in mind, however, that although in these circumstances optimality may be attained by setting up a price equal to the marginal congestion cost (at least in this short run during which we cannot increase the size of the collective asset) the fact that we can attribute a marginal *congestion* cost to a person does not conflict with our definition of a collective good. Even when congested, the highway and the park continue to be collective goods on our definition. For this marginal congestion cost is no more than a *reduction* in the collective benefits, or benefits simultaneously conferred on many persons, by the collective good in question. Once we allow for changes in the size (or other dimension) or in the servicing of the collective asset in the longer run, its marginal *production* cost cannot be attributed to any one person.

Let us dwell on this a moment longer. For it is just as demand, and therefore congestion costs, are increasing (with the given size of collective asset) that the decision whether to increase the size of the collective asset arises. As the congestion costs rise there comes a point at which it is cheaper to expand the size of the asset than to continue incurring congestion costs. In other words, we ought to change over to expanding the size of the asset once additional production costs become lower than additional congestion costs.

Before discussing an interesting implication of collective goods, it is worth drawing a number of conceptual distinctions that have caused confusion among students.

It is sometimes alleged that each of the beneficiaries of a collective good receive the same amount of the benefit. Possibly the writer who states this is thinking about the services of the armed forces which may be regarded as affording equal protection to all citizens. Even here, the proposition is more of a constitutional formality than one of exact description. Certainly the value that people put on such protection will vary, since some citizens will find it easier to escape a triumphant enemy or to come to terms with him. Thinking, however, of more ordinary collective goods, television transmitters, street lighting, parks, artificial lakes, wilderness areas, zoos, museums, and so on, it should be manifest that every one does *not* spend the same time using any particular collective good and certainly does *not* get the same enjoyment from it as every other person. Some people there are who never visit an art gallery or a wilderness area. Their consumption of such services is nil; which is to say their marginal valuation of the first unit of such services is nil.

What is more, once we introduce a distinction between *optional* collective goods (of which the above mentioned, excepting armed protection, are all examples) and *non-optional* collective goods, the differences in the benefit enjoyed can be more marked. As the term suggests, an optional collective good is one for which the amount taken by the individual is that which he himself chooses. In contrast, the amount received by him from a non-optional collective good is not of his choosing. The armed forces extend their protection to pacifists even though pacifists may view such protection as an affront and, therefore, as a 'disservice' to them. A less controversial example is the 'seeding' of clouds so as to precipitate rain over an area of farmland. The amount of rain received by each farmer differs and, clearly, he cannot control the amount falling on his land. Although to most of the farmers we can suppose the rain to be a boon, to others it may create more harm than good. And even among the farmers who benefit, the amount of rainfall they receive could well be more than the amount they would choose – which means that the *marginal* valuation of the rain received is negative. These negative marginal valuations of some farmers will have to be more than offset by the positive marginal valuations of other farmers if their algebraic total is to be positive and equal to the marginal cost so that an optimal amount of rain (assuming we have the technology to control it) may be precipitated on that area of farmland.

Another misconception is that – in the absence of congestion costs at least – the marginal cost of a collective good is always zero. Thinking in terms of parks, street lighting, radio transmitters, and other optional collective assets, this is correct only for such assets of given size, producing given services. Under these conditions additional persons availing themselves of the collective facilities do not add to the costs. In the radio-transmitter example, any number of people can settle in the area it serves (at their own expense) and listen to the programmes without raising the costs of transmission by a penny. The marginal cost per additional person is therefore zero only within that short period during which no alteration in the size or service of the collective asset takes place, and always provided that the additional numbers do not cause congestion costs.

In the longer period, say one during which specific capital is augmented or altered, capital costs are incurred. The marginal cost of such extensions is therefore positive. And the optimal size of the collective asset is, again, that for which the collective marginal valuation is equal to the (now positive) marginal cost.

The same principle holds also when the collective asset is designed to confer a number of different benefits. A river dam, for example, may be constructed to supply electricity and also to provide boating, fishing and swimming facilities. The collective marginal valuations of each of these four services have to be added together in comparing the community's marginal valuation curve for this multi-purpose facility with its marginal cost. At the same time, this project may inadvertently generate adverse spillovers also such as increasing the mosquito population or causing some ecological damage. Assuming these things can be foreseen, these collective marginal losses have to be subtracted from the collective marginal valuation curve (or added to its marginal cost curve). No new principle is involved, but the calculation is more difficult and costly.

Collective goods are troublesome to the economist because they do not lend themselves easily to production by competitive industry. A competitive industry is guided by prices: if the demand price of the good is above its unit cost the industry expands by attracting firms and *vice versa*. But for a collective good, the demand price is the sum of the individual marginal valuations, a datum that is not easy to guess at or experiment with. And even if it could be estimated by a private firm, it has no incentive to produce the collective good unless it is able to charge a number of people – perhaps a very large number – in order to cover its costs. But if the firm has no means of excluding people from enjoying the service once it is provided, people will have no incentive to pay.

It may seem that there is a case for the public ownership and provision of collective goods after all since the state can cover the total costs through taxes and, in the very short period, provide the service free – equal, that is, to its marginal cost (at least for optional collective goods). However, the collective marginal valuation curve is not easy to estimate, especially when the technique of sample surveys does not lend itself easily to instances in which it is difficult for the potential consumer to place a value on the service and/or when there is an incentive to misrepresent his true valuation of it.[4] A political decision also runs into difficulties. When the decision whether or not to build a collective asset is put to a vote, voters expecting to pay more tax than the good is worth to them have an incentive to vote against it, whereas those expecting to pay less tax than the good is worth to them have an incentive to vote for it.

In order for private enterprise to produce a collective asset, either it must have legal powers to charge the population, on some formula, for the collective good provided, whether this is street lighting, broadcasting services, or the services of a light house; or it must employ some device for exluding people from the service unless they pay a set price. This latter device is sometimes spoken of as 'building excludability into' the good. A simple example would be the installing of a coin-operated turn-stile at the entrance to a privately owned park. The box office at a cinema or theatre for charging admission is another instance of effective excludability built into a collective good. Provided that the cinema or theatre is not full, the actual marginal cost of an additional person for any given performance is zero. The optimal number of spectators would then be ensured by setting the price also at zero. Only as the house begins to fill up, and additional spectators get in the way of others can we speak of marginal congestion costs limiting the numbers who attend. Similar remarks apply to art galleries and museums.

Yet when they are run as commercial enterprises, as they usually are, theatres and galleries are unable to cover their costs unless they do charge the public no matter what the attendance. And if they are not to cause resentment or an uproar, they cannot discriminate by charging only customers who come in early, allowing late-comers in free (provided they do not cause congestion), in this way attaining an optimal number of spectators. For each class of seats, they are expected, as a matter of equity, to charge the one price, even if this implies that the numbers attending will often be smaller than optimal.

We may conclude that, in a short period, the use of excluding devices associated with an entry charge extends the benefit of the collective good to a number of people that is smaller than optimal – unless there is overcrowding in which case a positive charge is warranted.

However, the excluding device may not always be relatively inexpensive. One way of building excludability into a transmitting service is to use equipment to 'scramble' the signals, so that only by buying an 'unscrambling' device from the company can the owner of the television set receive the programmes. 'Cable' television is obviously another way of building excludability. A privately owned lighthouse, it has been suggested, can be designed so that its warning signals are received only by ships that buy the required apparatus from the owners. In sum, the costs of excludability, which may be a prominent feature under private ownership of collective goods, may not be necessary if they are placed under public ownership. Against the advantages of public ownership, however, have to be placed the costs incurred in raising additional taxes in order to finance the overhead resource costs of the collective good and also the current costs of its maintenance.

Finally, it should be recognized that a number of collective facilities proposed over the last few years are in fact no more than projects designed to remove or reduce the incidental collective bads (adverse spillovers) resulting from the spread of industry, the growth in populations and the introduction of new technological processes and their products. One thinks in this connection of the efforts of private organizations and the state to restore wilderness areas, to clean up and re-stock rivers and lakes, and to undertake research into antidotes to the adverse side effects of new drugs, pesticides and chemical fertilizers.

Further reading for Part Three

For a timely survey of the variety of pollutants in the modern world, and for a lucid exposition of the difficulties of applying the solutions favoured by academic economists, the reader is referred to Baumol and Oates (1979).

A popular version of externalities that are internal to cattle-grazing activity (formally the same model as the corn-growing example in Chapter 15) appeared under the title 'The tragedy of the commons' and has been reproduced in a book of readings by its author Garrett Hardin, and John Baden, entitled *Managing the Commons* (1977). The economics student might benefit from glancing through my 1971 survey of 'The postwar literature on externalities'.

Part Four

Resource allocation within a general context

19 Uses of a general economic context

Among the kinds of questions that the economist would most like to be able to answer are the more general ones; general in that they involve a comparison between alternative forms of organization of the whole economy. Popular examples are whether free trade (or some international trade, at any rate) is better for a country than 'autarky' or no international trade; whether a competitive economy is better than a monopolistic economy; whether some tax systems are better than others – where better is to be understood in terms of ranking according to the Pareto criterion. Again, if there are no unambiguous answers to such questions, is it possible for the economist to specify conditions under which answers to them will be unambiguous?

In order to be able to answer such questions, the analyses have to be developed within a general economic context. They are necessarily more abstract than those analyses employed to answer questions framed within a partial economic context. But they are not, repeat not, any more difficult. What is more, from my teaching experience I can assure you that students are apt to regard the exposition of propositions within a general economic context as the more fascinating part of normative economics. The ease with which seeming paradoxes are revealed, the simplicity of the syntheses effected – especially when the analysis is presented for the most part in the form of a two-good, two-person economy – seldom fails to delight the interested student. Prepare, then, for much intellectual enjoyment in working through this part of the book. The conclusions to be reached, moreover, are far-reaching and, in a negative way alas, quite devastating. No economist who has successfully assimilated this literature – which goes by the name of the New Welfare Economics, and addresses itself to criteria for ranking alternative economic organizations, in particular the Pareto criterion – emerges without his complacency being ruffled.[1]

Now in thinking about alternative organizations of the entire economy, we need, for the most part, only to visualize alternative collections of goods produced by the economy – by which I mean alternative amounts of a given number of goods that are produced and consumed by the members of the economic community. However, these alternative collections of goods which are to be compared are also to be conceived as alternative equilibrium positions of the economy. Thus for each collection of goods considered on its own, the amount of each of the goods being produced is exactly equal also to the amount being consumed at its prevailing price. Each set of goods in the collection is, then, associated with a corresponding set of equilibrium prices. And, what is very much to the purpose, as we shall soon discover, each collection of goods along with its equilibrium set of prices also entails a particular distribution of welfare (or 'real' income) among the members of the economic community.

It is customary also to suppose initially (a) that all factors are fully employed, (b) that the resource endowment of the economy (so many workers, so much land and so much capital) is fixed, and (c) that techniques of production remain unchanged. These three suppositions, however, are used only to simplify the exposition for the time being. Their removal would enable us only to extend the illustrations of our conclusions, not to invalidate them.

We come finally to the most incredible simplification of all, namely, that there are only two goods produced and consumed in the economy, goods x and y, these letters serving to identify either the particular good – say x is wheat and y is cloth – or else their respective amounts, according to the context. Yet you may take it for granted that the important conclusions we reach in discussing this two-good economy are valid also for an n-good economy (where n is any number greater than 2). In fact much of the journal literature on the subject has made use of a two-person two-good economy in reaching conclusions that are deemed to apply to an m-person n-good economy.

In Figure 30 we measure the amount of good x – say bushels of wheat per annum – along the horizontal axis, as we would be doing in the preceding Parts. But from now on, however, the vertical axis will be used *not* to measure price or cost, but simply to measure the amount of the other good y – say yards of cloth per annum. Thus a point such as Q_0, which happens to be inside the curved boundary

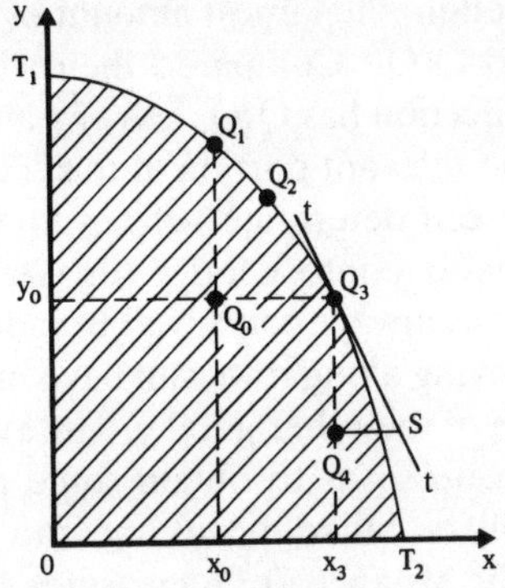

Figure 30

line T_1T_2, represents a collection of goods that consists of Ox_0 of good x and Oy_0 of good y. The point Q_3, on the other hand, represents a collection of goods that is on the boundary T_1T_2 and consists of Ox_3 of good x and Oy_0 of good y.

If we continue to assume continuity in goods space, there will be an unlimited number of different collections of goods, each one represented by a point such as Q_0 and each being producible with the resource endowment of the economy. Obviously, however, there are limits to the magnitudes of the collections that can be produced with the fixed endowment of resources. And once the techniques of production are given, as we suppose they are, the limits are unambiguously defined.

In Figure 30, the limits are defined by the boundary T_1T_2. All points within the striped area OT_1T_2 comprise the set of goods collections that can be produced by the economy in question. And when we say 'within' the area OT_1T_2 it is to be understood that we include the points along the boundary itself. Clearly the collection indicated by point O is to be included in the set since it is possible to produce nothing at all. Likewise the point y_0 is to be included since it is possible to produce Oy_0 of good y and nothing at all of good x. For the most part, however, we shall be paying attention to the points along the boundary itself, this boundary – T_1T_2 in Figure 30 – being referred to as the 'transformation curve' inasmuch as a movement along it from one point to another may be said to entail a transformation from one collection of goods to another. Thus a movement, say, from point Q_1 on the transformation curve to point Q_3 on it reveals that, for a reduction of Q_1Q_0 of good y from the original Q_1 collection, the largest amount of good x that can be produced is equal to Q_0Q_3. Compared then with the original Q_1 collection, the Q_3 collection has Q_1Q_0 less of y and Q_0Q_3 more of x.

By reference to the relevant portion of this transformation curve for the economy we can determine what is known as 'the rate of transformation' of good y into good x (or *vice versa*). Since the transformation curve is always conceived broadly as sloping down from right to left, moving along it we can have more of good x only by giving up so much of the other good y. The *average* amount of y that has to be given up so as to obtain some additional units of good x can reasonably be called the *average* rate of transformation of y into x. Thus, if the distance Q_0Q_3 measures 100 units of good x whereas the distance Q_1Q_0 measures 300 units of good y then in moving from collection Q_1 to Q_3 we effectively transform 300 units of good y into 100 units of x. The average rate of transformation in moving from Q_1 to Q_3 is therefore 300 of y divided by 100, or an average of 3 units of y per unit of x. We abbreviate this by saying the average rate of transformation in moving from Q_1 to Q_3 (or, for that matter, from Q_3 to Q_1) is 3.

The point Q_1 can, of course, be chosen as to be closer and closer to the point Q_3 and as it becomes closer this average rate of transformation of y into x generally alters. In the limiting case Q_1 is to be conceived as coinciding with Q_3, in which case we are talking of the 'average rate of transformation' at a single point Q_3. Economists call this rate of transformation at a single point on the transformation curve the *marginal* rate of transformation. And if we draw a straight line tt that is tangent to the transformation curve at point Q_3 we can measure the *marginal* rate of transformation of y for x from the slope of the line tt. Thus, if we drop vertically from point Q_3 to some arbitrary point Q_4 below it, and then draw a horizontal line from Q_4 to point S on the line tt, the ratio of the distance Q_3Q_4 to the distance Q_4S – which we may suppose is equal to 4 – measures the marginal rate of transformation of y into x as 4 at point Q_3.

It should be evident from the convex shape of the transformation curve in Figure 30 that the tangent at point Q_3 is steeper than the tangent at Q_1, from which it follows that the marginal rate of transformation at Q_3 is greater than at Q_1. For this shape of transformation curve (which is the one most commonly assumed by economists) successive movements along the transformation curve in the T_1–T_2 direction entail successively steeper tangencies – indicating successively higher marginal rates of transformation of y into x. In common sense terms, this amounts to saying that the more of x is produced by the economy the harder it becomes – that is, the more of y we have to sacrifice – to produce more x.

Since one of the fundamental assumptions of allocative economics is that more goods are preferred by society to less, society should never be satisfied with an 'interior' point such as Q_0 in Figure 30. By moving from Q_0 to any point on the transformation curve between Q_1 and Q_3 more of both goods can be produced with the same resource endowment available to the economy. By moving from Q_0 to Q_1 itself, we produce an additional amount of good y without having to produce any less of good x. On the other hand, if we move from Q_0 to Q_3 we produce an additional amount of good x without having to produce any less of good y. If finally, we move from this interior point Q_0 to any point Q_2 on the transformation curve between Q_1 and Q_3, we produce more of both goods x and y.

We might properly talk of any point on the T_1T_2 transformation curve as a production *optimum* inasmuch as – in contradistinction to an interior point such as Q_0 – it is not possible to produce more of *all* goods (more of both goods x and y in our simple model) with the resource endowment given to the economy. Once on the transformation curve, more of one good can be produced only by reducing the amount of the other good. Using analogous terminology, we should say that if the economy is producing a collection of goods that can be represented as a point along the transformation curve, goods are being produced *efficiently*. If, instead, the collection of goods being produced can be indicated by a point within the transformation curve, the economy can be said to be producing goods inefficiently.

A minute's reflection will convince you that an interior point such as Q_0 cannot possibly be a Pareto optimum (defined, remember, as a position from which it is impossible to make 'everyone' better off). For if we move from a point Q_0 to a point Q_2 on the transformation curve, the economy will be producing more of all goods: in this case more of both x and y. With more of all goods we can certainly make 'everyone' better off. Thus there can be movements from Q_0 that will indeed enable us to make 'everyone' better off – which, by definition, implies that an interior point such as Q_0 cannot be a position of Pareto optimality.

We might reasonably surmise therefore that a *necessary* condition, at least, for a collection of goods to be a Pareto optimum is that it be a point on the transformation curve itself. But is it a sufficient condition? There are, of course, an infinite number of points along the transformation curve. Are they all Pareto optimal? And if not, *can* they all be Pareto optimal under some conditions?

You may wonder why I am being so tentative. The reason is that there are pedagogic advantages in moving cautiously at this stage. So let us take our time and recapitulate the concepts introduced. First, there is the transformation curve itself which encompasses all the collections of goods producible with the economy's given endowment of resources at the current stage of technical knowledge. Second, there is the rate of transformation implied by the shape of the transformation curve, particular attention being paid to the *marginal* rate of transformation (say of good y for good x) associated with any point on it. And lastly, there are an indefinite number of points interior to the transformation curve that are not, by definition, production optima and – by inference – cannot be Pareto optima either, as a result of which we conclude that a *necessary* condition for a collection of goods to be a Pareto optimal collection is that it be a point on the transformation curve.

I will end the chapter by qualifying some of my assumptions in minor respects.

First, although the transformation curve is commonly drawn as it is in Figure 30 (convex from above) it can also be drawn as a straight line sloping downward from left to right, a construction that implies a constant rate of transformation, average and marginal. For that matter, it can also be constructed to be concave from above wherever powerful economies of scale in the production of each good are to be indicated. Thus, in contrast to the more familiar convex transformation curve, the concave tranformation curve implies that the more of x produced by the economy the 'easier' it becomes to produce more of x (that is to say, the marginal rate of substitution of y for x becomes *smaller*). A lot is sometimes made of such cases but the issues they raise are not basic.

Second, the assumption of a fixed resource endowment for the economy is not to be confused with the assumption of a fixed supply of the factors. The resource endowment is to be understood as the potential for productivity – so many workers, so much land of different kinds, so much capital, etc. And the longer the period envisaged, the more time there is for the retraining of labour and for the transforming of one kind of capital asset into another.

If we begin with the assumption of a given resource endowment, the supplies of factors forthcoming will, in general, vary with the factor prices – which factor prices, incidentally, will vary with the prices of the goods. If, for example, there is an exogenous shift in demand from cloth toward grain, the price of land (which is more important in grain production than in cloth production) will normally rise relative to the price of labour and, possibly, some land may be taken from non-productive uses and put to use raising crops while at the same time some labour may be withdrawn from the market.

The assumption of fixed supplies of factors is therefore a special case: the case in which the amounts of capital, land and labour put on the market do not alter irrespective of changes in factor prices. Extreme though it sounds, it is a useful special case for expository purposes, and one that is frequently adopted by economists. For our purposes in the following chapter we shall go along with this assumption of fixed factor supplies since, in any case, relaxation of this assumption – the adoption, instead, of the assumption of a given resource endowment – does not qualify our main conclusions.

20 Optimality for the economy

In this chapter we illustrate the facile and once standard demonstration that a Pareto optimal position for the economy is identified (geometrically) by a point of tangency of the price line with the transformation curve. Such a point is Q_2 on the transformation curve of Figure 31 since the price line p_2 is tangent at Q_2. A suboptimal, or nonoptimal position, in contrast, is identified by a point at which the price line intersects the transformation curve. Such a suboptimal position is shown at Q_1 in Figure 31. (Notice, however, that Q_1 is a point along the transformation curve, so that it is productively efficient in that more of one good cannot be produced without giving up some of the other good. An interior point

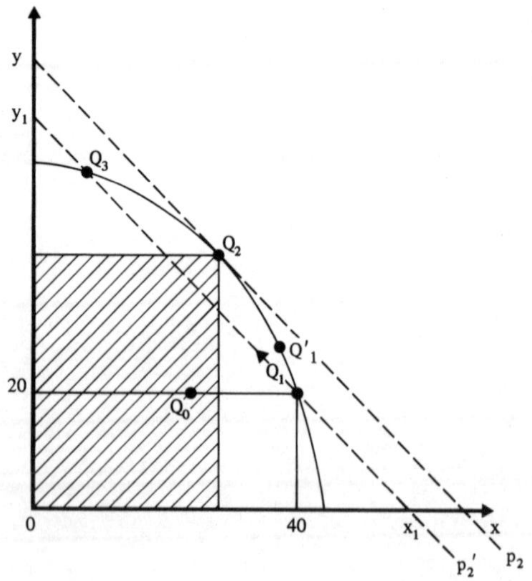

Figure 31

such as Q_0 inside the transformation curve is clearly one of productive inefficiency: a movement from Q_0 to some points along the transformation curve results in more of both goods being produced.)

To assert that an optimal position is superior to a suboptimal position along the transformation curve, as ranked by the Pareto criterion, might seem to be tautological – being true in virtue of the meaning of the terms optimal and suboptimal. Even if it were true, however, the comparison in Figure 31 of the optimal position Q_2 with the suboptimal position at Q_1 adds clarity to our understanding of the comparison.

Since this sort of comparison is standard theory, it is worth going over it more carefully using some numbers in order to make the conclusion more explicit.

Let us begin then with an equilibrium situation in which the amounts of the two goods consumed are known to us along with their corresponding prices. Unless otherwise stated, we shall suppose production always to be efficient. Thus the equilibrium collection of goods Q_1, a suboptimal position in Figure 31, is nonetheless a point along the transformation curve. The equilibrium prices are, we shall assume, \$6 per unit x and \$3 per unit y, as a result of which the price line p'_2, passing through point Q_1 is drawn with a slope of 2 (for at these price 2 units of y exchange for one unit of x). At these prices, the total value of the collection Q_1 is exactly \$300 since it comprises 40 units of x and 20 units of y as indicated in the figure. Clearly, \$300 can buy any other collection of goods indicated by any point along this price line p'_2 – including, at one extreme, 100 units of y alone given by point y_1, and, at the other extreme 50 units of x alone given by the point x_1 on the p'_2 line. We may then associate the distance of this p'_2 line with respect to the origin O, with a value of \$300. Any point along it, including the equilibrium collection Q_1, is valued at \$300.

A price-line p_2, having the same slope of 2 as p'_2 but to the right of it, will have a value of more than \$300; let us say it has a value of \$400. Thus with \$400 a person can buy, at most, Ox_2 of good x at the given prices, or else, at most, Oy_2 of good y, or else any combination of goods x and y given by a point along the p_2 price-line.

Suppose we happen to be consuming collection Q_1 on the transformation curve. The prices of the two goods are given to us, so we know that two units of good y exchange for one of good x. The slope of the transformation curve at point Q_1 is, however, steeper than the slope of the price line; let us say that the slope of the transformation curve at Q_1 is 3 – which means that, when Q_1 is produced efficiently, by producing one less of good x we can produce three more of good y. In brief, the rate of transformation of y into x, being equal to 3, is higher than the rate of substitution y into x (given by the slope of the price line) being equal to 2. Any discrepancy between the rate of transformation and the rate of substitution is a signal to the economist that the postion is suboptimal: that with the same resource endowment a greater value of goods is possible by choosing another collection on the transformation curve.

Thus, allowing that we can move freely along the transformation curve, we can avail ourselves of the greater amount of y which can be produced per unit x by moving upward along the transformation curve. For example, at the relative goods prices, given by the slope of 2 of the price line, a movement from Q_1 to Q_1' is an improvement inasmuch as Q_1' will be on a price line parallel to but to the right of p_2'. And this higher price line has a value greater than $300. We can continue moving up the transformation curve in this way, noting that successive collections have higher values, until we reach the collection indicated by the point Q_2 on the transformation curve. Through this point the price-line is p_2 which has a value, as indicated, of $400. Should we continue to move upward along the transformation curve, successive collections become worth less and less at the given goods prices. At Q_3, for instance, we are on the same price line p_2' as Q_1, with a value therefore of $300.

Since Q_2 is the collection having the highest value, equal to $400, it will appear as the point on the transformation curve through which passes the highest possible price line. This price-line, marked p_2 in Figure 31, is obviously tangent at Q_2 to the transformation curve. To the economist, such a tangency signals an optimal position – any movement along the transformation curve away from Q_2 cannot make 'everyone' better off since it necessarily reduces the total value of the goods.

Now since this price-line p_2 is tangent to the transformation curve at Q_2 it follows that the slope of the transformation curve at this point is exactly the same as the slope of the price line. Thus the rate of transformation at Q_2 must also be equal to 2 of y per unit x, the same as the rate of substitution given by the slope of the price line.

However, this rate of transformation of 2y per unit x can be translated into a ratio of the marginal cost of y to that of x. If the marginal cost of good y happens to be equal to its price, which is $3, then the marginal cost of x must be equal to $6. For with these marginal costs, $6 is the cost of one unit of x or, alternatively, of two units of y. It is possible, however, that the marginal cost of y is only $1, in which case the marginal cost of x has to be $2 in order for 2 units of y *in production* to exchange for one unit of x. Clearly, these proportionally lower marginal costs of goods x and y also entail a slope of the transformation curve of 2 at the point Q_2 – which meets the required optimal condition.

Hence, the tangency of the p_2 line to the transformation curve at Q_2 may be interpreted either in terms of the slopes – the rate of substitution (or market exchange) of y for x being equal to the rate of transformation of y for x – or, alternatively, in terms of ratios: the ratio of the market *prices* of x and y being equal to the ratio of the marginal *costs* of x and y – ratio equal to 2 in this example. The expressions are equivalent, though it is sometimes more suggestive to use one rather than the other.

You will recall, however, that in Part Three we reached the same conclusion in Chapter 12 – that optimality requires that the ratio of prices be equal to the ratio of their corresponding marginal costs – using, there, constructs appropriate to a *partial* economic context. In Figure 31, however, where this same condition is expressed by the tangency of the price line to the transformation curve, it appears not only as a necessary but also as a sufficient condition. No higher value for the economy is attainable. But this is simply the result of constructing our transformation curve convex from above – which is, nonetheless, the most reasonable and the most usual way of constructing it.

(Were we to construct this transformation curve, instead, as concave from above, the price line tangent to the transformation curve would *not* be the highest price line. The highest price line would be that which passed through the point at which the transformation curve touched either the x axis or else the y axis – a situation referred to as a 'corner solution' optimum. This solution has some mathematical interest but is not worth pursuing here if only because the implication of a corner solution – that the optimal position for society is one in which only one good is produced – is highly implausible.)

First, ask yourself what kinds of organization of the economy are consistent with the optimal position illustrated in Figure 31, that in which prices are proportional to marginal costs. Clearly universal perfect competition, defined as in the textbooks, is such an organization since, in the absence of excise taxes on some goods and in the absence of spillovers from some goods, prices everywhere are exactly *equal* to their corresponding marginal costs – which is a limiting case of prices being proportional to their corresponding marginal costs.

Now ask yourself what sort of organization would correspond – at least in the two-good economy – to the suboptimal position Q_1 in Figure 31 at which the price line intersects the transformation curve. The steeper the slope of the transformation curve at Q_1 compared with the slope of the price-line indicates that the rate of transformation of y into x through the productive process is greater than the market value of y in exchange for x. If, once more, we suppose that the transformation curve at Q_1 has a slope of 3 whereas that of the price-line is 2 then, in the simplest case in which the marginal cost of good x is equal to its price of \$6, it follows that the price of y has to be \$3 but its marginal cost \$2. This suboptimal position at position at Q_1 can therefore be the result of perfect competition in the x industry (price of \$6 there exactly equal to marginal cost of \$6) and of monopoly in the y industry (price of \$3 being 50 per cent above the marginal cost of \$2). Alternatively the suboptimal position Q_1 could represent an equilibrium in which both goods are produced by perfectly competitive industries yet either (a) industry y is subject to a stiff excise tax that raises its price to 50 per cent above its marginal cost, or (b) the production of good y is associated with a highly beneficial spillover so although, in equilibrium, price is indeed equal to marginal factor cost, its marginal social cost (which should properly be reflected in the shape of the transformation curve and, in particular, in the slope of the transformation curve at Q_1) is well below its marginal factor cost (by the value of the benefit conferred on the community by the marginal unit of y).

When you look back at this exposition and glance again at Figure

31, it must all seem devastatingly obvious. And once you accept it as being equally valid for an economy producing any number of goods you may be tempted to share for a while the complacency with which economists, until the 1940s, pronounced that perfect competition – or, given fixed supplies of factors, equi-proportional marginal cost pricing[1] – was allocatively ideal, at least in the absence of taxes and spillovers.

This point of tangency between the price line and the relevant transformation curve, which is identified with the optimality condition, can, however, also be constructed for the case of a domestic poll tax and for the case of free international trade. In the event, such constructions served to assure economists that free trade was best for the world as a whole and that, for a single country, free trade (or, at any rate, some foreign trade) was better than 'autarky' (no foreign trade at all); and that a poll tax (a tax on each income earner that does not vary with his earnings), though somewhat impracticable, was the best possible tax. Indeed, by introducing an additional special assumption or two, other normative propositions seemed to follow.

Those far-off innocent days, alas, are now over – though you wouldn't know it if you confined your reading of economics to some of the more popular newspaper and magazine articles. The sad fact is that these fetching little demonstrations will no longer do. Soon you will find yourself swimming in the waters of cynicism to emerge a chastened and wiser person.

Before taking the plunge, however, you are to be introduced to an important construct, one that will provide you with the key to unlocking a veritable Pandora's box; namely, the connection between distribution and relative prices.

21 What is an efficient distribution of goods?

You will have noted that we are not asking the question, what is an equitable or a just distribution. That is an entirely different and a more controversial question. We are asking a simpler question: what is an efficient distribution – efficient, that is, by reference to the Pareto criterion. And the answer to the question covers both the concept of efficiency in this connection and the conditions required for its realisation.

In order to answer the question, we have now to step back from our transformation curve diagram and focus attention on a single collection of goods whether the collection is produced efficiently or inefficiently (whether, that is, it is a collection identified as a point *along* the transformation curve or a collection identified was a point *inside* the transformation curve). Once we have settled our minds about this matter of an efficient distribution, we shall return to the transformation curve construction so as to assess the validity of comparisons made between optimal and nonoptimal positions for the economy as a whole.

In this attempt to assess the validity of optimal–nonoptimal comparisons we encounter a seeming paradox, and things really start to hum. As mentioned at the end of the preceding chapter, the key that opens the door to an understanding of this paradox is nothing more than the connection between particular distributions of a given collection of goods and their corresponding price ratios. This vital connection, then, is the subject of the present chapter.

First, a simple proposition which we illustrate below even though it is plausible enough. Wherever members of a community receive rations of a number of goods, some exchange of the rationed goods is likely to take place, especially if such exchanges are not illegal. If, to take an example from a prisoner of war camp, each prisoner receives a quarter of a pound of tobacco and three-quarter of a pound of sweets a week, sweet-toothed non-smokers would be glad to exchange their tobacco ration for sweets whereas tobacco addicts would be willing to give up their sweets for additional tobacco.

Sooner or later a common rate of exchange will emerge – say, one ounce of tobacco for two ounces of sweets – which can properly be said to reflect market values. Whatever the unit of account used, an ounce of tobacco will be worth two ounces of sweets. If tobacco itself were used as money, and therefore also acted as a unit of account, one ounce of sweets would be priced at half an ounce of tobacco. If a bar of soap each week were added to the ration, it also would acquire a price, say two ounces of tobacco. In terms of tobacco, one bar of soap is valued at twice as much as an ounce of tobacco, and an ounce of tobacco is valued twice as much as an ounce of sweets. We could switch the unit of account from tobacco to soap or to sweets, but the above price ratios would remain the same.

Now all we have to do is go over this more carefully so as to have a clear idea how a common price ratio, or rate of exchange, is established between traded goods. Provisionally, then, we forget about the production process and imagine that the two goods, x and y, drop like manna from heaven. Each Monday morning, individuals find parcels of goods x and y outside their front doors. These parcels could also be the same size for everyone, but it makes no difference to the exercise.

Since we have already used the word 'collection' of goods when thinking of total amounts of goods to be shared between the members of a community, we shall refer to the amounts of x and y received by each individual as a 'batch' of goods. Thus the point q_A in Figure 32(a) represents the batch of goods x and y received weekly by person A. This is made up of $O_A x_A$ of good x and $O_A y_A$ of good y. The striped rectangle marked A acts only to identify this particular batch accruing to person A.

We shall suppose that person A's tastes are such that with this q_A batch, he values an additional unit of x twice as much as an additional unit of y. In other words he is indifferent (given this q_A batch to start with) as between having one more unit of x and having two more units of y – or, for that matter, as between having one unit less of x and two units less of y. In the jargon, this is his subjective rate of exchange (or rate of substitution) *at the margin*. If he does acquire more x by giving up good y, or more of y by giving up good x, or indeed if he acquires more of both then his *marginal* rate of exchange, or *marginal* rate of substitution, is

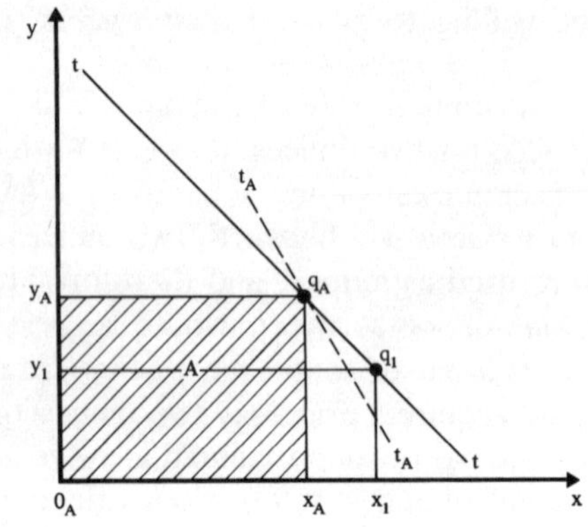

Figure 32(a)

likely to alter. It will be convenient to use the latter term which is, in any case, more conventional.

The marginal rate of substitution at q_A – two units of y per unit of x – is given by the slope of the price line t_At_A passing through the point q_A. Having indicated person A's tastes by the slope of this t_At_A line about the point q_A, we may now present him with an opportunity to exchange some y for x, or some x for y, whichever he prefers, at a *market* rate of exchange given by the new price line tt. In the limiting case, in which this market rate of exchange is exactly the same as his original marginal rate of substitution of two of y per unit x, there is no scope for gain: the market offers him two units of y per unit of x and, as we know, he himself is indifferent as between two units of y per unit of x. Any *other* market rate of exchange, however, does provide him with an opportunity for gain.

Let this market rate of exchange be one unit of x for one unit of y, a slope of 1 as in Figure 32(a). This is very different from his marginal rate of substitution at q_A of 2 units of y for one unit of x. Is there a reasonable presumption that person A has an incentive to avail himself of the opportunity presented by the market rate of exchange?

Person A does not have to be very bright to recognize that he can do well for himself by acquiring an additional unit of x by giving up only one unit of y. After all, with the batch of x and y given by point q_A, he is ready to give up, at most, two units of y for a unit of x. With the market rate of exchange that faces him, he can obtain an additional unit of x for only one unit of y. He is better off, acquiring an additional unit of x at the market rate, by the saving of one unit of y. Granted this much, you may well ask: How many additional units of x will he then want to buy at the market rate of exchange tt?

We should have to have more information to discover exactly how many additional units of good x he will acquire at the market rate tt. But it would be surprising if he acquired so much as to have to give up all of Oy_A, his initial amount of good y, and so end up consuming only good x. For as he acquires additional units of x, by giving up y, he is likely to value increments of good x less compared with good y: in other words, his marginal rate of substitution of good y for x declines.[1] At some point, at any rate, there will be no further advantage from his using the market rate of exchange tt in order to acquire an additional unit of x by giving up a unit of y – at which point it may be inferred that his marginal rate of substitution has fallen to one y per unit of x, equal, of course, to the market rate of exchange, tt.

The point at which he ceases to acquire additional units of x is indicated by the point q_1 along the tt line. As a result of being presented with the market rate of exchange, then, he ends up with O_Ax_1 of good x and O_Ay_1 of good y.

The situation for person B is depicted in Figure 32(b). With his initial batch of goods q_B the line t_Bt_B indicates B's indifference at that point as between a half unit of good y and a complete unit of good x; in other words, with the batch q_B, person B's marginal rate of substitution is $\frac{1}{2}$y for 1x.

Faced with the same market rate of exchange, indicated by line

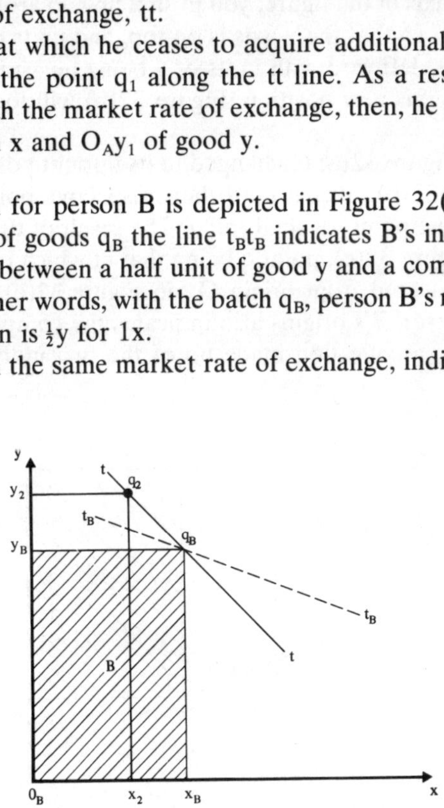

Figure 32(b)

tt, which offers him an entire unit of y per unit x, he is induced to acquire additional units of y until he reaches position q_2 on the tt line. This q_2 batch which he ends up with consists of O_Bx_2 of good x and O_By_2 of good y.

From these examples of the reactions of persons A and B we can generalize as follows: provided that the market rate of exchange differs from each person's initial marginal rate of substitution, he can improve his welfare by using the market rate of exchange either to obtain more of x in exchange for y or else more of y in exchange for x.

Having drawn a picture each for person A and B, it remains to put them together so as to have all the information in one picture. First, however, imagine that you have cut out Figure 32(b) from the page and stuck a pin through the origin O_B. With your finger under the x axis of the figure, you push it up and around, turning it through 180° so that the x axis is on top, and units of x are measured from O_B leftward with units of y being measured downward from O_B. In this new position, Figure 32(b) will look like Figure 32(b)′.

Leaving Figure 32(a) unchanged in its upright position, we now slide Figure 32(b)′ over it until their respective points q_A and q_B coincide at the point we shall call q. The result of this operation is shown as Figure 32(c), point q being that at which q_A touches q_B.

When measured from origin O_A in Figure 32(c), the point O_B (which is person B's origin) also indicates the complete collection of goods Q_0, a collection made up of the two individuals' initial

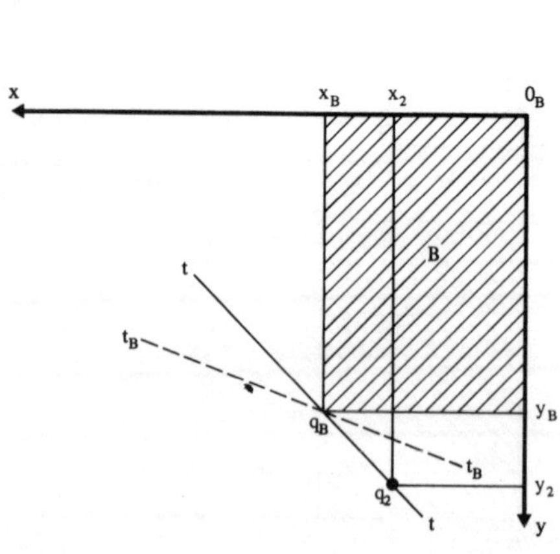

Figure 32(b)′

batches q_A and q_B. These two initial batches are easily identified in Figure 32(c) by the two striped rectangles marked A and B which correspond with those shown in Figures 32(a) and 32(b) respectively.

Now in moving from initial position q to q_1 on the tt line, person A is *giving up* units of y in order to acquire additional units of x at the tt market rate of exchange of one unit of x per unit of y. Bearing in mind the inverted position of person B's origin O_B, his movement from his initial position q to q_2 along tt reveals that B *acquires* additional units of y by giving up units of x.

If the tt line were some arbitrary rate of exchange set up, say, as an experiment, it would be something of a coincidence if q_1 and q_2 were the same point. It would be much more likely that they were different points along tt as in the figure, where q_2 is below q_1. This means that with the exchange rate given by the tt line, person B chooses to acquire more of good y that person A chooses to give up. Clearly, this is not an equilibrium situation since at this rate of exchange there is an excess demand for good y (equals – at the tt prices – an excess supply of good x). And, indeed, with the fixed amounts of x and y that together form the collection Q_0 such choices for A and B cannot be realized.

An equilibrium rate of exchange of y for x has to be such that the amounts persons A and B wish to exchange match up exactly: that is to say, the amount of good y that person B chooses to acquire at that rate of exchange must equal exactly the amount of y

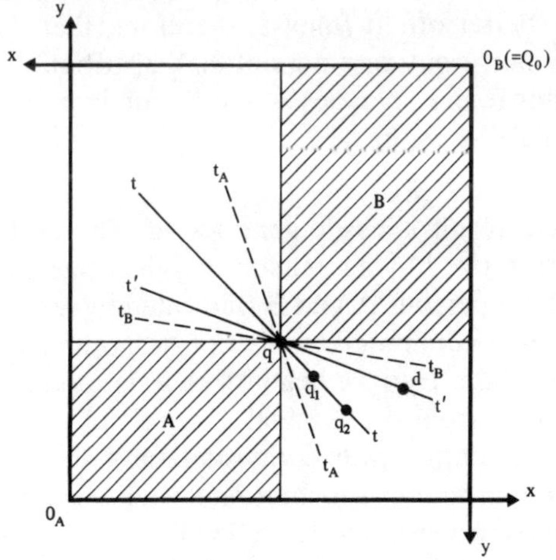

Figure 32(c)

that person A chooses to give up (in order to acquire additional x units). There will, generally, be such an equilibrium rate of exchange of y for x (or ratio of prices) such as t′t′ in Figure 32(c) – which rate of exchange t′t′ is one that offers a unit x for somewhat less than a unit of y – which meets the required equilibrium condition. Along t′t′, the choices of person A and B coincide at point d, since the amount of y that A wishes to give up at this t′t′ rate of exchange is exactly equal to the amount of y that B wishes to acquire.

This point d, then, marks the resulting equilibrium division of the Q_0 collection of goods as between persons A and B. In comparison with the initial position, before any exchange takes place, this equilibrium division is one for which person A has more of x and less of y whereas person B, in contrast, has more of y and less of x. But both persons are presumed to be better off with this equilibrium d division of collection Q_0 than they were with the initial q division since, of their own volition they chose to move from the q division of the Q_0 collection to the d division of it when they were faced with the equilibrium rate of exchange shown by t′t′ in the figure. What is more, given this collection Q_0, there is no mutually advantageous movement possible from d (that is, no other division of the Q_0 collection can be found) that will make both A and B better off.

Such a division may properly be called an *efficient* distribution of the Q_0 collection of goods as between persons A and B. It is efficient in the sense that it is a Pareto optimal distribution of the goods collection; no other distribution of Q_0 being able to make both persons better off. It follows, therefore, that the original q division is an inefficient, or a nonoptimal, distribution of Q_0 since, as we have shown, both persons A and B gain in moving from q to the equilibrium d division.

This important result is easily generalized. The optimal point d, which is characterized by a common marginal rate of substitution of y for x to both persons A and B (indicated by the slope of t′t′ at d) is only one of an unlimited number of such optimal distributions of the Q_0 collection. Had we begun with a nonoptimal division of Q_0 very different from the original nonoptimal division given by point q, the resulting optimal division (and the corresponding common marginal rate of substitution) would also be very different from that shown at point d. To be more exact, beginning with any given nonoptimal distribution of the Q_0 collection movements can take place to any one of a range of alternative optimal distributions, each being marked, in general by a different common marginal rate of substitution.

All possible optimal distributions of the Q_0 collection would – assuming continuity – take the form of a locus of such points plotted as a slightly wavy line joining origin O to Q_0 in Figure 33 – its being understood from now on that, for the two-person case, person A's origin is at O and person B's origin is at the point Q_0. Such a locus goes by the name of the *contract curve*, and it is drawn in this wavy way as a reminder that its actual shape will depend upon the peculiarities of the tastes of persons A and B.

You will notice that 3 possible optimal distributions of Q_0, d_1, d_2, and d_3, have been indicated in Figure 33, each with a line of different slope passing through it in order to remind us that, in general, the common marginal rate of substitution is different for each optimal distribution of the Q_0 collection.

If the optimal, or efficient, distribution of Q_0 happens to be d_1, the common marginal rate of substitution indicated by the slope will, in a market economy, be expressed by the price ratio of the two goods. (If there are more than two goods, the resulting common marginal rates of substitution correspond to the set of market prices.) Since a given economic situation is characterized not only by a given collection of goods by also by an equilibrium set of prices, an efficient distribution of the collection of goods is implied.

Thus a comparison of two alternative economic situations can be represented as in Figure 34. One situation is given by the goods collection Q_1, which consists of Ox_1 of good x and Oy_1 of good y, along with a price ratio indicated by the slope of the line passing through Q_1 (say $1y = 5x$, so that the price of y is five times that of x). This price ratio, however, corresponds with the marginal rate of

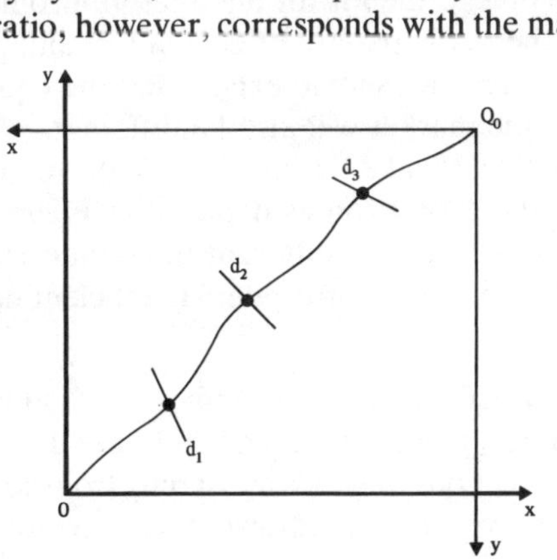

Figure 33

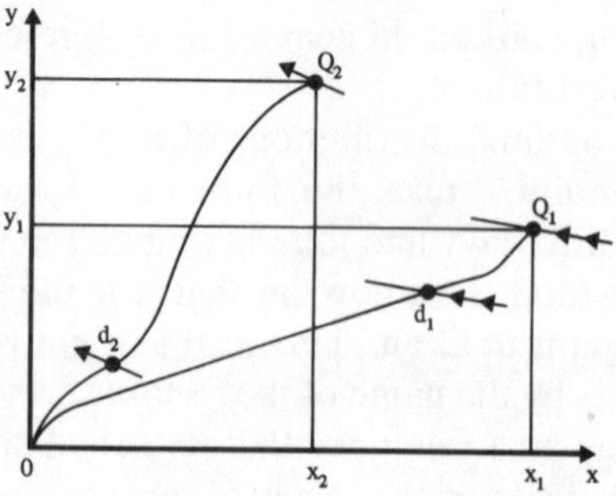

Figure 34

substitution common to both persons as between whom collection Q_1 is shared, the particular efficient distribution being d_1 along the contract curve of this Q_1 collection.

The alternative situation shown is the Q_2 collection, comprising Ox_2 of good x and Oy_2 of good y, having a price ratio indicated by the slope of the line passing through Q_2 (say $\frac{1}{2}y = 1x$), which is reflected by the common marginal rate of substitution at d_2, this being the corresponding efficient distribution of the Q_2 collection.

So much for the important connection I want to establish, that between a particular efficient distribution of a collection of goods and the corresponding price ratio of those goods. If my account of the matter looks a bit long-winded, chalk it up to conscientiousness. If you are a little uncertain of the logic of the connection, a second reading of this chapter should secure it for you. At all events, the connection I am trying to drive home is summed up by the construction of Figure 34 above. It is, moreover, plausible enough once you ponder on it. Allowing that people have different tastes (and incomes), then if for any reason incomes are redistributed among them, the pattern of demand resulting will be different. In consequence, we should expect that the equilibrium prices established by the market will also be different.

If you are willing to take this much on faith, you need only keep in mind its visual expression as depicted in Figure 34, particular attention being paid to the different price-ratio slopes of collections Q_1 and Q_2 and their corresponding efficient distributions, d_1 and d_2.

An inconsequential qualification and a brief addendum before ending the chapter. In Figures 33 and 34 I have drawn the contract curves of the collections of goods as running from corner to corner. The contract curve is often drawn this way for convenience, although it is perfectly possible to have the curve begin at some distance from either or both corners. Anything that looks a little odd, like this possible construction, can be counted upon to fascinate some economists. But such a possible construction will not have the least effect on the broad conclusions we are to reach in this Part of the book.

Addendum. We can interpret Figure 32(a) somewhat differently in order to gain some additional insight. We suppose that person A has a given money income per week. Let the price of good x be the same as that of good y, say $3. The line tt can then be regarded as person A's 'budget line' – being the locus of all possible batches of goods x and y that may be bought each week, at these market prices, with an income of $300 a week. If person A were made to spend his $300 income on the q_A batch, he would not be as well off as he might be, a statement which implies that his marginal rate of substitution with the q_A batch (given in the figure by the slope of line t_At_A) *differs* from the rate of exchange of y for x given by the market (the slope of line tt). Allow person A to choose a batch at the market prices and, as we know, he will choose batch q_1.

Now suppose, instead, that market prices are now reflected by the slope of line t_At_A, and person A chooses batch q_A. After this choice has been made, the market prices alter so that his new budget line is given by tt, and the individual now chooses batch q_1. It is easy to show that the change in market prices that induces him to choose batch q_1 must make him better off – or, at the very least, no worse off than before. For the intersection of the new tt line with the original t_At_A line at point q_A implies that the part of the tt line below the intersection at q_A is to the right of the part of the t_At_A line below q_A. And this presents him with a locus of batches that were unavailable to him with his original t_At_A budget line. Person A can, of course, continue to take the q_A batch with his new tt budget line, in which case he is no worse off than he was with the original t_At_A budget. But if from the new locus of batches he chooses one, say q_1, we may reasonably infer that he does so because he prefers it to the q_A batch which, as mentioned, is still available to him.

We may, then, generalize as follows: given a person's money income unchanged, any alteration of the market prices that does not preclude his buying the original batch cannot make him worse off and may make him better off. (If he chooses to buy a different batch in these circumstances we may properly infer that the alteration of market prices does indeed make him better off.)

22 Economic efficiency: a paradox

Instead of using the words 'economic efficiency' in the chapter title I could have used 'the Pareto criterion', which I have been using (and will continue to use) as a synonym for a *potential* Pareto improvement. For as I pointed out earlier, the academic economist's notion of economic efficiency invariably turns on this Pareto criterion. In short, an economic situation II is said to be more efficient than another economic situation I if the change from I to II is one that meets the Pareto criterion. And it is sufficient for this criterion to be met if the value of the *collection of goods* II (which is the most common interpretation of an 'economic situation' II) is higher than that of collection I. For if collection II has a higher aggregate value than collection I there must be some division of this II collection that can yield every one a batch of goods higher in value than the batch he has in the original I collection. What we are to illustrate in this chapter is the seeming paradox that arises in the application of this apparently straightforward Pareto criterion.

This basic paradox in the application of the concept of economic efficiency cannot be too heavily stressed. There are many economists around who, not taking a close interest in the normative economics literature, are still under the impression that although abstract and elusive subtleties abound in normative economics, these have no bearing on the familiar and sturdy concept of economic efficiency itself. The use of the words 'economic efficiency' in the chapter title is chosen, therefore, as a device to arrest the attention of any reader browsing through the book who is still under this misapprehension.

We start then with the simple mechanics of an application of the Pareto criterion which is, as I repeat yet again, the economist's criterion of economic efficiency. Thus, as indicated above, a movement from a collection of goods Q_1 to a collection Q_2 that has a higher value than Q_1 is a movement that increases economic efficiency.

Such a movement is depicted in Figure 35 where collection Q_2 is chosen so as to have more of good y but less of good x than the Q_1 collection. The *value* of Q_2, however, is indicated by the distance of the p_2 price-line (which passes through Q_2) from the origin O, the relative prices of goods x and y being represented by the slope of this p_2 price-line. Notice also that this p_2 price-line passing through Q_2 is drawn well above the parallel p_2' price-line passing through Q_1. Thus, whether we measure the values of the two collections in terms of x alone (treating x as numeraire) or of y alone (treating good y, instead, as numeraire), the Q_2 collection is clearly worth more than Q_1 collection.

We can write this result in shorthand as $p_2Q_2 > p_2Q_1$ . . . . (1) where p_2 stands for the set of p_2 prices (here only two prices corresponding to our two goods x and y, although the expression is valid for the prices of any number of goods). These p_2 prices are, incidentally, those prevailing in the equilibrium situation associated with the Q_2 collection. The sign $>$ stands for 'greater than' (the reverse sign $<$ standing for 'less than'). The *inequality* $p_2Q_2 > p_2Q_1$, therefore, tells us that when the amount of each good in the Q_2 collection is multiplied by its corresponding p_2 price, and similarly for the Q_1 collection with respect to the p_2

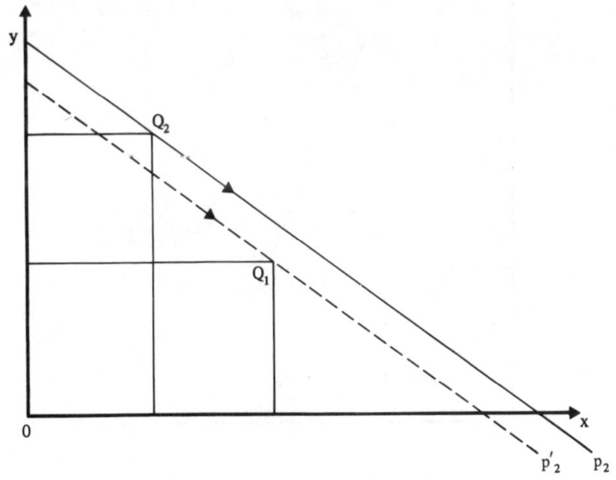

Figure 35

prices, the Q_2 collection has a higher aggregate value than the Q_1 collection.

Now for the apparent paradox. I add the word *apparent* because the way I approach the problem here it hardly looks paradoxical at all. In contrast, the manner in which the problem was originally stated, it did indeed look somewhat disconcerting.[1]

Figure 36 reproduces exactly the same two collections of goods Q_1 and Q_2. But now they are being valued at the p_1 set of prices, which prices are those that happen to prevail in the Q_1 equilibrium. It is evident from the figure that the steeper slope of the p_1 line (compared with the slope of the p_2 price-line of Figure 35) – indicative of a higher price of x relative to y (more of y per unit x) – completely changes the picture. For the p_1 price-line passing

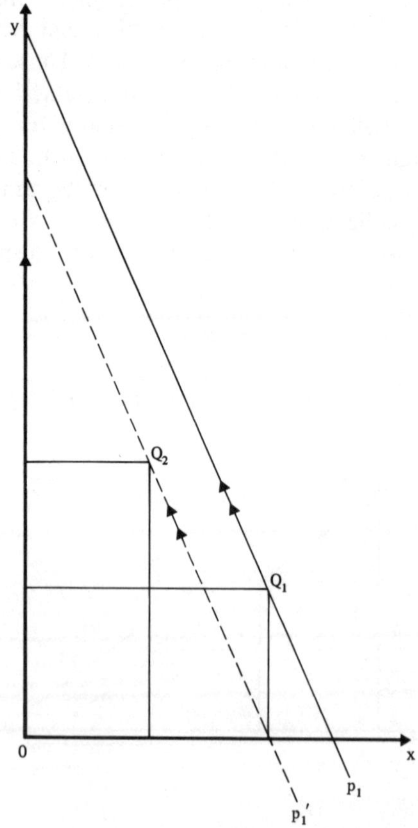

Figure 36

through Q_1 is above the parallel p'_1 line passing through Q_2, indicating that the value of Q_1 is above that of Q_2. By analogy with the preceding case, this result can be written as $p_1Q_1 > p_1Q_2$ . . (2).

This inequality tells us that valued at the p_1 price set, the Q_1 collection has a greater aggregate value than the Q_2 collection.

If we compare the inequalities (1) and (2), and bear in mind the corresponding constructions of Figures 35 and 36, we are not likely to feel that any real contradiction is involved. Inequality (1) ranks the two collections by valuing them at the p_2 prices whereas inequality (2) ranks them by reference to the p_1 prices. It is obvious then that the two different price ratios, p_2 and p_1, is the crucial factor.

For all that, should an economist wishing to compare the worth of the two collections happen to use the available set of prices in the Q_2 equilibrium,[2] he could easily overlook the possibility of a contrary result arising were he, instead, to compare the two collections by reference to some other set of prices, in particular the p_1 price set that prevails in the Q_1 equilibrium. The same remarks apply if, in contrast, the comparison were to be based on the p_1 price set associated with the Q_1 equilibrium.[3] When, later, it was shown that opposite results could be reached by adopting, actually or in effect, the other price set the reaction of many economists, especially of those who were not much interested in, or who did not much approve of normative economics, was that there was something paradoxical about such demonstrations. They were inclined to think that demonstrations revealing contrary results were economic curiosa, and not to be taken too seriously by the practising economist.

Since the simple constructs of Figure 35 and 36, however, have been distilled from what were once relatively complex models, you, the reader, are not prone to these evasive rationalizations. The seemingly contrary results arise quite clearly from the device of adopting two different price sets p_2 and p_1. There is, in fact, only one question left that is worth considering: Why should the set of prices be different for the two collections in question? Is it plausible that they should be different, and plausible also that they should be so different as to yield these contrary results?

The answer to the first part of the question follows from our discussion in the preceding chapter. Figure 37 reproduces the collections Q_2 and Q_1, along with the p_2 price-line passing through Q_2 and the p_1 price-line passing through Q_1. The contrary results

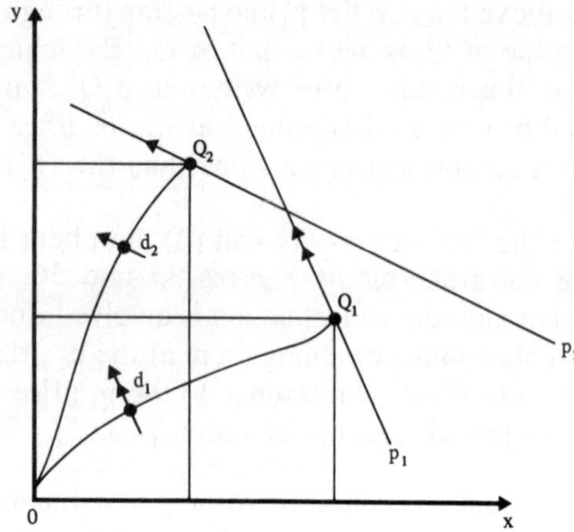

Figure 37

reached from ranking Q_2 and Q_1, first with the p_2 price set and then with the p_1 price set, necessarily implies an intersection of the two price-lines somwhere between points Q_1 and Q_2. (If these price-lines did *not* intersect in this way, then for both price lines the same collection would be the higher valued one.)

You will also notice that I have drawn the contract curves for each of the two collections in Figure 37 and, what is more to the purpose, indicated the actual distributions of Q_2 and Q_1 by points d_2 and d_1 respectively. Observe particularly the slope of the small line drawn through d_2, which is the same as the slope of the p_2 price line passing through Q_2; also the slope of the small line drawn through d_1, this being the same as the slope of the p_1 line passing through Q_1.[4] We may reasonably suppose that the change in the equilibrium market prices of Q_2 and Q_1 is associated with a change in the efficient distributions. More generally, we should not expect to move from some equilibrium position (represented, say, by a collection Q_2 and its equilibrium p_2 price set) to an alternative equilibrium position (represented by collection Q_1 and its equilibrium p_1 price set) *without*, in the process, generating a change of factor prices. This change of factor prices itself alters the distribution of income and, consequently, also alters the equilibrium set of goods prices from p_2 to p_1.

You will see that I have so drawn Figure 37 that the d_1 distribution of the Q_1 collection is much more favourable to person B than is the d_2 distribution of collection Q_2, which latter clearly favours person A. This marked difference in the efficient distributions of the two goods collections has been chosen so as to make the pronounced change in the price ratios (indicated by the marked change in the slopes of price-lines p_2 and p_1) appear more plausible. But you must recognise that the choice in Figure 37 of the slopes of the p_2 and p_1 price-lines, and of the positions of the distributional points d_2 and d_1, are arbitrary. The figure is drawn in this way simply in order to exhibit clearly what is in fact no more than a possibility; the possibility, that is, of contrary results arising from valuing the two collections in turn by their respective market prices. We cannot say without empirical knowledge just how important this possibility is for a particular change in any actual economy.

Bearing in mind the extraordinary variety of finished goods in a modern economy, even where broadly classified, it may transpire that the sort of policy changes that can be associated with movements from Q_1 to Q_2 are such that the accompanying distributional changes are relatively minor or that, even if these distributional changes are large, the corresponding change in market prices are small – small enough, at any rate, to ensure that one collection is valued above the other whichever set of market prices is used. None the less, we cannot rule out *a priori* the possibility that in some policy changes involving a movement from collection Q_1 to Q_2 the distributional changes will be large. Nor can we rule out the possibility either that some small distributional changes will issue in critical changes in market prices as to produce those seemingly contradictory results illustrated in Figure 37.

For the arguments of the following chapter, however, the important thing is not so much the actual relationships in the economic universe but the possibility we have uncovered. This is because, irrespective of the relevant economic facts that may yet be unearthed, those elegant demonstrations of general propositions – concerning the economic superiority of a competitive economy, of free trade, or of a system of poll taxes – can no longer be upheld. All such demonstrations are flawed in as much as their analyses hinge on the use of a single set of prices.[5]

The exposition so far has ignored the public sector of the economy which is, alas, growing in size and complexity. Of the goods produced, or directly controlled, by the government, a large proportion will be services most of which are not priced, their costs being covered by tax revenues. Although priced at zero, they may not be freely available to the public, and they are often rationed to those citizens legally entitled to receive them. To that extent it is correct to say that many goods prices in the economy do not change even though important policy changes take place.

On a theoretical level two methods are favoured by economists for dealing with the public sector. One is to imagine that the resources used by the government are subtracted from resources available to the entire economy, and to confine attention to those resources left to the private or market sector of the economy. The other is to suppose that whatever tax proceeds are collected, they are returned to citizens in the form of unconditional payments from the government. This latter method implies that the government does not itself engage in the production of any goods but simply acts as an agency for redistributing incomes – notwithstanding which the relative prices of goods in the private sector can be affected by this form of government intervention according to the structure of excise taxes and even income taxes. Neither of these devices is wholly satisfactory, if only because they may leave the impression that the size of the public sector of itself is of small importance.

Nevertheless, in comparing the net national products of a country in two different years, or in comparing the net national products of two countries, a common set of goods prices is used. These estimated prices, however, will also vary within one country as between two periods, or within a given period as between two countries. The ranking of the net national products being compared may then vary according to which price set is adopted. In so far as those public sector goods that are priced at zero are included in the comparisons, growth of the public sector acts to reduce variations in the price sets that accompany changes in economic policy.

Finally, and of incidental interest only in this connection, wherever a batch of goods q_2 is that chosen by an *individual* in the new situation, the observation

$$p_2q_2 > p_2q_1 \quad \text{(i)}$$

precludes the observation that

$$p_1q_1 > p_1q_2 \quad \text{(ii)}$$

For the inequality (i) tells us that although batch q_2 costs him more at the new p_2 prices than his original q_1 batch (which he bought at the p_1 prices), the individual chooses q_2 rather than q_1 – from which observed choice we must infer that he prefers batch q_2.

The inequality (ii), on the other hand, tells us that at the old p_1 set of prices, the individual took batch q_1 even though it cost him more at that price set than the q_2 batch, implying a clear preference for the q_1 batch.

Inasmuch as we are abiding by the assumption of unchanged tastes, consistency requires that observation (i) precludes (ii), and *vice versa*. For the individual, that is, inequalities (i) and (ii) cannot prevail simultaneously.

In contrast to the above conclusion for the individual, however, for a *community* of at least two persons, in which a change of market prices is accompanied by a change of distribution – and in which the criterion of 'better off' for the community is that of a potential Pareto improvement – it is possible, as already shown in this chapter, for the observation that $p_2Q_2 > p_2Q_1$ to be wholly consistent with the observation that $p_1Q_1 > p_1Q_2$.

23 Pareto optimality: an empty vessel

Figure 38 reproduces the main features of Figure 31 in Chapter 20. The Pareto optimal situation at Q_2 is identified by the tangency of the p_2 price-line with the transformation curve at that point. The suboptimal situation is that shown by the intersection of the p_2' price line with the transformation curve at Q_1. In Chapter 20 we concluded tentatively – indeed, with deliberate naiveté – that the optimal position at Q_2 was Pareto superior to (or more efficient than) the suboptimal position at Q_1.

The first thing to emphasize is that, although Q_2 appears in Figure 38 as an optimal position it is not *the* optimal position. There can, in general, be an indefinite number of such optimal positions. For instance by choosing a different market price ratio, one given by the slope of the p_1 price-line in Figure 39, its tangency to the unchanged collection Q_1 on the transformation curve renders the position at Q_1 a Pareto optimal one. On the other hand, the position at Q_2, which is intersected in Figure 39 by the p_1'

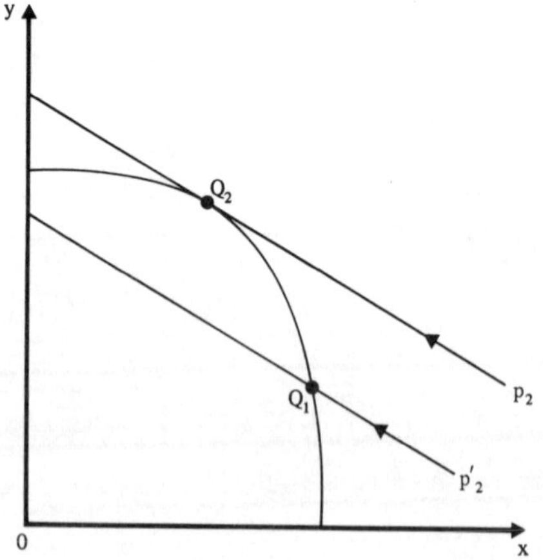

Figure 38

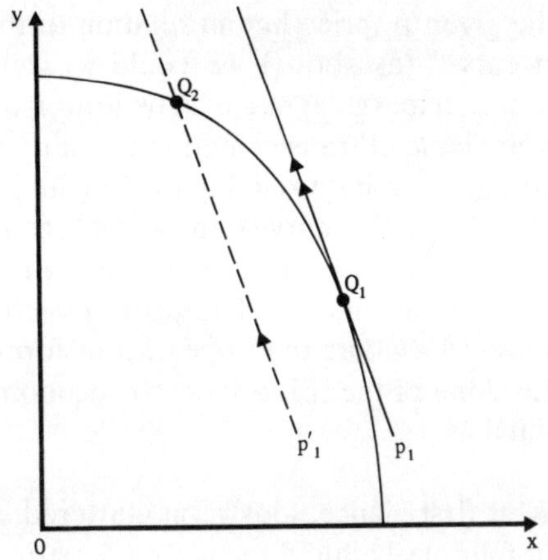

Figure 39

price-line (parallel and to the left of p_1) becomes suboptimal. A simple change in market prices appears to be enough to reverse the relation of optimal to suboptimal: with the p_2 price set Q_2 is economically more efficient that Q_1 whereas with the p_1 price set Q_1 is economically more efficient than Q_2.

On the face of it, however, there does not seem to be any way of comparing alternative optimal positions. We could not, for example, show that the optimal position at Q_2 with the p_2 price set as in Figure 38 is Pareto superior to the optimal position at Q_1 with the p_1 price set as in Figure 39.

The second thing to be emphasized is that, once we construct a transformation curve – regarded as a locus of efficient production possibilities open to the economy – the comparisons we make are no longer merely those between collections of goods. What we have to compare are economic *situations*, or economic *positions*, which term includes both the goods collections being compared and also their corresponding cost–price relation. Thus, in Figure 38, the economic *situation* at Q_2 embraces both the point Q_2 itself (representing the Q_2 collection) and also, at that point, the slope of the given p_2 price-line in relation to the slope of the transformation curve. Inasmuch as we are assuming that the distribution of the Q_2 collection between persons A and B is efficient, their respective marginal rates of substitution of good y for x must be the same and, in equilibrium, equal to the market rate of exchange given by the slope of the p_2 price-line. It follows that instead of referring to 'the *slope* of the given p_2 price-line in relation to the *slope* of the transformation curve' (as above) we could as well refer to the community's common marginal *rate* of substitution of y for x to the economy's marginal *rate* of transformation of y into x. Where these are equal, as they are at point Q_2 in Figure 38 (the price-line being tangent to the transformation curve), an optimal economic situation is identified. Where, instead, the common marginal rate of substitution differs from the marginal rate of transformation as at point Q_1 in Figure 38 – where the slope of transformation curve is steeper than the slope of the price-line – the economic situation is clearly suboptimal.

Figure 40 does, at first glance, look a bit cluttered up. But with a little patience it falls easily into a recognizable pattern. For it is no more than the result of superimposing Figure 39 upon Figure 38 *plus* the addition of a couple of points on each of the contract curves of collections Q_2 and Q_1.

Consider first the distributional points d_2 and d_1. The point d_2 on the contract curve of the Q_2 collection is one particular efficient distribution of the Q_2 collection between person A and B. It is particular in that it is consistent with the market equilibrium. This entails that the common marginal rate of substitution of y for x (given by the slope of the line through d_2) is the same as the market rate of exchange of y for x (given by the slope of the p_2 price-line). It goes without saying that the slope of the line through

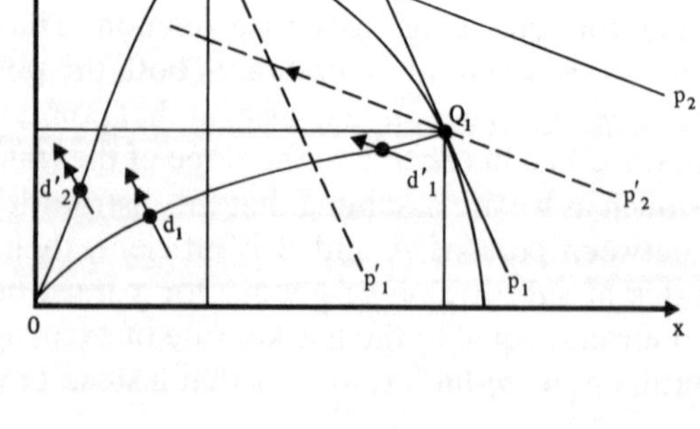

Figure 40

the distributional point d_1 on the Q_1 contact curve, being equal to the slope of the price-line p_1, carries the same implication.

In effect, we could say that the distribution d_2, which prevails in the Q_2 equilibrium and results in the marginal rate of substitution given by the slope of the p_2 price-line, is that efficient distribution of Q_2 which – given the shape of the transformation curve – renders the point Q_2 an optimal position. Similarly, the d_1 distribution is that efficient distribution of the Q_1 collection which – given the shape of the transformation curve – renders the point Q_1 an optimal position.

Let us now consider at leisure the apparent contradiction that an unsophisticated economist would discover by supposing his starting point to be the *sub*optimal position at Q_1 where it is intersected by the p_2 price-line. This nonoptimal position at Q_1 is the result of the efficient distribution of Q_1 being d_1' (*not* d_1), which d_1' distribution is consistent with an equilibrium rate of exchange of y for x given by the slope of the p_2' price-line, one that cuts the transformation curve at Q_1. Being unsophisticated, our economist pays strict regard to the existing price set (as given by the slope of p_2 or p_2'). Having determined that, with respect to these prevailing p_2 prices, the Q_1 economic position is suboptimal he determines the optimal position at Q_2. With the original p_2 prices it is clear that no collection on the transformation curve will have a higher aggregate value than Q_2. The economist accordingly recommends that the economy be reorganised so as to attain the Q_2 position.

To expose his predicament without more ado, let us suppose that this recommended economic reorganization is accomplished at negligible cost and that very soon Q_2 is the new equilibrium position on the transformation curve. But once Q_2 has been reached, our hard-working economist observes, to his chagrin, that the p_2 prices no long prevail. Instead the *equilibrium* price set is that given by p_1. The resulting slope of the p_1 price-line is one that cuts the transformation curve at Q_2. The economist is impelled to recognize that this new Q_2 position has turned out to be a suboptimal one. (Notice that the efficient distribution of Q_2, when the resulting *equilibrium* price set is given by the slope of p_1', is shown by d_2', this being the distribution of the Q_2 collection that – with respect to the existing transformation curve – renders the situation suboptimal.)

Our unsophisticated economist may be baffled but determined. He observes that the equilibrium prices are now the p_1 prices.

Accepting them as a datum, he discovers that the optimal position is at Q_1, this giving the highest aggregate value of any collection on the transformation curve. Undeterred by the fiasco of his first recommendation, our economist now attempts to persuade society to shift back to the earlier Q_1 equilibrium in the belief that this must be the true optimum after all.

Of course, we know just what will happen if society hearkens yet again to his recommendations. We can therefore suppose that any further to-ing and fro-ing is cut short when our hapless economist is pensioned off, so providing him with the leisure necessary to read up the literature. If he does so he will eventually realize that, wherever the characteristics of the economy are like those depicted in Figure 40, the *apparent* optimum at Q_2 cannot in fact be attained. For once Q_2 is reached, the equilibrium produces a set of prices that are at variance with the corresponding marginal costs: Q_2 therefore sheds its optimal characteristics.

Before taking the final step in this seeming paradox, we should mention, for the sake of completeness, the opposite predicament that our unsophisticated economist might have fallen into; namely, that of being unable to avoid an optimal position as between the alternatives being considered. The initial equilibrium position, that is, may now be at Q_2 with the efficient distribution d_2 being such as to render it an optimal position. Given the slope of the p_2 price-line, collection Q_1 is clearly a nonoptimal position and has a lower aggregate value than Q_2. But if, by some accidental nudge, the economy got shifted to the Q_1 equilibrium along with the resulting p_1 prices, it would be apparent that Q_1 was an optimal position, the p_1 price-line being tangent to the transformation curve at Q_1. At these prices, Q_2 would have a lower aggregate value than Q_1 as shown by the p_1' price-line passing through Q_2 being below the parallel p_1 price-line passing through Q_1.

In neither of these cases then were we able to compare an apparent optimal position with an apparent suboptimal position. In our first case, the movement from the initial suboptimum at Q_1 to the expected optimum at Q_2 resulted in an *equilibrium* at Q_2 having market prices p_1 that incidentally destroyed its optimal characteristics. In our second case, a tentative movement from the optimum at Q_2 to the alternative (and seemingly) nonoptimal position at Q_1 produced an *equilibrium* at Q_1 with market prices p_1 that incidentally destroyed its nonoptimal characteristics, so resulting in an optimal position there.

We conclude that, in general, we cannot compare at the initial price set either an existing nonoptimal position with what looks like an optimal (since in the movement to the seeming optimum, the equilibrium price set will change) or an existing optimal position with what looks like a nonoptimal position for the same reason.

Of course, empirical research may yet reveal limitations on the extent of the change in distribution and the change in the set of equilibrium market prices that actually accompanies any movement from one economic situation to another. There may, therefore, be occasions in the real economy when a particular collection of goods on the transformation curve can be valued higher than another collection at either set of prices. We can afford to be open-minded about further developments and bide our time. What is significant about the above analysis, however, is that those elegant and facile demonstrations about the Pareto superiority of the several economic institutions already mentioned can no longer be upheld. For all such demonstrations hinged upon the deployment of but a single set of prices.[1]

Another firm step on the road to scepticism before ending the chapter. In the exposition so far, all our economic positions have the saving grace, at least, of being collections of goods situated along the transformation curve. Whether optimal or suboptimal, the collections were therefore produced efficiently: more of one good in the collection could not be produced without producing less of some other good(s). Were any collection to be produced inefficiently, it would be represented by an interior point – one inside the transformation boundary, as is the point Q_1' in Figure 41.

You might well think that a nonoptimal position that is also an interior point is, compared with an optimal point such as Q_2 in the figure, at a double disadvantage. You might reasonably expect to be able to show that such a poor economic position is somehow Pareto inferior, or less efficient, than an optimal position at Q_2. Yet a glance at Figure 41 will convince you otherwise.

The actual equilibrium position at Q_2 is shown as an optimum in Figure 41, the set of market prices corresponding to the distribution of Q_2 between persons A and B being those represented by

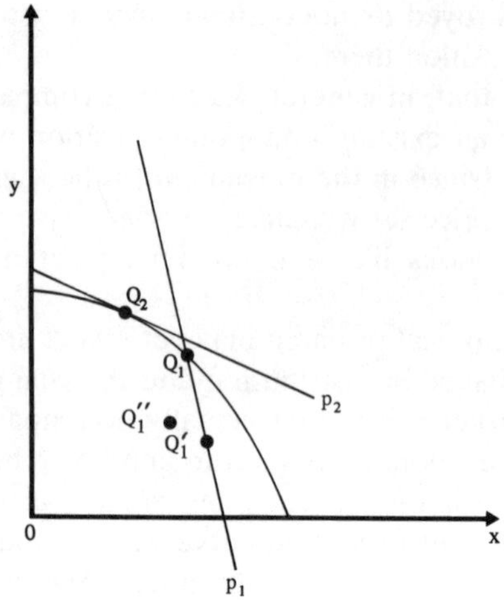

Figure 41

the slope of the p_2 price-line. In constrast, the actual equilibrium position of Q_1 on the transformation curve is a nonoptimal one, the set of market prices corresponding to the distribution of Q_1 being represented in the figure by the p_1 price-line which cuts the transformation curve at Q_1.

At the p_2 market prices, corresponding to the Q_2 equilibrium, it is clear that the Q_2 collection is optimal and has a higher value than the Q_1 collection. Thus, at the p_2 prices, Q_2 is Pareto superior to – or more efficient than – Q_1.

It is, however, equally clear that at the p_1 market prices, corresponding to the Q_1 equilibrium, the Q_1 collection – although nonoptimal – has a higher value than the Q_2 collection. Thus at the p_1 prices Q_1 is Pareto superior to – or more efficient than – Q_2.

But now look at the inefficently produced collection Q_1', correctly shown as an *interior* point in the figure. Being a point along the p_1 price-line, however, it has exactly the same value as does the efficiently produced collection Q_1. It follows that a comparison at the p_1 prices of the interior point Q_1' with the initial optimal point Q_2 also reveals the interior point Q_1' to be Pareto superior to Q_2 (For that matter we could have chosen a collection Q_1'', yet having a higher value than Q_2 at the p_1 prices.)

We cannot, then, be too emphatic about the verdict we pass on all the so-called demonstrations of the superiority of an optimal position, actual or anticipated. For, to repeat, all such general demonstrations of the Pareto superiority of the optimal position in question over the alternative nonoptimal position(s) have tacitly built into them the assumption that the respective valuations are to be compared by reference to the set of prices prevailing in the optimal position. This tacit assumption, though convenient, is arbitrary and has no normative sanction.

24 Resolving the apparent paradox

You may think that enough has been said to damp any one's enthusiasm for Pareto optimal positions. At any rate you will, I hope, have followed the argument well enough to understand that once account is taken of alternative price sets, associated with the alternative situations being compared, any general proof of the superiority of the optimal position cannot be demonstrated.

But there is one more trick in the bag, one that has to be played before ending this Part of the book since it marks the culmination of the allocation game and is the necessary and logical sequel to the preceding two chapters. What is more, in knitting it all together without much effort, it also issues in a surprise conclusion, one that may afford you some intellectual pleasure.

As pointed out in Chapter 21, for any particular distribution along the contract curve of a collection of goods there corresponds a particular price ratio (or common marginal rate of substitution of y for x), one that is usually (though not necessarily) different from the price ratios of different distributions. This being so, we begin this exercise by arbitrarily choosing two distributions d_1 and d_2 along the contract curve of the collection of goods shown by point Q_3 in Figure 42. To the distribution d_1 there corresponds the p_1 price set, indicated by the p_1 price-line passing through Q_3. To the distribution d_2 there corresponds the p_2 set of prices indicated by the p_2 price line passing through Q_3.

In terms of good x, the value of Q_3 given by the p_1 price-line is equal to Ox_1. In terms of good y, on the other hand, the value of Q_3 given by the p_1 price-line is equal to Oy_1. Thus any collection of goods along the p_1 price-line has a value equal to Ox_1 in terms of good x or alternatively equal to Oy_1 in terms of good y. Since the collection Q_1 is a point along the p_1 price-line it, too, must have exactly the same value as Q_3.

With respect to the p_2 price-line, on the other hand, the Q_3 collection is valued as equal either to Oy_2 of good y or else to Ox_2

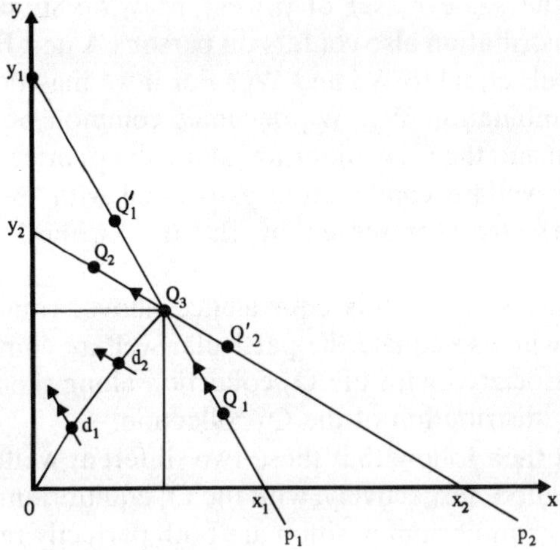

Figure 42

of good x. And, again, any other point along the p_2 price-line will have exactly the same value. The Q_2 collection is, of course, just such a point.

Before going a little further, let us recall from Chapter 22 that, by reference to the Pareto criterion, there can be no unambiguous ranking of collection Q_2 on the p_2 price-line and collection Q_1 on the p_1 price-line (by reference to the p_2 prices collection Q_1 is Pareto superior; by reference to the p_1 prices collection Q_1 is). It is this paradox that we are now to resolve.

We mentioned above that with respect to the p_1 price line Q_1 has exactly the same value as Q_3. But the prices represented by the p_1 price-line is the result of the d_1 distribution of Q_3.

We now broach the critical part of the argument and I require your unswerving attention for about five minutes. Since along the p_1 price-line that is common to both collections, Q_3 has exactly the same value as Q_1, it is possible to make each person as well off with the Q_3 collection as he is with the Q_1 collection. But, when Q_3 is valued by reference to this p_1 price-line, the actual d_1 distribution between person A and B also entails a distinct level of welfare for each person, say W_A' for person A and W_B' for person B. Thus, the d_1 distribution of Q_3 can also be regarded as the welfare combination W_A' and W_B'.

What about the particular distribution of the Q_1 collection that results in the same p_1 set of prices? May we suppose that this resulting distribution also confers on persons A and B respectively welfare levels equal to W'_A and W'_B? For if we may do so, then the welfare combination W'_A, W'_B becomes common both to the Q_1 equilibrium and the Q_3 equilibrium along the p_1 price-line. In other words, the welfare combination associated with the Q_1 position is also perfectly represented by the d_1 distribution of the Q_3 collection.

If we may suppose this equivalence above, considerations of symmetry will also equate the particular welfare combination, say W''_A, W''_B associated with the Q_2 collection along the p_2 price-line, with the d_2 distribution of the Q_3 collection.

It would then follow that these two different welfare combinations associated, respectively, with the Q_1 equilibrium position and with the Q_2 equilibrium position are both perfectly represented by the d_1 and d_2 distributions of the Q_3 collection.

We should be able, therefore, to conclude at once that, even where the collections Q_1 and Q_2 on the transformation curve cannot be ranked unambiguously on a Pareto criterion (as illustrated in Chapter 23), it is entirely possible to rank Q_1 and Q_2 on a *distributional* criterion. For a ranking of the two welfare combinations, associated respectively with Q_1 and Q_2, reduces to no more than a ranking of alternative (efficient) distributions of collection Q_3.

Bearing in mind that person A's origin is at point O in Figure 42, and that person B's origin is at point Q_3, then clearly person A is better off with the d_2 distribution than with the d_1 distribution of Q_3. Provided the community has a distributional criterion, one that is applicable at least to the ranking of d_1 and d_2, the Q_1 and Q_2 equilibria can be ranked on distributional grounds, and on distributional grounds only. If, on the other hand, the community has no distributional criterion, or one that is not applicable to the ranking of the d_1 and d_2 distributions of Q_3, then there is no way of ranking collections Q_1 and Q_2.

Before we conclude on this provisional note, it should be evident that although we began the exercise with an *actual* Q_3 collection valued by two alternative price lines from which we selected two *hypothetical* collections Q_1 and Q_2, we could just as well have started the other way round. We could, that is, have begun instead with two actual collections Q_1 and Q_2 having distributions that generated, respectively, the p_1 and p_2 price-lines, and taken as a hypothetical collection Q_3 the point of intersection of these two price-lines. The structure of the diagram is unchanged. And if we continue to suppose the equivalence suggested above (to which we have now to turn), then distributions d_1 and d_2 of this hypothetical Q_3 collection represent exactly the respective welfare combinations associated with the actual Q_1 and Q_2 equilibria.

On the assumption that the suggested equivalence holds our conclusion is as follows: wherever the equilibrium price-lines associated with two collections of goods Q_1 and Q_2 intersect, and consequently an unambiguous Pareto ranking is not possible, the comparison of Q_1 and Q_2 boils down to that of a possible distributional ranking of a single hypothetical collection Q_3.

We have not, however, actually *proved* the suggested equivalence; namely, that when the values of Q_1 and Q_3 are the same, the welfare combination given by the equilibrium distribution of Q_1 is the same as the welfare combination given by the d_1 distribution of the Q_3 collection (and similarly for Q_2 and Q_3). In order to prove this, we should have had to develop the 'community indifference curve' construction to which I have been making discrete footnote references. This construction presents no intrinsic difficulties. But it takes a little time, and so would prevent us from getting to the core of the allocation problem with a minimum of fuss.[1] Had we used this construction, we should have correctly located the required hypothetical Q_3 collection, *not* at the actual intersection of the two price-lines, as conveniently assumed in the preceding exposition, but at a point a little to the right of Q_3 in Figure 42. (However, the closer are Q_1 and Q_2, the closer is the required hypothetical collection Q_3 to the point of intersection of the two price-lines.)

Allowance being made for correctly locating the required hypothetical collection Q_3, the above conclusion is surprising. Indeed, it is rather more devastating than it seems on first reflection. For if you ask anyone, even an economist, if a collection Q_2' having more of every good than an alternative collection Q_1 is socially to be preferred to Q_1, he will almost certainly say yes. After all, however the Q_1 collection is distributed, it is always possible to divide up the Q_2' collection so as to give more goods to every one – in this way making everybody better off with the Q_2' collection than he is with the distribution of the Q_1 collection. Indeed, a collection Q_2' that has more of every good than a Q_1

collection surely meets the Pareto criterion irrespective of the actual (or hypothetical) distribution of Q_1.[2]

But now look again at Figure 42, where Q_2' is located northeast of Q_1 (and therefore has more of both goods x and y). If we could see no more of the picture than Q_1 and Q_2', we might feel thoroughly satisfied in ranking Q_2' above Q_1. Once we are able to see the larger picture, and therefore become aware of the intersection of the two price-lines that pass respectively through Q_1 and Q_2', we realize, to our chagrin, that the same conclusion above holds in this case also: that, in fact (since the welfare combination at Q_2' is identical to that of the d_2 distribution of Q_3 when it is priced at the p_2 prices of the Q_2' equilibrium, and also that the welfare combination at Q_1 is identical to that of the d_1 distribution of Q_3 when it is priced at the p_1 prices resulting from the Q_1 equilibrium) Q_2' and Q_1 can also be reduced to the two different distributions d_2 and d_1 of the single hypothetical Q_3 collection. There can, therefore, be an unambiguous ranking, if at all, only along a distributional scale. A similar conclusion is reached in the attempt to rank Q_2 and the collection Q_1' that has more of every good than Q_2.[3]

You will recall that in the preceding chapter we demonstrated that an optimal position such as Q_2 in Figure 43 could not be said to be unambiguously Pareto superior to a nonoptimal position such as Q_1 even when Q_1 is an interior point (being inefficiently produced). For when valued at the p_1 prices, the Q_1 collection would have been higher value than the Q_2 collection.

In the light of the results reached in the present chapter, which are always applicable to cases of intersecting price-lines, the above conclusion about the ambiguity of ranking on the scale of efficiency has to be transformed into the conclusion that the two positions in question can be ranked (if at all) only on a distributional scale.

Thus, in the case depicted in Figure 43, the conclusion merely that optimal position Q_2 and nonoptimal position Q_1 cannot be ranked unambiguously on a Pareto criterion does not go far enough. Since there is a hypothetical Q_3 collection along whose contract curve the actual welfare combinations associated with the Q_2 and Q_1 positions can also be identified as the distributional points d_2 and d_1 (not shown in the figure) respectively, these origi-

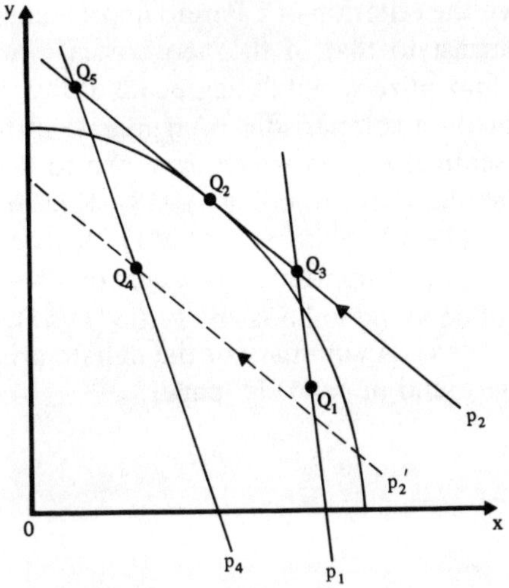

Figure 43

nal situations Q_1 and Q_2 lend themselves only to a distributional ranking.

What is no less interesting is the case where the collection in the optimal position Q_2 is Pareto superior to the collection in a nonoptimal position Q_4 whether valued at the p_2 prices associated with the Q_2 equilibrium or whether valued instead at the p_4 prices associated with the Q_4 equilibrium. Indeed, it is possible that for all conceivable prices the Q_2 collection is valued higher than the Q_4 collection – notwithstanding which an unambiguous efficiency ranking is not possible, since the welfare combinations associated with the Q_2 and Q_4 positions can be identified as alternative distributions d_2 and d_4 respectively (not shown in the figure) of the hypothetical Q_5 collection.

Further reading for Part Four

The 'New Welfare Economics' was regarded as new in that, as distinct from the neoclassical normative economics, it jettisoned the concept of an inverse relation between income and the marginal utility of money (and therefore the implications drawn from that relation about the desirability of an equal distribution of income between the members of society). Moreover the goal of the New Welfare Economics was that of attaining a Pareto optimal position, hence the criterion of a Pareto improvement. This overall goal is in contrast to that of the neoclassical normative school, which was to maximize society's aggregate utility, hence the criterion used turned on comparisons of aggregate utility.

The more seminal papers which gave rise to the New Welfare Economics are those of Hotelling (1938), Kaldor (1939), Hicks (1939), Hicks (1940), Scitovsky (1941), Kuznets (1948), and Samuelson (1950). Important critiques of the New Welfare Economics can be found in books by Little (1957), Graaff (1957), and by Nath (1964). A summary of the debate arising from these sources can be found in my 1965 paper.

Part Five

Sources of economic failure in a technological age

25 Introductory remarks

Although there are interesting comparisons to be made as between capitalism and socialism, as between private and public enterprise, as between centralized and decentralized planning, and as between a highly competitive economy and an economy of cartels and monopolies, we shall not consider these issues any further in this final part. We shall be concerned entirely with sources of economic failure – of those losses of social welfare that escape the conventional economic calculus and, until very recently, the attention of economists also. Such sources of economic failure are common to all modern industrial societies irrespective of their economic and political organization. In the event, we might as well assume the best about such a society and (from a libertarian economist's point of view at least) imagine it to be a Western-type liberal democracy having a private sector of the economy that is large and highly competitive.

Perhaps the caveat that follows is unnecessary for most readers, though impatient and impetuous students should heed it. There is a (possibly apocryphal) story told that Nero agreed to act as judge in a competition between two Roman lute players. After hearing only the first player, he gave the prize to the second. The moral of the story in this context is this: any effective criticism of the modern economy does not, of itself, warrant our support for any proposed alternative kind of economy. The alternative itself has to be tested through experience. The prudent policy would be to recognize the more glaring deficiencies of the existing economy – and of the existing society – and in so far as they appear to be incapable of remedy within the existing system to bear 'the ills we know than to fly to others we know not of'. We may well conclude that modern man, being avaricious, impatient, and short sighted, things are more likely than not to get worse over time. Yet, being cynical, we may also believe that no sweeping revolution is likely to make things better. The ideal is the enemy not only of the good, but of the tolerable, and, indeed, of the seemingly intolerable yet somehow viable.

Having made it clear that I have little sympathy with what the young today refer to euphemistically as 'direct action' in the endeavour to topple the 'bourgeois' civilization in which they are enmeshed, I return to the description of my thesis. It can be put as follows: despite continuing economic growth or, better still, continuing growth of per capita 'real' income (as conveniently measured), despite well functioning markets, and despite increasing attention to the cannons of allocative efficiency, it is more than just possible that the experience of well-being in the economically advanced countries has been declining over the last thirty years. There are a number of economists who would think that if such were indeed the case, the causes should be sought in the massive expansion of government bureaucracy since the second world war, and the consequent diminution of private enterprise and competition. Although I go along with them in deploring these developments, the thesis I am to expound, if valid, would be also independent of these developments

At all events, this thesis or, if you like, conjecture is not intended to cast doubt on the endeavours of economists or on the power of the human intellect. The declining trend in social well being that I surmise arises primarily from the very nature of scientific and technological innovation; from the physical and social environment it brings into being.

The main emphasis in what follows is on the impact of such innovation on the state of information, on people's tastes (which we have so far accepted as an exogenous datum), on the biases of the market, on the range of the new spillovers for which economists cannot prescribe, and on the genesis of an increasingly 'pluralistic' and 'permissive' civilization. The reader will understand that in order to discuss these various themes, and to reflect seriously on the contribution that the study of economics can make to the welfare of ordinary people, we have to move away from the conventional economic framework – in which, however, there are problems enough, as already revealed in the chapters of Part Four.

Much of what I have to say, therefore, necessarily represents a personal interpretation of the many characteristic features of our age, an interpretation that is not by any means shared by all academic economists. My excuse for raising such polemical issues is simply that they are, I believe, the really crucial issues. Think of it, if you will, as a search to ask the right questions about the impact of economic growth over the last few decades on the cohesion, character, and felicity of society – a search, however, that is conducted by means of persistent conjecture about causes of the growing sense of unease and malaise so repeatedly articulated by concerned and perceptive writers.

26 The folklore of the market 1

In this chapter we shall look at some of the more manifest failures of the market to promote economic efficiency, equity and expansion of choice even though, as measured by conventional indices, per capita real income continues its upward trend.

But first let us ask what is a market. It is often understood as a place where trading takes place, as a mart or medieval fair. The economist likes to define it in terms of voluntary exchange between persons or groups. If two peasants haggle over the price of a pig, they can be said to form a market. More generally, however, a larger number of people are involved in forming a market. And a market so constituted need not be confined to a particular location. Markets in staple commodities such as wheat, coffee, sugar, coal, steel, gold or cotton, are world markets, the product of a network of continuous communication between centres all over the globe.

In its common manifestations, the market may be regarded as a natural institution in that, in the absence of prohibitions, it comes into being wherever there are opportunities for mutually gainful exchange. In a thoroughgoing communist economy, and even in a private enterprise economy during a crisis, coercive powers are needed to prevent the emergence of a market in some or all goods. In so far as such powers fail to prevent them, the resulting markets are dubbed black markets in recognition of their illegality. And it is a tribute to the unquenchable desire for gain in some men that, notwithstanding the direct penalties for trading in forbidden merchandise, such black markets have flourished in all ages and civilizations.

There are, of course, costs in setting up and maintaining an organized market, or system of markets, in a free enterprise system. Apart from the costs of premises where traders may gather, officials are needed to ensure the enforcement of contracts and, where necessary, to set up arbitration procedures and to disseminate information. Liberal economists believe that such costs are well worth incurring in view of the disadvantages they associate with the alternative of bureaucratic planning. In contrast to the latter, the free market is held to offer the citizen greater choice. It is held also to be far more economic in effecting savings in information costs and in the costs of bureaucratic planning and enforcement. Nor is the market so prone to corruption, nepotism, and other abuses as is a powerful bureaucracy.

Again, switches from one pattern of production to another comes about easily enough, and without any need for central direction, in a market economy in response to changes in the conditions of demand and supply. The economy is not prone to abrupt changes that result from the overthrow of one power group by another within a centralized economy. Moreover, in a well functioning market system – one functioning in the absence of prolonged unemployment or inflation or one under the continual threat of disruption – resources flow easily into the production of goods for which demand is growing and away from the production of goods for which demand is declining.

Finally, in so far as the market sector is powerful, people tend to accept the verdict of the market as expressed in the set of resulting prices. And there will be less grievance against a government whose control of economic forces is believed to be limited (as indeed it was before the second world war, and was more so before the turn of the century). In these circumstances the government is absolved from any duty to determine what is just or fair. Indeed, this obsession with what is just and fair has grown during the post-war period along with the growth of government, and the even faster growth of governments' illusions (until the last few years) about its ability to control the over-all performance of the economy and the direction of its development.

It cannot be too often stressed however that the market economy, left to operate according to its own internal logic, is not to be regarded as a mechanism for producing equity. It does not, nor can it be expected to, resolve questions bearing on social justice. Claims for the virtues of the market – and these are not small virtues – include that of conferring economic freedom of choice: the freedom to enter or leave an occupation on the terms prevailing, the freedom to introduce new products or new methods of production, and the freedom to buy and sell goods at the prices emerging from the interaction of market forces.

Although it may not be historically inevitable, economists have pointed to a strong connection between capitalism, especially a competitive market capitalism, and individual freedom. For those thinkers who view the state, not so much as an instrument for promoting the social good but rather as a force that threatens the economic freedom and, by extension, the political freedom of the citizen, the post-war expansion of government activity in Western democracies has been viewed with increasing dismay. The articulate and persuasive monographs bearing on the strong connections between capitalism and freedom, both economic and political, written by Hayek (1944) and Friedman (1962) are highly recommended to readers, particularly to those who continue to favour socialist solutions. I am, myself, impressed with the following passage by Friedman (1962, p. 15):

> . . . the fundamental threat to freedom is the power to coerce, be it in the hands of a monarch, a dictator, an oligarchy or a momentary majority. The preservation of freedom requires the elimination of such concentration of power to the fullest possible extent and the dispersal and distribution of whatever power cannot be eliminated – a system of checks and balances. By removing the organization of economic power from the control of political authority, the market eliminates this source of coercive power. It enables economic strength to be a check to political power rather than a reinforcement.

I confess that I am in sympathy with the broad sweep of this type of argument. Nevertheless, while remaining highly critical of, and antagonistic to, the expansion of government power, it is possible also to exaggerate the power for good inherent in a decentralized private enterprise system. It may be useful therefore to list those conditions that if met would be sufficient for the market to bear good fruit in the form of a steady improvement in social welfare or, more modestly, an expansion in the area of choice available to the community during a period of rapidly advancing technology, the hallmark of our present civilization.

First, the familiar condition already laboured in earlier chapters, that the economy should be competitive in all its branches of activity to the extent of prices everywhere tending to their corresponding marginal costs.

Second, in so far as a more egalitarian distribution of the national product is regarded as an important ingredient of social welfare, the apparent rise in per capital real income over time must not be accompanied by a less egalitarian structure of income.

Third, and drawing on our conclusions in Part Three, the direct effect on other persons arising in the production or use of any good (that is, those effects that escape the price mechanism) have to be brought into the cost calculus. How they are brought into the calculus is of the essence. With respect to the magnitude of transactions costs, for instance, a sufficient condition for ensuring that, on balance, society is not made worse off is that property rights in environmental amenity be invested in citizens.

To these three conditions that suffice within the conventional economic framework, four more have to be added once we move away from its unavoidable limitations.

Fourth, the consuming public has to be fully conversant with the comparative qualities and performances of all new goods appearing on the market, otherwise its subsequent disappointment and disillusion may result, on balance, in a diminution of welfare.

Fifth, that citizens, in their capacity as workers, do not over time become worse off as a result of having to adapt themselves to new techniques of production.

Sixth, that the so-called Jones Effect, in an extreme form at least, is not operative.

Seventh, and most important of all, that the welfare experienced by men from sources other than the goods produced by the economy is negligible or, if not negligible, is not declining.

Though it hardly needs saying, none of these conditions is likely to be met in any existing Western economy. The last five conditions, which have particular relevance for today's wealthier countries, are unlikely to be met or even approached.

27 The folklore of the market 2

We now turn to some of the other welfare issues in connection with the operation of a competitive market economy. I do not allege that many economists have claimed or would claim merit for the market in all the respects I am to mention; only that these issues have not received enough emphasis by the profession. Since some economists are likely to find my brief reflections on these issues controversial, I list them in the form of questions.

Has the market a consumer bias?

Suppose there is a shift of expenditure from consumption of good x to consumption of good y which, in due course, is followed by a movement of 1000 workers from industry x to industry y as a result of which equilibrium is restored in both industries. But the welfare of the workers may easily be overlooked. The 1000 workers moving from x to y may well prefer to continue working in x and to remain in their original neighbourhood. Of their own volition they would not have moved into industry y unless they were adequately compensated.

But we cannot realistically suppose that they will always be attracted into industry y by payment there of higher wages or bonuses. They may simply be discharged by industry x as being 'redundant'. To that extent they suffer a loss of welfare that has to be compared with the gain to the consumer from being able to buy more of good y at much the same price.

Bear in mind in this connection that the surplus of a dollar gained or lost by the consumer is likely to have less welfare significance than the rent of a dollar gained or lost by the worker – a difference that has nothing to do with their respective earnings. The average consumer in a wealthy country is faced with a wide range of goods, substitution as between which may cause him a modicum of inconvenience but certainly no hardship. In fact a good proportion of his purchases is aptly described as 'impulse buying' – being the result of a successful advertising campaign, or of observing such an item in a friend's house, or of a momentary fascination with novelty, or of a sudden whim or caprice or of the excitement of a bargain. Although any frustration of his preferred purchases at such moments may elicit a protest, the hardship endured is negligible. In contrast, the loss of welfare borne by workers who, in consequence of these shifts in consumer demand, can suffer temporary unemployment and may eventually have to move from the familiarity of their workplace and neighbourhood, can reasonably be described as hardship.

Such considerations permit us to describe the operation of the market to be consumer-oriented. The importance of this notion, however, depends upon the vicissitudes of consumer demand and the extent to which, through subsequent successions of redundancies and family movements, hardships are inflicted on citizens *qua* workers. Increasing affluence, which entails a growth in what are called luxuries (often better described as 'expendables' or even 'regrettables') and novelties, and which strengthens the trend toward impulse buying, is likely to increase the threat to the security of workers unless there are countervailing forces at work. Such countervailing forces are associated with the rise of the welfare state and also with the power of the labour unions – which unions occasionally seek to control employment as well as wage rates. Both these developments, however, interfere with the smooth functioning of the market mechanism. With the growth of affluence, the dilemma is perhaps inevitable.

Can the market produce too much variety?

The question is all but rhetorical. Up to a point an increase in variety can be assumed to increase satisfaction. Beyond that point, the costs of choosing rationally rise and can eventually overcome the advantages of a wider range of goods of each type. Information, even where it is available when needed, is time-consuming and often indigestible.

It may be argued that the consumer always has the option of not troubling himself with the new range of goods; that he may continue to buy the same batch of goods as he used to and, therefore, be no worse off – always assuming the older goods will not be withdrawn from the market. But if we are concerned, as we are, with the actual effect on people's welfare of the growth of variety, the question is whether in these circumstances this option is usually exercised; indeed, whether it can be exercised. For existing brands and models are, within a few short years, entirely superseded by new brands and new models. And as often as not, by the time a reliable consumers' report appears a number of the models and brands that have been recommended are no longer available.

Is the assumption of given tastes reasonable?

This question is evidently related to the preceding one. In a traditional society in which staple items form the bulk of consumer purchases, the assumption of unchanged tastes over time is reasonable. In such a society we can discount the prevalence of any Jones Effect and suppose that an increase of goods per capita raises people's welfare. In a modern affluent society, on the other hand, even the proportion of income spent on broad categories of goods – food, clothing, shelter, transport, recreation, medical treatment and so on – tends to alter over time. And within these broad categories, the range of goods, and their brands and models, alter more rapidly. Perforce, consumers tastes cannot remain constant for long.

Neither is expenditure on commercial advertising designed to stabilize tastes. Nor, as sometimes alleged, may they be regarded as information – unless by semantic licence we include persuasive appeals as a form of information and refuse to draw a distinction between partial information and impartial information.[1]

Thus, contrary to the gratifying vision of the market mechanism operating to direct scarce resources to satisfy given wants, the reverse may be closer to reality in the modern economy: scarce resources continually being employed in advertising campaigns that are designed to create *dissatisfaction* with existing wants. A cynic might be forgiven for detecting a transposition of ends and means: of people's consumption being encouraged by industry in order to serve the ends of production. In other words, the prevailing rationale of the system seems to be that of using the consuming public as a means of realizing the expansionist aims of industry.

Does the growth of spillovers act to reduce choice?

Even where we restrict ourselves to environmental spillovers and, in addition, make the simplifying assumption that transaction costs are not large enough to prevent optimal outputs being attained in all spillover-generating activities, the answer must be an unambiguous yes.

The proponents of the virtues of the market economy never tire of pointing out that the more the public sector takes over from the private sector the smaller the choice remaining for the individual. His money is used allegedly on his behalf in the production of those goods that could well be left in the private sector, such as education, medicine, insurance, and recreation. The amount and the quality of such goods are then no longer determined by the individual himself. They are determined for him by enlightened bureaucrats.[2] What these same proponents of the competitive market fail to observe is that this resulting diminution of choice, this individual frustration, arises also and in a more pernicious and pervasive form in an age of rapid technological innovation. In the last three decades, in particular, we have witnessed an unprecedented proliferation of new spillovers from new gases and toxic wastes to radiation hazards and thousands of new synthetics and chemicals.

What becomes a public good is, generally, a matter of social choice. What turns out to be a collective bad is not – at least if we accept the presumption in favour of economic 'progress' and expansion.

To take a more homely example, when a person complains of smog or of aircraft noise, it is not much to the purpose to expatiate on the impressive growth of the auto industry or of the increase in opportunities for air travel – even though the person himself creates some of the smog, or uses the facilities for air travel or other noise-creating goods. In any case, there is no incentive for him to desist from such activities since the effect of his own forbearance on the ambient environment would be virtually nil. Thus in the prevailing circumstances he is rational to avail himself of all goods whose collective disamenity he has in any case to live with. Given any choice in the matter, however, he might choose *not* to avail himself of these spillover-generating goods provided that he himself could escape all the spillovers. But, of course, he does not have this sort of choice. Whether or not such spillovers are 'corrected' to their optimal amounts (according to the economist's criterion) each person in the community has no choice in the matter: he is effectively compelled to accept a 'package deal' – for instance, aircraft noise plus the opportunity of travel, or gas-filled cities along with the opportunity of car travel – that, on balance, may make him much worse off.

The point is far from being trivial. The advantages of individual choice claimed for the market is warranted only in so far as the market succeeds, so to speak, in 'decomposing' what would otherwise be composite packages of both goods and bads – packages that result from the increasing prevalence of collective goods and bads – into their constituent goods and bads among which the individual may exercise effective choice.

In the nature of things, however, it is not possible to set up a spillovers market, one in which each person can also decide for himself just how much of the damaging spillover he will absorb at the market price. He may choose only the amounts of the *market* goods that generate the spillovers in question and has to put up with whatever amounts of the *collective* bads that alight upon him – incurring some expenditures perhaps to mitigate their effects on him.

The importance of this limitation wrought by spillovers on the virtues of the market clearly depends upon the impact on individual wellbeing of the range and nature of the spillovers in question. Considering the pace and scale of modern technology, the power of industry, the vested interests of the scientific establishment, and the fascination of the modern consumer with the cornucopia of modern gadgetry, it would be optimistic to anticipate any decline in the growth and spread of spillovers over the future. At best we can expect new spillovers for old. Some of the more pervasive spillovers, such as noise, visual distraction, urban filth and litter, congestion of traffic and of people along with the 'uglification' of our cities, are not likely to diminish over the next decade.

Bearing in mind the inertia of the political process, the financial interests vested in many of the environmentally damaging industries – including, above all, the tourist industry – it is not too cynical to conclude that, notwithstanding the operation of free competitive markets, in all that is relatively trivial the individual today has ample choice, indeed, too much choice, whereas in all that is vital to the state of his wellbeing, in particular the environment in which he is immersed, his choice is being steadily eroded.

Can the market control world population?

Economic forces certainly play an important role in birth and death rates, but the relationships are by no means straightforward. In countries where the bulk of the population live near the margin of subsistence, a rise in living standards will initially increase the population. It will act to reduce the mortality rate and is likely also to increase the birth rate. In the affluent West, on the other hand, an increase in living standards has recently been associated with a decline in the growth of the indigenous population. True, to the extent a family is better off it can afford to have more children. But, at the same time, the cost of children happens to have risen disproportionately. A child today entails numerous restrictions on an increasingly mobile society. And once technology has freed women from the home, the opportunities she forgoes in the form of industrial earnings and status are a heavy part of the cost of rearing children.

In the meantime, the overt disparity in living standards between East and West (or, as we now tend to say, between North and South) has produced waves of massive migration from poor to rich countries, by far the greater part of which, I suspect, is illegal.

Economic forces are obviously at work. But there is no market mechanism that can be counted upon to bring about some ideal world population however understood. We are far from being sure today that Malthus was too pessimistic in believing that, in the absence of voluntary controls, population would ultimately be held in check by war, famine and plague. Of course, the revolution in science and technology over the last 200 years or so has also multiplied the size of the world's sustainable population,[3] at the same time enabling living standards to rise to near-profligate levels in about a third of the world's population. But this seeming success – in numerical terms at least – may be no more than a transitional phase, one preparatory to some global catastrophe.

In broad perspective, science and technology may be viewed as the main instrument in man's struggle to prevent his living standards from sinking under the weight of expanding population. But apart from the very real hazards of self-destruction, there can be no assurance of success in this historical venture. World net reproduction rates are still positive. World population is still growing and spreading, and migrating in increasing numbers to the more affluent countries. Assuming that by some miracle we survive the perils of the new technology, the end result of this millennial development could be nothing better than an outlandish world population precariously dependent upon the ceaseless efforts of science and technology.[4]

28 Economic expertise in an age of rapid innovation

Notwithstanding the limitations of the market in promoting welfare, discussed in the preceding chapter, the belief that economic expertise – which term comprehends familiarity with the norms of allocative efficiency and proposals for their application – can make a substantial contribution to human betterment is one that dies hard in the profession. Among the disinterested, however, it may die more easily, particularly if they reflect on a number of considerations I invoke in this and the following two chapters. In this present chapter I restrict myself to two observations that, if I interpret them aright, act to weaken the confidence that can be reposed in economic calculation that informs public policy, in particular the evaluation and ranking of public projects. In the chapter that follows, this iconoclasm is carried further in a more radical critique of the general presumption favouring economic growth.

In order to simplify the discussion of the allocative implications of adverse environmental spillovers, we assumed that we had the necessary knowledge of their consequences; that is, knowledge of the extent and physical nature of the damage inflicted directly or indirectly on humans, knowledge of ways of measuring the damage and where necessary, knowledge also of the statistical probability of the damage occurring. Even for the more familiar forms of pollution, knowlege of this sort tends to be shaky and subject to wide margins of error. For this reason, the procedure favoured by democratic governments, and also by many economists, is that of setting environmental standards, or of setting limits to the levels of various forms of pollution, rather than that of attempting to calculate an ideal effluent tax. The economist's role is thus reduced even in circumstances where, in principle, he should be able to offer more detailed allocative advice.

Since the second world war, however, a new class of environmental spillovers has come into prominence, one that the economist finds difficult if not impossible to cope with. These are the multifarious side-effects of recent innovations having in common certain characteristics that separate them from the conventional spillovers such as smoke, noise, effluent and congestion, which feature so large in the conventional economic literature. The chief of these characteristics that appear to render this new class of spillovers intractable to economic calculation are the following.

First, since many new industrial processes being introduced bear little relation to known industrial processes, and many of the new products being created are synthetics that are foreign to the ecological system, there is no experience of the nature or incidence of their side-effects. The consequence for the environment, and therefore for humanity, of the continuance and spread of these new processes and products remain for some time under a gigantic and threatening question mark. Specific effects, or a range of possible effects, are sometimes suspected by scientists and give rise to speculation and controversy. For the rest, it is expected, and feared, that novel and unwelcome effects will emerge over time.

Second, there is, in such cases, some apprehension that the spillovers in question may take the form of large scale disasters possibly having global dimensions.

Third, the damage caused, which may be ultimately fatal to humanity and other forms of life, could turn out to be irreversible.

Fourth, some of these as yet imperfectly understood spillovers take the form of effects that accumulate over time so as to imperil the health and lives of future generations. And there can be no presumption that safe technological methods for dealing with them will be discovered in time.

In the face of these characteristics, the question is whether the economist, or any kind of scientist for that matter, can produce figures purporting to be an economic contribution to the political decision-making process.

A number of current hazards including the possible escape of a synthetic virus against which man has no defences, the dissipation of a critical proportion of the earth's ozone mantle through the continuing use of chlorfluoromethanes and other gases, the danger to life from the accumulation of radioactive wastes, illustrate the quite terrifying outcomes that cannot, at present, be dismissed as being beyond the pale of likelihood.

The conscientious and sober economist has to recognize the hopelessness of trying to calculate the economic cost of these new spillovers. In the circumstances, the crucial question is that of the policy to be followed during the period necessary for knowledge to accumulate to the extent needed for a decision to be taken with respect to the innovation in question.

Two diametrically opposed responses, or rules of procedure, may be suggested. Rule A would countenance the initiation and continuation of an economic activity involving novel processes or products until the evidence that it was harmful or risky had been established 'beyond reasonable doubt'. Rule B, in contrast, would prohibit the activity in question until evidence that it was safe had been established 'beyond reasonable doubt'. The qualifying phrase 'beyond reasonable doubt' can, of course, excite a great deal of controversy. But however the phrase is interpreted, the distinction between the alternative procedures remains the crucial issue.

Which rule will, in the event, prevail depends upon the institutions and attitudes that reflect the ethos of the particular form of society. On the other hand, which rule *ought* to prevail should depend among other things upon the state of material wellbeing of the members of society as well as upon the peculiarities of the hazards feared. In this connection, I would hazard the opinion that inasmuch as the history of industrial innovation over the last thirty years or so does not read exactly like a success story, the wisdom of continuing to allow ourselves to be guided, in the main, by rule A is no longer self-evident.

The second observation that, if valid, weakens the foundations of economic expertise in the area of resource allocation is the apparent erosion of an ethical consensus. I argued in Chapter 4 that in order for allocative propositions to have prescriptive force independently of political decisions, the maxims on which an allocative economics is founded must conform with the ethics of the society for which such allocative economics is intended. I remind you briefly that these maxims are (1) that the welfare only of the individuals comprising society is to count; (2) that only the individuals' own valuations of the change in question are to be used; and (3) that with respect to a choice as between alternative economic situations, the Pareto criterion (translated as the algebraic aggregation of all individual losses and gains) is to be employed as a ranking device.

It follows that if these maxims do not accord with the ethics of the society in question then an economic judgement that some allocations are more or less efficient than others cannot be vindicated. In the event, the role of the economist in the area of allocation loses its prescriptive aspect. It is reduced to that of gathering information specified as relevant by the political decision-making body whose authority for pronouncing upon and resolving allocative issues is no longer constrained by considerations of economic efficiency and is, therefore, beyond challenge.

Already we have had occasion to reveal some exceptions to society's acceptance of the second maxim – the requirement that in any economic calculation the individuals' own valuations alone are to be used. Thus in Chapter 17 on non-environmental spillovers, I suggested that individual valuations that arise, in the main, from unwarrantable prejudice, from envy, from spite or from sadism, may well be rejected by society in its ethical capacity. And if so, such valuations ought not to be entered into the economic calculation. Such exceptions imply that a number of economic reorganizations that apparently meet a Pareto criterion, or even entail an actual Pareto improvement (each person affected by the change being made better off) may yet be repudiated on ethical grounds by society.

But we need not stop at non-environmental spillover effects. By extension, individual valuations placed, say, by consumers on a range of private goods, or even collective goods, might also be rejected by reference to an ethical consensus. The inferred motives of consumers or producers may be thought detestable. The goods in question may be regarded as appealing only to perverted desires or instincts that ought actively to be discouraged, or the goods may be thought to be pernicious to the health or character of the members of society. For example, there may be a broad consensus that the valuations placed by some individuals on tobacco products, on bugging devices, or on obscene or violent entertainment ought not to enter an economic calculation at individual valuations, ought not to be entered at all or, if entered, should carry a negative valuation.

A final and more disturbing extension of this line of thought is that in a number of important respects there no longer seems to be an ethical consensus and, therefore, no virtual constitution by reference to which the economist can justify his economic calculations, his particular recommendations, or any general normative propositions. Thus, although the economist might be able to disregard those non-environmental spillovers that society as a whole would stigmatize as arising from unworthy motives, and to deal in some specified way with goods which society believes conducive only to instability or decadence, he would be much harder put to prescribe for a society that has, at some stage in its development, become intricately discriminating in its ethical capacity. The strain of doing so, however, though considerable, might not deter him altogether. He could always console himself with the hope that his errors of oversight will not always be such as to nullify the value of his calculations and that, with opportunities over time for a better understanding of the pattern of the ethical consensus, his calculations will improve.

What is far more destructive for any normative economics is the incipient ethical fragmentation exhibited in the affluent societies of the West whose economic growth is powered by continuing technological innovation. If such a society, euphemistically and misleadingly referred to by myopic optimists as 'pluralistic', becomes divided in its ethical judgement on issues involving taste, propriety, and decency; divided, moreover, in its convictions about the significance to be attached to individual valuations in the presence of rapid change and the consequent belatedness of reliable information; and divided, finally, about the validity of individual valuations in the presence of widespread commercial advertising and in the presence also of a division among experts and the public about the value to be placed on a wide range of depleting natural resources and species of fauna and flora – if such is the case, and casual observation appears to confirm it – then there can be no consensus whatever about *which* individual valuations are to count and how. Calculations of economic efficiency raised on a Pareto criterion carry no prescriptive force in a fragmented or 'pluralistic' society.

Indeed, on a more general level toward which we move in the following chapters, this difficulty is compounded by doubts increasingly expressed over the last two decades whether, as economists have traditionally assumed, more goods are always better than less for the individual and for society.

At all events, we are compelled to conclude that under conditions of consensual collapse, and of the growing doubts among segments of society about the value of more goods, the task of the normative economist is practically impossible to discharge conscientiously. His criterion for determining the economic efficiency of alternative policies or projects has all but evaporated. Only in a traditional society, perhaps, can his calculations and normative propositions have the sanction of an ethical consensus.

29 The limits of abundance: a conservative critique 1

For many generations now, humanists, socialists, libertarians, economists, radicals and advanced thinkers in general – an assortment of intellectuals that may be referred to as the Established Enlightenment – have shared a number of basic beliefs, among which I single out one: that economic progress (in the shape of rising per capita 'real' income) is one of the chief components that contribute to improving the quality of life.[1]

I should add, in passing, that the critique of economic progress (or rising per capita 'real' income) which follows is independent of the many possible refinements that can be made to the economist's conception and definition of economic progress or economic growth. For the purpose in hand, however, you may conceive economic progress or economic growth as an outward movement over time of the transformation boundary (illustrated in Figure 30 and described in Chapter 19) as it faces each individual. The conventional economic opinion has it that, as compared with preceding generations, the position today of this transformation curve – at least for us lucky ones who live in the West – is such that it is legitimate to assert that the age we live in is an age of plenty.

Manifest doubts about some features of this sovereign age of plenty are not to be allowed to mar this glowing vision of expanding opportunities for the multitude. Dedicated growthmen, aware of the general rumbling and misgivings, exhort the public on the imperative need for faster economic growth in order to deal with those pressing problems that are, apparently, the products themselves of rapid economic growth. Alternatively, they take refuge in metaphors about babies and bathwater or in inspiration about man's unconquerable spirit, and are more likely than not to culminate with that much-favoured injunction: not to jettison economic growth but to give it 'a new direction'.

Put in its strong form, as it often is, per capita 'real' income is said to be the single most important measure of social welfare. If we believe in this positive relation between 'real' income and social welfare or – to vary the language – between 'real' income and human happiness, we are impelled to conclude that the age we live in, the very decade we live in, is the happiest ever experienced by man – which, if it were true, would make earlier ages seem bleak indeed. But although production statistics, cost of living comparisons, infantile mortality figures, epidemiological data and the like are agenda for the modern welfare state, and the pure pap of life for echelons of experts gainfully employed in producing them, their relation to people's actual experience of well-being is questionable.

Without being historically naive, is it possible to assert that, in a comparison of two periods, the one having a higher per capita 'real' income (and, for that matter, a more equally distributed income) must necessarily be the happier time to live? At the turn of this century, for instance, the British were surely the proudest and most confident of people. Their island home was guarded by the greatest navy the world had ever known. They ruled the greatest empire in history. Their institutions were – or, at any rate, the British people believed they were – the envy of the rest of the world. Bank tellers paid out in jingling gold sovereigns. Income tax was never more than a shilling in the pound. Food was cheap and plentiful. The British were the world's greatest trading nation. And as the international currency *par excellence*, sterling was a synonym for absolute security.

True, there were slums as well as pomp and pageantry. But poverty is not among the worst social evils. As a people the British were known to be proud, resourceful and confident.

Compare the British today. *Per capita* 'real' income, according to the indices, is about three times as high as it was then. Income is more equally distributed, and the welfare state and its army of social workers is on tap at all time. Yet – permitting myself a little journalistic licence – what a sorry lot we have become. Pride, patriotism, confidence have long flown from these islands. In their place sit cynicism, avarice, envy and resentment. As a people we are plunged into internecine turmoil, squabbling incessantly for the spoils of industry, members of each organized occupation ready at an opportune moment to blackmail the community in the hope of swelling its pay packet. To boot, we have been described as a nation of tax-fiddlers. And, as a result of a mass of indigestible economic legislation brought in by successive governments, we are fast acquiring an uncontrollable contempt for the law itself.

You may say I exaggerate. We need not, however, resolve our differences in judgement about the respective merits of these two periods of British history before proceeding. Enough can be salvaged from the comparison to make credible the reflection that it is not by goods alone that people live and rejoice.

Although modern life is currently characterized by much vexation and disamenity, it is not because we lack material resources. Rather the contrary. As our wealth has grown we have contrived to use technology to make life increasingly complex, frantic, and wearing. Indeed, the ideals by which scientists and engineers rationalize their freedom to experiment and innovate – that of removing physical hardship and promoting ease and mobility – are themselves responsible.

In the larger vision of life, what does it avail to smooth the edge of nature, to shut out the draughts and even the temperature? Can there be any true fulfilment without some prior frustration? Can there be any welcome of comfort without prior hardship? Living at the margin of surfeit is hardly better than living at the margin of subsistence. Indeed, humanly speaking, it is worse. For in a world of ample provision, in a world of perfect adjustment, in a world of instant gratification, there can be no self-denial and therefore there can be no romantic love. There can be no conflict, and therefore no drama. There can be no suffering and therefore no tragedy. There can be no passion and therefore no poetry. And there can be no sacrifice and therefore no heroism. The wonderful irony of Aldous Huxley's *Brave New World* is that in it, in this comically colourless and unheroic society, in this subtopia of emotional cretins, have the dreams of countless humanists and reformers been finally and fully realized.

Of course, we have far far to go ere we reach this devoutly desired consummation. There can be reasonable doubt that – even should we survive the lengthening gauntlet of hazards – we shall ever approach a Brave-New-World civilization. Present trends indicate that life, instead, is becoming increasingly frenzied and frustrating. A high consumption society is also a high tension society. Tension arises from conflict between two powerful social objectives; on the one hand, that of a meritocracy inspired by the ideal of efficiency and, on the other, that of an all-embracing welfare state inspired by the egalitarian ideal. And the competition for status grows more intense as the hopefuls in the race also find themselves locked in political struggle with populist demands for greater sharing of the spoils. Tension arises because the proliferation of goods presses harder against the scarcity of time available for their use. Tension arises also because the commercial promotion of hedonic pursuit breeds anxiety and discontent.

30 The limits of abundance: a conservative critique 2

Enough has been said in the preceding chapter to suggest that although the process of economic growth is the outcome of men's choices – albeit choices that are profoundly influenced by existing institutions and belief systems – the economist's adopted dictum that men know their own interests best is far too simple to be serviceable once we are free to reflect seriously about the consequences of continued economic growth.

Scepticism about this dictum which, were it regarded as a truism, would go far toward rationalizing a presumption in favour of economic growth as a self-evident social goal, may be fortified by reversing the direction of arguments we began with. Instead, that is, of tracing and appraising the consequences of economic growth we could begin by explicitly listing some of the chief constituents of the good life in the attempt to determine whether or not they are likely to be fostered by continued economic growth in already affluent societies.

My belief that the six attributes mentioned below are among the more pertinent conditions for a good life rests to some extent on a judgement of fact, that the capacity of ordinary people both to imbibe high culture and to resist corruption is limited. More generally, I subscribe to the conservative view that – acting within the area of choice conferred on them by civilization – men are indeed imperfect creatures, intellectually and morally. There will, I hope, always be a number of saints among us here on earth. But they are sure to be heavily outnumbered by fools and knaves.

The selected constituents of a good life on which I shall comment briefly are as follows:

1 Personal freedom
2 Love and trust
3 Self-respect
4 Security

5 Contentment
6 Sense of purpose

In a short chapter, my comments on each of them are sure to appear either more complacent or more provocative than I intend. None the less, they may serve to illustrate the advantage of this approach to the economic growth debate.

1 The interpretation I place on *personal freedom* accords with that described by libertarian writers, the emphasis being on the protection of the citizen from the power wielded by the state. No other politically fashionable 'freedom' is intended, least of all those embodied in currently popular declarations of entitlement such as 'freedom from want', 'freedom from unemployment', 'freedom from sickness', 'freedom from exploitation', to mention some of the less exotic varieties. Certainly one of the consequences of a political determination to implement such asserted 'freedoms' would be an expansion of bureaucractic intervention and coercive powers, which is obviously constrictive of that personal freedom sought by libertarians which is held to be essential to the good life.

So much by way of clarification. We now raise the question: Is sustained economic growth likely to promote personal freedom? I believe the contrary is more likely.

Within a Western democracy, economic growth acts in two distinct ways to enlarge the area of government control. The first operates through specific technological innovations that produce either or both of the following effects: (i) they generate conflicts of interest within society, usually by creating new opportunities for one group that unavoidably damage the amenities once enjoyed by another group, or (ii) they expose large segments of the population to unprecedented hazards arising from new technologies. Whether (i) or (ii) occurs, the consequences include a public demand for government intervention and, therefore, an eventual increase in legislation and government controls.[1]

The second way economic growth acts to increase government controls operates through the so-called permissive society. In a traditional society, at least one with a fairly fixed pattern of consumption, a rising level of output would eventually press against limits of satiety. The expansion of industry would eventually be curbed. Nothing, then, could be more providential for the expansionist tendencies of modern industry than the growth of the permissive society – an unrooted society, one freed from the restraints of accepted rules of propriety and encouraged to engorge its appetites and revel in self-indulgence, one in which the moral order is disintegrating and is being replaced by an ethic described as 'doing one's own thing'. In this new dispensation, 'anything goes' and therefore virtually anything sells. Inanities abound, exhibitionism is endemic, extravagances become a cult, and porno-erotic literature and entertainment flourish.

But the growing demand for novelty, excitement, and instant gratification, accompanied as it is by an impatience of traditional fetters, also fosters an increasingly ungovernable populace. One person's 'own thing' is some other person's 'anti-thing'. Appetites whetted to the point of being insatiable turn to wierd and anti-social outlets. The erosion of the moral order poses an increasing threat to the social order. But as the moral restraints upon which any viable civilization is founded are scrapped in the name of unlimited emancipation for the individual so, in the name of (and the need for) public security, the state has to expand its powers.

Thus, as the individual's *internal* repressive mechanisms are eroded so, in its struggle for survival, is society impelled to erect collective and *external* repressive mechanisms. The permissive society, it may be concluded, is the precursor of the totalitarian state.

2 For those who come to feel that life has cheated them of *love*, no compensations suffice. Yet if it is a fact that the bonds of mutual affection take years to form, and are strengthened by long familiarity, there are grounds for concern. For it is too much to expect that such bonds will be formed in a highly mobile society, in a hedonic society impatient of personal commitment, and in a technological society in the throes of rapid change.

Worse, there is the consequence flowing from the seemingly inevitable trend in labour-saving innovation. Such innovations act to reduce human contact over time, and to reduce the need for mutual help once characteristic of small communities. This vital area of direct communication between people has declined since the second world war with the establishment of supermarkets, automatic elevators, turnstiles, vending machines, transistors, television, and the spread of automobilization. And it will continue to decline with the growth of automation in industry and commerce, with office computers, with computerized diagnosis and patient-monitoring machines, with closed-circuit television instruction and teaching machines, and with automated travel.

We are entering an era of incredible artifice in the purveying of services and entertainment, a veritable push-button world in which – overlooking the vexations of lengthening queues and service breakdowns as capacity is continually being over-reached – basic psychic needs are neglected as people adapt and re-adapt to a changing pattern of life that is, seen in historic perspective, little more than a by-product of compulsive technological innovation. Disoriented, they come increasingly to seek to gratify commercially inspired appetities. The thought of such a world, an admass world incessantly clamouring for more man-made goods, may elate the businessman and the technocrat. But, in such a world, the direct flow of communication and sympathy between persons becomes ever thinner and, to that extent, the quality of their lives that much poorer.

3 *Self-respect* comes to a man with the assurance that his person and his services are valued by the community. The pre-industrial economy based on farming and communities of craftsmen changed its methods of production over time very slowly. With the rapid expansion today of scientific and technical knowledge, the grown man cannot be sure from one year to the next whether his hard-earned skills are about to become obsolete, or so obsolete that no retraining at his stage of life will avail. He can, of course, always join with others in demonstrating and asserting his right to work. The organization may even continue to employ him. In the last resort there is the welfare state to fall back upon. But neither his alleged rights nor state aid can compensate him for the mortifying realization that, in ways beyond his control, he has now become expendable.

4 Although the word *security* comprehends a number of factors, that of personal safety alone will be touched on here. Since the second world war, and contrary to the high hopes entertained by nineteenth century visionaries in the sovereign and meliorative powers of economic progress and universal education, the crime statistics in all the economically advanced countries (and especially those of violent crimes) have climbed relentlessly. For the sociologist, there are always explanations – in the main sympathetic to the criminal. On a more general level, however, the basic causes for this trend may be found in economic growth itself.

Characteristic of the latter part of the twentieth century are the immense built-up urban areas, ideal for large scale criminal organizations. Such areas would not be possible without the technical know-how that feeds economic growth. The recent advances in small weapons technology, and in ancillary facilities, tend to make the modern criminal more effective and dangerous. What is more, developments in nuclear and chemical science have made the metropolitan area increasingly vulnerable to blackmail and terrorist tactics.

To this expanding horizon of criminal opportunity there has to be added the encouragement afforded by the 'permissive' ethic that is so assiduously cultivated by the expansionist tendencies of modern commerce.

5 A pre-condition of sustained economic growth is *sustained discontent*. To be inveterately dissatisfied with existing methods of production, with existing scientific knowledge, with existing levels of output and consumption, and above all with one's income, status and present prospects, has for long been regarded as the supreme virtue in the Pantheon of the Established Enlightenment. It is a virtue that has so thoroughly suffused the character of modern man, and has become so ineradicable a response to the external world, that it is today actively inimical to his sense of well-being. This socially conditioned discontent with his material lot, moreover, acts to keep his eyes perpetually focused on the future – on the morrow, on the coming weeks, and the years to follow – effectively dissipating the vital sense of the here and now that is essential to the sharpness and richness of experience.

6 Finally, *sense of purpose*. The advance of knowledge, especially scientific knowledge that is, for economic growth, the prime mover, entails a continuing secularization of society and, consequently, an erosion of the great myths which – though at times subverted to fanatical ends – offered solace and hope to the greater part of mankind for millennia.

But the loss to humanity does not end there. The experience of history suggests that without a belief in its divine origin, the moral code itself cannot survive. Humanistic ideals may serve for the few, especially if these few are in professions where they are wholly absorbed in adding their mite to the mountain of modern knowledge. But for the ordinary mortal, the dawning realization that God is no more, that neither is there a hereafter, nor is there any transcendental purpose in the universe, is one that is oppressive to his spirit, the more so as he ages.

In moments of sober reflection, modern man sees himself as no more than an inconsequential flicker of life soon to be expunged by a freezing eternity. Well may he wonder why he should forbear from any desperate venture knowing that he is immersed in a spiritual void bequeathed to him by science and rationalism. Why should he not steep himself in the goods and pursuits offered by affluent society, no matter how ephemeral and meretricious!

Hence this final consideration reinforces the first. For this unavoidable process of secularization[2] that erodes the moral foundations upon which the civic order ultimately rests is itself a powerful contributory factor in generating our 'permissive' society, the necessary response to which, as already indicated, is the repressive state.

31 Concluding remarks

Although it is not possible to end on a promising note, the study of normative economics is a fascinating one. It is fascinating to discover how writers have been tempted into adopting particular simplifications in the endeavour to reach sweeping conclusions, whether positive ones or negative. And it is a fascinating study for its being so tantalising and elusive, and also for its offering so much scope for invention, insight and elegance.

Aside from the intrinsic interest and challenge of normative economics, it is a valuable discipline to be exposed to. Students of the subject are much less likely to fall into vulgar error than are intelligent citizens even when they are interested in economic affairs, and less likely also to fall into sophisticated error than those students of economics who specialize in its positive and quantitative aspects. It is important even for those citizens and students who are already prone to be cynical about economic prescription and about official estimates of net benefits of particular projects. Rather than continue to cultivate an attitude of vague contempt and impatience of what they conceive to be bogus expertise they could become more articulate critics of such expertise by seeking instead to develop a more coherent understanding of the implicit assumptions on which such policies and economic calculations are premised.

Moreover, an introduction to normative economics that is directed primarily to dissecting the critical relationships at the core of the subject offers considerable advantages to the economics student purposing to read the literature on normative economics or the literature, both theoretical and applied, on familiar normative techniques such as cost–benefit analysis and mathematical programming. With respect to the general normative economics literature, a basic introduction to the critical relationships will enable him to place any particular contribution within a broader framework, to accord it proportionate emphasis, and to resist being disoriented by pages of mathematical foliage which, more often than not, is the first refuge of trivial thought and threadbare theorizing. With respect to the literature on normative techniques he is unlikely to be over-impressed by the methods for capturing essential data or by quantitative results since he will be aware constantly of the tacit and often fragile assumptions on which it all rests.

Finally, in spite of the meagre harvest of dependable propositions it yields, this branch of economics does have some application to the real world, though perhaps more to the poorer countries of the world than to the richer ones.

In order to assess the value of these applications better, I remind you of the distinction that economists, even normative economists, have failed to make clear: that between a normative economics proper as described in this volume and a positive study of social welfare.

The former rests among other things on an ethical consensus, assuming there is one. The latter does *not* rest, *inter alia*, on an ethical consensus: it rests, indeed, on factual judgements of the effects on social welfare of alternative economic organizations. (The *inter alia* clause has reference to the behavioural, technical and institutional assumptions that may be common to both a normative and a positive study of social welfare.)

It is far from impossible that general and conditional propositions, or particular proposals, emerging from each of these distinct studies should coincide – in particular where the ethical consensus is one that embraces a potential Pareto improvement and is also shaped by convictions that are widely held (or were until recently) among civilizations of the Western world. But there is no reason to expect this coincidence to prevail generally. In the absence of this coincidence, then, and assuming there is indeed an ethical consensus, and also some realism in the conventional economic assumptions, a correctly drawn economic prescription could have the incidental effect of making society worse off. Yet this possibility does not of itself invalidate a prescriptive economics. For society, like the individual, may be assumed to cherish the freedom conferred by its ethical consensus to risk making a bad choice rather than have a good choice imposed upon it.

For poorer countries, where goods are really 'goods' for most people – in the sense that, irrespective of the material position of others, additional goods make a significant contribution to the welfare of most individuals – there is more likely to be an unfragmented consensus. Thus, apart from distributional questions, the goods currently being produced there are not likely to be thought 'regrettable' or 'inimical' by a significant proportion of the population. What is more, the behavioural assumptions at least – and they are the more crucial ones – are not at all unrealistic. In more traditional societies, the assumption of unchanging tastes over the relevant time period is plausible enough. Even if settled norms of behaviour and taste did not exist, the time needed to raise the bulk of the population from its current near-subsistence standards to standards approaching those prevailing in the Western world would be such that, for practical purposes, tastes may be assumed not to change. It follows that familiar allocative propositions can be taken more seriously and, further, that an overall expansion of output, or a movement of resources to places or uses where the value of their outputs is greater, is likely enough to raise society's well-being.

There are, as is well known, quite a number of policy proposals for improving the material prospects of poorer countries in the so-called development literature. They include suggestions for increasing incentives among the mass of people, for increasing rural employment at low cost, for controlling population, for increased self-sufficiency and for retarding and reversing the flow of labour from the villages to the cities. But although allocative conclusions may have to be modified or carefully interpreted in view of the particular institutions of poorer countries, they are nonetheless more pertinent to such countries than they are to affluent industrial countries.

Turning to these affluent industrial countries of the West, where incipient fragmentation of an ethical consensus is already evident, and where – in view of the rapidity of innovation and the craving for novelty – the supposition of unchanging tastes is unrealistic, the many applications of normatively based economic techniques may continue to attract attention simply because a technological society, by its nature, is impressed by quantitative techniques. But the contribution to social welfare of these applications is much more dubious for reasons mentioned in the preceding two chapters.

Nevertheless, under restricted conditions, certain projects that could meet a cost–benefit criterion might well make a modest contribution to social welfare. The creation of recreational centres, of pedestrian precincts within towns and cities, and of amenity areas for more sensitive members of the community, are worth considering in this connection. But for the rest, my sceptical opinion is that the current and intense research devoted to the discovery of economic strategies for combining price stability with high employment is about the only way open for economists to make an unambiguous and significant contribution to social welfare.

Be that as it may, once we stand back from the current preoccupation with the daily bread of our economic afflictions – with unemployment, inflation, the balance of payments, industrial conflicts, and the like that fill the columns of our quality newspapers – and find time to reflect on the big question of society's overall welfare and on the relative helplessness of the economist to influence its direction, the considerations raised in Chapters 29 and 30 become the dominant ones. Indeed, one is led to wonder seriously whether the industrial and scientific progress over the last two hundred years or so has been worth it. It would be futile to attempt a balance sheet of a historical development so complex. All one can say is that misgivings continue to gather in the minds of thinking people. It cannot be denied, at least, that the growth of the commercial ethos, and the universal diffusion of the scientific method and attitude, which have endowed our civilization with incalculable powers both of production and destruction, has also taken all the magic out of our lives and has begun to undermine men's faith in the transcendental value of their humanity. It is, perhaps, not too imaginative to say that people today seem to be struggling desperately, almost hysterically, against a chilling sense of purposelessness.

Seen in historic perspective, even the positive material achievement of the last two centuries may be destined to be ephemeral. World population is increasing at over 2 per cent per annum and has begun to spread – mainly through illegal immigration – from South to North, from poorer countries to richer ones. The neo-Malthusian pessimism evinced by David Wilkinson's *Poverty and Progress* is far from being untimely. If improved technology is, in the last resort, a response to population expansion and the threat of scarcity, and population expansion itself is, in large measure, a response to improved technology, the high living standards currently enjoyed by the West may not endure long. On this conjecture, they mark only a short phase in a historic process that is destined to culminate in a teeming world population which – if it does not destroy itself through mischance, fanaticism, or despair – must return to a material condition bordering on bare subsistence.

Notes

Chapter 1: Introductory observations

1 Among the best known essays on this and related themes are those of Hayek (1944) and Friedman (1962).

2 In a number of papers some of which have appeared in Hayek (1952).

3 A paragraph from a bank review I happen to have by me will illustrate this sort of personal political economy:

> Protectionism, old and new, ignores the dispassionate activity of the market-place to promote competition, specialization, and efficiency. When governments resort to import restrictions, they utilize subjective criteria that may be neither equitable nor effective in increasing real national income. The more imprecise the rules enforcing pursuit of a liberal international order, the more likely it is that political discord and economic waste will ensue. It would be folly to allow these negatives to bedevil an international system increasingly dependent on multilateral cooperation to solve problems and achieve progress. [S. Cohen, 'Coping with the new protectionism', *National Westminster Bank Quarterly Review*, November 1978, p. 15]

The factual and value judgements of the writer are plain enough in this passage – which is not to say, however, that his advice is not well taken or that a large number of economists would not go along with him. But the arguments are quite different from the style of explicit analysis associated with the professional academic literature.

4 For an example, see Chapter 3, note 1.

5 The inquisitive student familiar with symbolic logic is referred to a survey of the literature on what is now sometimes called Social Choice Theory by J. S. Kelly (1978).

Chapter 3: The nature of the economist's efficiency criterion

1 An example of a political criterion that, in some circumstances, can produce for society an intransitive ordering is that of majority voting when there are more than two alternatives to rank. To illustrate, suppose there to be three alternatives, I, II and III, and the community to comprise three persons, identified as A, B and C. Their respective orderings are to be read from top to bottom below:

A	B	C
I	II	III
II	III	I
III	I	II

The voting as between alternatives I and II gives a majority for I (both persons A and C rank I above II, while B ranks II above I). As between alternative II and III, there is a majority for II (both persons A and B rank II above III, while C ranks III above II). We should conclude that, using majority voting, society ranks I above II, and II above III. *A fortiori*, society ranks I above III. Yet you will find that majority voting also ranks III above I (both persons B and C rank III above I, while person A alone ranks I above III).

Chapter 4: The rationale of the economist's efficiency criterion

1 Some writers have used the term 'Pareto Criterion' to indicate an *actual* Pareto improvement, while I and others have used it as shorthand for a *potential* Pareto improvement. Since allocation propositions turn almost always on the algebraic magnitude of V alone, which is rationalized by a potential Pareto improvement, it is more economical to use the term Pareto criterion as a shorthand for a potential Pareto improvement criterion, as in the text.

2 The specialized economics student interested in the course of the debate might like to glance through Mishan (1965).

3 Sometimes referred to as the Cambridge School of thought, and in all that concerns allocation associated with such illustrious names in the recent history of economic doctrine as Marshall, Pigou and Robertson.

Chapter 6: The basic economic assumptions

1 The specialized economist who is inquisitive about these problems, which centre about the use of a discount rate applied to benefits over a period that spans a number of generations, may like to glance at Chapter 69 in Mishan (1981).

Chapter 7: Uses and limitations of a partial economic context

1 These and other problems particular to cost–benefit analysis are treated at length in a number of modern textbooks. Mishan (1981) is fairly detailed on concepts. Students who fear they are being subjected too heavily to my prejudices may like to consult Sugden and Williams (1978). There are a number of other textbooks, especially some on

project appraisal for Third World countries, such as Little and Mirrlees (1974) and Dasgupta *et al*. (1972). But such textbooks adopt methodologies and carry political overtones that are highly controversial. (Reasons for so regarding them are given in Mishan (1974).)

2 A technique which falls into the category of comparative statics, known as linear programming (which is the more commonly used branch of mathematical programming), is not dealt with in this introductory text. One version of a linear programming problem is rather like the problem of a miniature economy in which there are available fixed amounts of different factors. If we are given the prices of a number of goods, the object becomes one of maximizing the total value of goods that can be produced with these fixed amounts of factors, bearing in mind that each good can be produced by combining factors in one or several different ways. I do not treat it even briefly in this book because its interest resides chiefly in its technique for solving specific sorts of economic problems. Although it has some heuristic value for students of economics, it does not introduce any essential new concept or principle. In fact, its use unavoidably bypasses the really crucial and fascinating problems we shall be facing in this and the following two parts of the book. (Inquisitive students might like to glance at a well-known introductory text on linear programming by Throsby, 1970.)

Chapter 8: The key concepts of social value and social opportunity cost

1 This distinction arises also in another connection; namely when it is necessary to calculate the opportunity cost to a country of increasing its imports of some good X from abroad. Should the government specify that the foreign currency to pay for the additional X imports be raised only by forgoing the necessary amount of some other imported good Y, then the actual opportunity cost of these additional X imports is equal to the domestic value of the amount of Y that has to be forgone. Again, if the government instead chooses to raise the necessary foreign currency by increasing the exports of a good Z, the actual opportunity cost of the extra X imports is equal to the domestic value of the amount of Z that is withdrawn from the domestic market. (In both instances spillover effects have been ignored.)

Chapter 9: Consumer surplus: a measure of welfare change

1 Textbooks and articles usually represent measures of an individual's consumer surplus on an 'indifference curve' diagram. This has some heuristic advantage. But for practical purposes, consumer surplus is calculated as the relevant area below the market demand curve.

2 The MV_1 curve is accordingly referred to as an individual's 'compensated demand curve' for the straightforward reason that moving along it from left to right he fully compensates (by paying the most for each unit) so as to offset any increase in his welfare. The MV_2 curve is also a compensated demand curve, but one corresponding to a higher level of welfare.

Chapter 11: The allocative virtues of a competitive economy

1 The case for a competitive capitalism economy is argued with persuasion and lucidity by Milton Friedman (1962).
2 If you would like to, however, consult Hicks (1956) or my elaborate plagiarization of Hicks in Mishan (1980), ch. 25.
3 A reminder by a fellow student would be enough to induce him to revise the ideal-output rule to that of price equal to *social* marginal cost in order to take care of any non-market costs such as environmental costs.

Chapter 12: Marginal cost pricing

1 If, instead, we were expanding the output of x beginning at a smaller output than OQ_1 the segment of the marginal opportunity cost of x would run from left to right, passing through $C''C'C$, again therefore cutting the x demand curve at C'.
2 Nothing but a *caveat* would emerge from exploring this further although, in view of estimates of 'producer surplus' made by economists who treat such upward sloping supply curves as if they were marginal factor cost curves, it is worth discussing in a cost–benefit context. The student who is interested in this misuse of what is misleadingly called producer surplus is referred to Mishan (1980), ch. 30.

Chapter 13: Second best and third best

1 The student with a smattering of maths (especially determinants) might want to check on our results by reading H. A. J. Green (1962).
2 Nor need we stop here. We might reasonably surmise that the p/c ratio to be adopted as the third best rule should be closer yet to the hypothetical ideal second best rule if it were calculated as a *weighted* average of the p/cs within the deviant Y sector. Thus, if the value added by the output of y_1 having a p/c of 1.5, and the value added by the output of y_2 having a p/c of 2.0 is each 5 per cent of the total value added by the Y sector, this leaves y_3 with its p/c of 2.5 having 90 per cent of the total value added by the Y sector. If we multiply the p/cs of each of these three y goods by their respective weights, the resulting p/c will be about 2.4. This figure is close to the p/c of the y_3 good itself,

which is by far the more important good in the Y sector. Adopting a p/c of 2.4 as our third best rule, and so applying it to all goods in the X sector, ensures that all the important goods have the same p/c: only two relatively unimportant goods, y_1 and y_2 have lower p/cs. We cannot then be very far from a Pareto optimum, and we should come closer yet as the values of y_1 and y_2 dwindled.

Further refinement is possible once we distinguish between goods that are substitutes (like butter and margarine) and those that are complements (like bread and butter). But enough has been said to illustrate the rationale of a third best rule.

Chapter 14: Can the market cope with externalities?

1 Although for expositional purposes it is convenient to raise the cost per ton of the original 100 tons of fish caught by the original 100 boats by $2\frac{1}{2}$ per cent (by assuming each of the boats fishes for a longer time each day), the conclusions remain the same if each of these 100 boats chooses, instead, to fish no longer than before and, therefore, to bring in a somewhat smaller catch of fish each day. For their aggregate loss of fish has now to be attributed to, and therefore added to the cost of, the fish caught by the new boat.

2 The actual case that engaged Marshall's attention was in fact the reverse of that in the text, the externality that is imposed by marginal firms on the industry being beneficial – an 'external economy' rather than (as above) an 'external diseconomy'. Thus in Marshall's case, the supply curve of the competitive industry is downward sloping in consequence of these external economies, internal to the industry but external to the firm. This supply curve,however, is an average curve, with the marginal curve to the industry lying below it. The equilibrium output is therefore below the optimal output at which the industry's marginal cost is equal to the price.

Chapter 15: Diminishing returns to agriculture as an instance of externalities

1 Even if the farmer owns his land, he knows the price it will fetch on the market. Therefore if he does not elect to sell his land to another farmer but to till it himself, he will include the price forgone (the rent of his land) as a cost that also has to be covered. It enters into his average cost along with the price of labour, which average inclusive cost in equilibrium is just equal to the price of corn.

Chapter 16: Environmental spillovers: what difference does the law make?

1 In a perfectly competitive constant cost industry, the area under this

DM curve would be equal to the consumer surplus from introducing x at a price equal to the (constant) unit cost.

2 As proposed in Mishan (1967b).

3 The minimum cost way of combining different methods of pollution-reduction is treated in Mishan (1980), ch. 58.

Chapter 17: Non-environmental spillovers: some ethical questions

1 For the transfer from A of $1 gives him 15 cents of satisfaction in knowing that it will be received by B. The *loss* to A is therefore only 85 cents ($1 less 15 cents), therefore, there is a social gain of 15 cents from the transfer – $1 gain to B and 85 cents loss to A.

2 This particular notion of a merit good appears in Dasgupta *et al.* (1972), in Little and Mirrlees (1974), in Sugden and Williams (1978), to name those authors that come to mind.

3 My own views on the subject can be found in Mishan (1974).

4 Alternatively, the curve of collective payments for marginal increases in a merit good (instead of being added to the market demand curve to give the social marginal valuation curve) could be *subtracted* from the marginal cost curve to leave us with the *social* marginal cost curve. Clearly, the optimal output is the same whether we equate social marginal valuation to marginal factor cost or whether instead we equate the demand price (or market value) to social marginal cost.

Chapter 18: Favourable spillovers and collective goods

1 For examples of how it has misled economists see Mishan (1969a).

2 If variable factor prices change as aggregate honey output expands then (under fairly common assumptions) the cost curve to each farmer will shift upward. This upward shift in the individual cost curves is translated into a rise of the supply price of honey. As a result, the curve S′S′ in Figure 28 becomes steeper than that shown.

3 As indicated earlier the original concept of externalities, introduced by Marshall (1930), was that of external economies that were *internal* to the industry (though external to the firms of the industry). It was devised as an explanation of the downward-sloping supply curve of a competitive industry.

4 Bohm (1973) has proposed some tentative schemes in an attempt to surmount this difficulty.

Chapter 19: Uses of a general economic context

1 Surprisingly, however, very few economists, even among those who specialize in resource allocation, appear (at the time of writing) to have

fully mastered the essential implications of the New Welfare Economics. This observation may seem controversial if not invidious. But I do not make it lightly. I make it only after serious reflection on a number of recent journal articles written upon the subject by otherwise competent economists.

Chapter 20: Optimality for the economy

1 By 'equi-proportional marginal cost pricing' I mean that for all goods prices are x per cent of their corresponding marginal costs (where x is any positive number).

Chapter 21: What is an efficient distribution of goods?

1 The student of economics will realize that this last sentence is a reference to the individual's indifference map. He will also realize that it is not necessarily true that in moving down the line q_At, the slope of successive indifference curves cutting that line will initially be flatter (declining marginal rate of substitution of y for x). I have decided to forgo the use of individual and community indifference curves in this introductory treatment of the subject in the hope that their omission would simplify the exposition without in any way impairing the essential argument – though I admit I could be wrong about this.

Chapter 22: Economic efficiency: a paradox

1 Of this the reader may convince himself by reading Kaldor (1939) followed by Scitovsky (1941). In addition, he should read Samuelson (1939) and Hicks (1940) followed by Kuznets (1948).

2 As indeed did Samuelson (in 1939) and Murray Kemp (as late as 1962).

3 Implicit in the original Kaldor Note (1939) was a comparison based on the p_1 price set.

4 If we allow that each person buys all he wishes of the two goods at the prevailing market prices then the marginal rate of substitution of y and x for each person, being the same as the market exchange of y for x, must also be equal – this equality being a sufficient condition for an efficient distribution of the collection of goods.

5 Or on a construct similar in its effect to the use of a single set of prices. Such a construct could be a single 'community indifference map' or, at least, the tacit assumption of 'Pareto comparable community indifference curves'. The economics student seeking further light on this subject could make a beginning by glancing through Mishan (1980), ch. 43.

Chapter 23: Pareto optimality: an empty vessel

1 Alternatively, such demonstrations depended upon the employment of a single set of 'community indifference curves'. The interested economics student is referred to Mishan (1980), part 4.

Chapter 24: Resolving the apparent paradox

1 Using the community indifference curve construction, the proof of this conclusion appears in Mishan (1973). However, a somewhat simpler version is given in Mishan (1980), ch. 48.

2 The criterion Q_2' meets when compared with Q_1 is the strongest form of the Pareto criterion, one that is sometimes referred to as 'the Samuelson criterion' (see Samuelson, 1950). Such a criterion is met in moving from a situation I to II *only* when II is ranked Pareto superior to I *for every conceivable distribution* of the collection in the I situation.

3 Although everything follows neatly enough, I can imagine some of you wondering uneasily about the resolution of a paradox which resolution itself seems puzzling. You may reason correctly as follows. If Q_1' has the same welfare combination, say C_1, as Q_1, and if Q_2' has the same welfare combination, say C_2, as Q_2, then below the intersection at Q_3, the Q_2' collection having more of all goods than Q_1, this welfare combination C_2 is surely to be preferred. Above the intersection Q_3, on the other hand, the Q_1' collection, having more of all goods than Q_2, the welfare combination C_1 is to be preferred. Clearly both welfare combinations cannot be simultaneously preferred.

I recognize that this does look a bit puzzling at first (indeed it partakes of the flavour of the original discovery of the paradox, of which the above paragraph is really a variant). But it will be less puzzling once you remind yourself that C_1 and C_2, which are the welfare combinations respectively of the d_1 and d_2 distributions of the Q_3 collection, are *not* directly Pareto comparable; that is, the movement from d_1 to d_2 cannot make *both* persons A and B better off (or both worse off). The movement makes person A better off at the same time as it makes person B worse off.

This also means, of course, that Q_1 and Q_2' are *not* Pareto comparable, and neither are Q_2 and Q_1': points such as Q_1 and Q_2' can never be compared directly in that sense. The Pareto criterion we have been using throughout has been explicitly defined in terms of a *potential* Pareto improvement – we ask the question, can Q_2' be so redistributed as to make every one better off that he is with the actual distribution of the Q_1 collection? And an affirmative answer to that question is entirely consistent with the fact that the actual welfare combinations associated with Q_2' and Q_1 (identical respectively with the distributions d_1 and d_2 of Q_3) are *not* Pareto comparable.

Chapter 27: The folklore of the market 2

1 Readers interested in a critique of the arguments advanced by some economists tending to justify commercial advertisements are referred to Mishan (1969b), ch. 9.
2 See for example Harris and Seldon (1970).
3 The apparently irresistible propensity of world population to expand is viewed by some scientists as the chief cause of the environmental disorders that threaten our civilization. This view is argued forcefully by Ehrlich and Ehrlich (1973).
4 A thesis similar in import and foreboding is conveyed with relish by David Wilkinson (1972)

Chapter 29: The limits of abundance: a conservative critique 1

1 I give only glancing footnote attention to the no less tenaciously held belief that a more equal distribution of the national income is a legitimate aim of enlightened economic policy. At the best of times and in the best of company, debates about basic beliefs are difficult, depending as they must on appeals to reason, to experience, to history, and to imagination. And the best of times to question the value of the egalitarian ideal is certainly not an age in which the tide of populist sentiment flows so strongly as it does today – an age in which any serious charge of 'privilege' or 'discrimination' can be depended upon to raise storms of protest.

So many of the present generation have accepted the priority of income and wealth equalization as a norm of economic policy that serious attempts to compare different historical epochs, or different civilizations, on some overall quality-of-life scale are inevitably stultified. Once the distribution of income and wealth is regarded as the touchstone or the one essential ingredient of social justice, it follows that no matter what considerable virtues might be possessed by earlier civilizations, any evidence of their unconcern with inequalities is enough to mark them in modern eyes as irredeemably flawed.

Compared with our self-conscious endeavours to promote the eventual establishment of a welfare planet, one in which no single person is to be left to imagine he suffers frustration or deprivation, other ages are seen as fatally deficient in 'compassion', that overly institutionalized good in which our own age claims to excel – as evidenced in every Western country by the growing scale and variety of 'hand-outs' supported by a rising flow of revenue from a tax-evading public, and administered by an expanding army of bureaucrats.

Chapter 30: The limits of abundance: a conservative critique 2

1 A careful examination of this trend can be found in Mishan (1976).

2 I am aware that – apart from the increasing fascination in the West with the occult, with yoga, with gurus, and with 'self-realization' cults – revivalist religions are growing, especially in America. They gather strength from the distress and despair of the masses of people who live today in an agnostic universe and in an anonymous society. The pain of purposelessness, the pain of loneliness, makes people gullible to what are in effect highly organized religious circuses. Relief is sought in collective affirmation and chanting and in sometimes hysteric invocation. But these forms of solace and therapy have little affinity with that quiet but unshakeable conviction in the omnipresence of a personal God that characterized the faith of man before the advent of modern science-based civilizations.

Bibliography

ALLEN, R. G. and HICKS, J. R. (1934), 'A reconsideration of the theory of value', *Economica*

ARCHIBALD, G. C. (1959), 'Welfare economics, ethics, and essentialism', *Economica*

ARROW, K. J. (1951), *Social Choice and Individual Values*, New York

ARROW, K. J. and SCITOVSKY, T., eds. (1969), *Readings in Welfare Economics* London

AYRES, R. V. and KNEESE, A. V. (1969), 'Production, consumption and externalities', *American Economic Review*

BARONE, N. (1935), 'The ministry of production in the collectivist state', in F. A. Hayek (ed.), *Collectivist Economic Planning*, London

BAUMOL, W. J. (1965), *Welfare Economics and the Theory of the State*, 2nd edn, London

BAUMOL, W. J. and BRADFORD, D. (1970), 'Optimal departures from marginal cost pricing', *American Economic Review*

BAUMOL, W. J. and OATES, W. E. (1975), *The Theory of Environmental Policy*, New Jersey

BAUMOL, W. J. and OATES, W. E. (1979), *Economics, Environmental Policy and the Quality of Life*, New Jersey

BECKERMAN, W. (1972), 'Economists, scientists, and environmental catastrophe', *Oxford Economic Papers*

BERGSON, A. (1938), 'A reformulation of certain aspects of welfare economics', *Quarterly Journal of Economics*

BERGSON, A. (1966), *Essays in Normative Economics*, Cambridge, Mass.

BOHM, P. (1974), *Social Efficiency*, London

BUCHANAN, J. and STUBBLEBINE, W. M. (1962), 'Externality', *Economica*

BUCHANAN, J. and TULLOCK, G. (1965), *The Calculus of Consent*, Michigan

BURNS, M. E. (1972), 'A note on the concept and measure of consumer's surplus', *American Economic Review*

COASE, R. H. (1960), 'The problem of social cost', *Journal of Law and Economics*

CURRIE, J. M., MURPHY, J. A. and SCHMITZ, A. (1971). 'The concept of economic surplus and its use in economic analysis', *Economic Journal*

DALY, G. and GIERTZ, J. F. (1972), 'Benevolence, malevolence and economic theory', *Public Choice*

DASGUPTA, P. *et al.* (1972), *Guidelines for Project Evaluation*, New York

DAVIS, O. and WHINSTON, A. (1962), 'Externalities, welfare, and the theory of games', *Journal of Political Economy*

DAVIS, O. and WHINSTON, A. (1965), 'Welfare economics and the theory of second best', *Review of Economic Studies*

DAVIS, O. and WHINSTON, A. (1967), 'Piecemeal policy in the theory of second best', *Review of Economic Studies*

DEMSETZ, H. (1971), 'Theoretical efficiency in pollution control: comments on comments', *Western Economic Journal*

DOBB, M. A. (1969), *Welfare Economics and the Economics of Socialism*, Cambridge

DOLBEAR, F. T. (1967), 'On the theory of optimal externality', *American Economic Review*

DORFMAN, R., SAMUELSON, P. and SOLOW, R. (1958), *Linear Programming and Economic Analysis*, New York

DOWNS, A. (1957), *An Economic Theory of Democracy*, New York

DUESENBERRY, J. (1949), *Income, Saving, and the Theory of Consumer Behaviour*, Cambridge, Mass.

EHRLICH, P. R. and EHRLICH, A. H. (1973), *Human Ecology*, San Francisco

FISHER, A. C. (1973), 'Environmental externalities and the Arrow–Lind public investment theorem', *American Economic Review*

FOSTER, C. D. and NEUEBERGER, H. L. (1974), 'The ambiguity of the consumer's surplus measure of welfare change', *Oxford Economic Papers*

FRIEDMAN, M. (1952), 'The welfare effects of an income and excise tax', *Journal of Political Economy*

FRIEDMAN, M. (1953), *Essays in Positive Economics*, Chicago

FRIEDMAN, M. (1962), *Capitalism and Freedom*, Chicago

GLAISTER, S. (1974), 'Generalised consumer's surplus and transport pricing', *Economic Journal*

GRAAFF, J. DE V. (1957), *Theoretical Welfare Economics*, Cambridge

GREEN, H. A. J. (1962), 'The social optimum in the presence of monopoly and taxation', *Review of Economic Studies*

HARDIN, G. and BADEN, J. (1977), *Managing the Commons*, San Francisco

HARRIS, R. and SELDON, A. (1970), *Advertising and Competition*, London

HARROD, R. F. (1938), 'Scope and method of economics', *Economic Journal*

HAUSE, J. C. (1975), 'The theory of welfare measurement', *Journal of Political Economy*

HAYEK, F. (1944), *The Road to Serfdom*, London

HAYEK, F. (1952), *The Counter-Revolution of Science*, Glencoe, Ill.

HAYEK, F. (1967), *Studies in Philosophy, Politics and Economics*, London

HICKS, J. R. (1940, 'The valuation of social income', *Economica*

HICKS, J. R. (1944), 'The four consumer's surpluses', *Review of Economic Studies*

HICKS, J. R. (1946), *Value and Capital*, 2nd edn, Oxford

HICKS, J. R. (1949), 'The foundations of welfare economics', *Economic Journal*

HICKS, U. (1947), *Public Finance*, New York

HOCHMAN, H. and RODGERS, J. (1969), 'Pareto optimal redistributions', *American Economic Review*

HOTELLING, H. (1938), 'The general welfare in relation to the problems of taxation and of railway and utility rates', *Econometrica*

JOHNSON, H. G. (1954), 'Optimum tariffs and retaliation', *Review of Economic Studies*

JOHNSON, H. G. (1973), *Man and His Environment*, British North American Committee

KAHN, R. F. (1935), 'Some notes on ideal output', *Economic Journal*

KAHN, R. F. (1948), 'Tariffs and the terms of trade', *Review of Economic Studies*

KALDOR, N. (1939), 'Welfare propositions in economics', *Economic Journal*

KELLY, J. S. (1978), *Arrow Impossibility Theorems*, London and New York

KEMP, M. (1962), 'The gains from international trade', *Economic Journal*

KLAPPHOLZ, K. (1964), 'Value judgments of economics', *British Journal of Philosophy*

KNEESE, A. V. (1977), *Economics and the Environment*, Baltimore, Md

KNEESE, A. V. and SCHULTZE, C. (1975), *Pollution, Prices and Public*

Policy, Washington, DC

KNIGHT, F. (1924), 'Some fallacies in the interpretation of social cost', *Quarterly Journal of Economics*

KNIGHT, F. (1933), *Risk, Uncertainty, and Profit*, London

KRUTILLA, J. A. and FISHER, A. C. (1975), *The Economics of Natural Resources*, Washington, DC

KUZNETS, S. (1948), 'On the valuation of social income—reflections on Professor Hicks' article, part 1', *Economica*

LERNER, A. P. (1946), *The Economics of Control*, New York

LERNER, A. P. (1970), 'On optimal taxes with an untaxable sector', *American Economic Review*

LIPSEY, R. G. and LANCASTER, K. (1957), 'The general theory of second best', *Review of Economic Studies*

LITTLE, I. M. (1957), *A Critique of Welfare Economics*, 2nd edn, Oxford

LITTLE, I. M. and MIRRLEES, J. A. (1974), *Project Appraisal and Planning for Developing Countries*, New York

MCKEAN, R. N. (1958), *Efficiency of Government Through Systems Analysis*, New York

MARGOLIS, J. (1955), 'A comment on the pure theory of public expenditure', *Review of Economics and Statistics*

MARSHALL, A. (1930), *Principles of Economics*, 8th edn, London.

METZLER, L. A. (1949), 'Tariffs, the terms of trade and the distribution of the national income', *Journal of Political Economy*

MISHAN, E. J. (1957), 'A reappraisal of the principles of resource allocation', *Economica*

MISHAN, E. J. (1959), 'Rent as a measure of welfare change', *American Economic Review*

MISHAN, E. J. (1960), 'Survey of welfare economics: 1939–1959', *Economic Journal*

MISHAN, E. J. (1962), 'Second thoughts on second best', *Oxford Economic Papers*

MISHAN, E. J. (1965), 'The recent debate on welfare criteria', *Oxford Economic Papers*

MISHAN, E. J. (1967a), 'Pareto optimality and the law', *Oxford Ecnomic Papers*

MISHAN, E. J. (1967b), *The Costs of Economic Growth*, London

MISHAN, E. J. (1969a), 'The relationship between joint products, collective goods, and external effects', *Journal of Political Economy*

MISHAN, E. J. (1969b), *21 Popular Economic Fallacies*, London

MISHAN, E. J. (1971), 'The postwar literature on externalities: an interpretive essay', *Journal of Economic Literature*

MISHAN, E. J. (1973), 'Welfare economics: resolution of a paradox', *Economic Journal*

MISHAN, E. J. (1974), 'Flexibility and consistency in project evaluation', *Economica*

MISHAN, E. J. (1976), 'The road to repression', *Encounter*

MISHAN, E. J. (1977), *The Economic Growth Debate: An Assessment*, London

MISHAN, E. J. (1980), *Introduction to Normative Economics*, New York

MISHAN, E. J. (1982), *Cost-Benefit Analysis*, 3rd edn, London

MUSGRAVE, R. A. (1959), *The Theory of Public Finance*, New York

MYINT, H. (1948), *Theories of Welfare Economics*, London

NATH, S. .K. (1964), 'Are formal welfare criteria required?', *Economic Journal*

NATH, S. K. (1969), *A Reappraisal of Welfare Economics*, London

NG, K. Y. (1976), 'Toward a theory of third best', *Public Finance*

NORDHAUS, W. and TOBIN, J., 'Is growth obsolete?', in *Economic Growth* (National Bureau of Economic Research), New York

OLSON, M. (1965), *The Logic of Collective Action*, Cambridge, Mass.

PAGE, T. (1976), *Conservation and Economic Efficiency*, Baltimore, Md

PARETO, V. (1909), *Manuel d'Economie Politique*, Paris

PIGOU, A. C. (1946), *The Economics of Welfare*, 4th edn, London

PLOTT, C. (1966), 'Externalities and corrective taxes', *Economica*

RAWLS, J. (1971), *A Theory of Justice*, Cambridge, Mass.

RIDKER, R., ed. (1972), *Population, Resources, and the Environment*, Washington, DC

ROBBINS, L. (1931), *The Nature and Significance of Economic Science*, London

ROBBINS, L. (1938), 'Interpersonal comparisons of utility', *Economic Journal*

ROBERTSON, D. (1962), 'Welfare criteria: a note', *Economic Journal*

SAMUELSON, P. A. (1939), 'The gains from international trade', *Canadian Journal of Economic and Political Science*

SAMUELSON, P. A. (1950), 'Evaluation of real income', *Oxford Economic Papers*

SAMUELSON, P. A. (1954), 'The pure theory of public expenditure', *Review of Economics and Statistics*

SAMUELSON, P. A. (1958), 'Aspects of public expenditure theories', *Review of Economics and Statistics*

SCHALL, L. (1971), 'Technological externalities and resource allocation', *Journal of Political Economy*

SCITOVSKY, T. (1941), 'A note on welfare propositions in economics', *Review of Economic Studies*

SEN, A. K. (1970), *Collective Choice and Social Welfare*, Edinburgh

STIGLER, J. G. (1943), 'The new welfare economics: a communication', *American Economic Review*

STOPLER, W. F. and SAMUELSON, P. A. (1941), 'Protection and real wages', *Review of Economic Studies*

SUGDEN, R. and WILLIAMS, A. (1978), *The Principles of Practical Cost–Benefit Analysis*, Oxford

THROSBY, D. (1970), *An Introduction to Mathematical Programming*, New York

THUROW, L. (1971), 'The income distribution as a pure public good', *Quarterly Journal of Economics*

TIEBOUT, C. (1956), 'A pure theory of local expenditure', *Journal of Political Economy*

TINBERGEN, J. (1952), 'The influence of productivity on economic welfare', *Economic Journal*

TURVEY, R. (1963), 'On divergences between social and private cost', *Economica*

VICKREY, W. (1948), 'Some objections to marginal cost pricing', *Journal of Political Economy*

VINER, J. (1953), 'Cost curves and supply curves', reprinted in *Readings in Price Theory*, New York

WEISBROAD, B. A. (1968), 'Income redistribution effects and benefit–cost analysis', in S. B. Chase (ed.), *Problems in Public Expenditure Analysis*, Washington, DC

WILKINSON, D. G. (1973), *Poverty and Progress*, London

WILLIG, R. D. (1976), 'Consumer's surplus without apologies', *American Economic Review*

WINCH, D. M. (1971), *Analytic Welfare Economics*, Harmondsworth

WISEMAN, J. (1957), 'The theory of public utility price—an empty box', *Oxford Economic Papers*

Index